Why Knowledge Matters in Curriculum

What should we teach in our schools and vocational education and higher education institutions? Is theoretical knowledge still important?

This book argues that providing students with access to knowledge should be the *raison d'être* of education. Its premise is that access to knowledge is an issue of social justice because society uses it to conduct its debates and controversies.

Theoretical knowledge is increasingly marginalised in curriculum in all sectors of education, particularly in competency-based training which is the dominant curriculum model in vocational education in many countries. This book uses competency-based training to explore the negative consequences that arise when knowledge is displaced in curriculum in favour of a focus on workplace relevance.

The book takes a unique approach by using the sociology of Basil Bernstein and the philosophy of critical realism as complementary modes of theorising to extend and develop social realist arguments about the role of knowledge in curriculum. Both approaches are increasingly influential in education and the social sciences and the book will be helpful for those seeking an accessible introduction to these complex subjects.

Why Knowledge Matters in Curriculum is a key reading for those interested in the sociology of education, curriculum studies, work-based learning, vocational education, higher education, adult and community education, tertiary education policy and lifelong learning more broadly.

Leesa Wheelahan is an associate professor in adult and vocational education at the L. H. Martin Institute for Higher Education Leadership and Management, at the University of Melbourne, Australia. Her research interests include vocational knowledge in curriculum, and tertiary education policy and social justice. She is a regular commentator for *Campus Review*, Australia's weekly tertiary education newspaper.

New studies in critical realism and education

A Critical Realist Perspective of Education
Brad Shipway

Education, Epistemology and Critical Realism
David Scott

Why Knowledge Matters in Curriculum
A social realist argument
Leesa Wheelahan

Knowledge and Knowers
Towards a realist sociology of education
Karl Maton

Why Knowledge Matters in Curriculum

A social realist argument

Leesa Wheelahan

Routledge
Taylor & Francis Group

LONDON AND NEW YORK

First published 2010
by Routledge
2 Park Square, Milton Park, Abingdon, Oxfordshire OX14 4RN

Simultaneously published in the USA and Canada
by Routledge
711 Third Avenue, New York, NY 10017

Routledge is an imprint of the Taylor & Francis Group, an informa business

First issued in paperback 2012

© 2010 Leesa Wheelahan

Typeset in Goudy by Glyph International Ltd.

British Library Cataloguing in Publication Data
A catalogue record for this book is available from the British Library

Library of Congress Cataloging-in-Publication Data
Wheelahan, Leesa.
Why knowledge matters in curriculum: a social realist argument/
Leesa Wheelahan.
    p. cm.
Includes bibliographical references and index.
1. Critical pedagogy. 2. Critical realism. 3. Curriculum change.
4. Bernstein, Basil B. I. Title.

LC196.W54 2010
375'.006–dc22   2009030102

ISBN 13: 978-0-415-48318-6 (hbk)
ISBN 13: 978-0-415-52200-7(pbk)
ISBN 13: 978-0-203-86023-6 (ebk)

For the men in my life – my partner and muse Gavin,
my sons Tim and Lachlan and their father Jamie
and my brother Roger

Contents

Acknowledgements

I owe an enormous debt of gratitude to my 'social realist' colleagues Michael Young from the Institute of Education, University of London, Rob Moore from the University of Cambridge, Johan Muller from the University of Cape Town and Karl Maton from the University of Sydney for their support and encouragement in preparing this book. The development of the social realist perspective in education has been a collaborative process and all have been generous in sharing their ideas and in taking the time to debate, consider, refine and elaborate various ideas and concepts. I am particularly grateful to Michael Young for writing the foreword to this book. Michael has also been a mentor and I value his encouragement and support more than I can say. Rob Moore provided me with an opportunity of a lifetime by allowing me to use his office at Homerton College when he was on study leave from the University of Cambridge. It is the nicest bunker I have been in and am ever likely to be in. I am very grateful and I will always remember his friendship and support and the time I spent at Cambridge. I also appreciate the support I received from those associated with the International Basil Bernstein symposiums who provided me with an opportunity to test and develop my ideas. The first symposium I attended in 2006 in Newark, New Jersey, was a defining moment in the evolution of the ideas and arguments in this book.

This book is part of the Routledge critical realism and education series edited by Roy Bhaskar and David Scott, both from the Institute of Education, University of London. I would like to thank them both for their support for this book – it would not have been published otherwise.

I am very grateful to Simon Marginson from the University of Melbourne and Trevor Gale from the University of South Australia. Both have supported me in the evolution of this work from PhD to book. Simon was my principal supervisor throughout my PhD and he was always generous with his support and with encouraging me to take intellectual risks. Trevor became one of my supervisors in the last year of my PhD when the supervisor's workload is most onerous, not least because they have to deal with prickly students.

My previous employer, Griffith University, provided me with the opportunity to work on this book and it would not have happened otherwise. I would also like to thank my colleagues, Stephen Billett, Ann Kelly, Ian James, Ray Smith and Fred Beven in adult and vocational education at Griffith University for their support. I will always be grateful to the Faculty of Education at the University of Cambridge for inviting me as a visiting scholar while I was on study leave so I could work with Rob Moore and on this book. John Beck from Homerton College at the University of Cambridge was our cultural guide and interpreter and was very generous with his time and ideas.

Stephanie Allais and I somehow got in touch when she was doing her PhD in South Africa when I was doing mine in Australia and our collaboration has subsequently become closer through our shared interests and perspectives. I would like to thank her for her support. Pat Forward from the TAFE division of the Australian Education Union (which covers TAFE teachers in Australia – the analogue of further education teachers in England) has become a good friend and intellectual collaborator and has helped me to think through the implications of the arguments developed in this book and what it means for TAFE teachers in the classroom.

Finally, I would like to thank my partner Gavin Moodie for his love, support and encouragement. He also is an intellectual collaborator and has helped me to think through, justify and most importantly to clarify the arguments in this book. He also generously and under enormous time constraints edited the whole draft – there is no greater love!

Some of the material in Chapter 8 appeared in an earlier form in 2009 in my article 'The problem with CBT' (and why constructivism makes things worse) in the *Journal of Education and Work* Vol. 22, (3), pp. 227–42.

I thank Taylor and Francis for permission to reproduce:

Table 4.1: The domains of the real, actual and empirical on page 56

This is reproduced from:

Archer, M.; Bhaskar, R.; Collier, A.; Lawson, T./ and Norrie, A. (eds) (1998) *Critical Realism: Essential Reading,* London: Routledge, p. 41.

Leesa Wheelahan
Brisbane, Australia
July 2009

Foreword

In starting her book from the premise that theoretical knowledge is, among other things, 'society's way of having a conversation with itself', Leesa Wheelahan picks up what was, like so many of his most powerful insights, one of Basil Bernstein's almost casual observations. It is this starting point that not only goes to the heart of what her book is about but enables her to make a crucial link between two issues that have all too easily been kept apart (or even seen in opposition to each other) in educational studies and the sociology of education in particular. I am referring of course to the commitment to access, equality and distribution of life chances on the one hand and to taking seriously the issue of what counts as knowledge in the curriculum on the other. *Why Knowledge Matters in Curriculum* makes a convincing argument that they are inescapably related. One of its signal achievements and why it is a book for graduate students as well as researchers is its success in making use of Bernstein's original but often elliptical and sometimes contradictory ideas. The book is a good example of following a dictum of Bernstein's that he himself did not always follow – theory is about formulating problems and asking questions, not finding new perspectives that merely re-describe the world (this is my formulation of what he wrote). As a concrete exemplar of 'doing Bernsteinian sociology of education', Wheelahan's book stands up well and can be compared favourably to the chapters in Rob Moore's more theoretical *Education and Society*.

Wheelahan's argument is that if, in our policies and practices, whether for school, vocational and professional, adult or higher education, we deny learners access to theoretical knowledge, we are effectively denying them access to those 'conversations about society and where it is going' to which Bernstein was referring. To put it even more starkly, in supporting such a denial, we are systematically undermining the possibilities of democracy. Her argument about knowledge that is drawn from critical realists such as Sayer and Bhaskar as well as from Bernstein, is sophisticated and closely reasoned. Furthermore, as I am sure she would expect, it will be hotly debated. She does not shirk the difficult issues that her 'social realist' concept of knowledge raises. In particular she focusses on the way that 'progressive' educational theorists, many of whom identify with the Left, have, in adopting, implicitly or explicitly, some form of constructivism, colluded with the forces of 'conservative modernisation' and neo-liberalism that they would doubtless oppose politically – at least in theory.

Why Knowledge Matters in Curriculum presents a sociological and philosophically grounded theory of knowledge as a basis for any curriculum; however, this argument is exemplified through the case of vocational education. This is important for a number of reasons. Firstly, with the one exception of Dewey, most educational theorists (and certainly most sociologists of education) have given very little attention to the vocational curriculum.

Wheelahan's book reminds us that, in the broadest sense, all education is vocational – and increasingly so as we try to prepare the next generation, whatever they are studying, for the complexities of building a safer, fairer and more sustainable world. Secondly, we are reminded that if vocational education programmes are to be 'educational' and not mere training, they also have the responsibility to provide students with access to the 'conversations about society' to which Bernstein referred. In making this argument her book provides powerful arguments to counter those who claim that a focus on young people's experience can be the basis for greater equality and a focus on specific workplaces on their own can be the basis for educating the future workforce. Thirdly, she makes a clear and important distinction between traditional curricula which treated knowledge (whether subjects or disciplines) as given and embodying certain notions of authority and social order which learners had to accept and her concept of 'theoretical knowledge' which is also largely based on disciplines but is always open and fallible and always needs to be questioned. In other words 'theoretical knowledge', whether in the form of literature, mathematics or engineering is never 'for its own sake' entirely – it too embodies purposes beyond itself – it too is 'vocational'.

There is another theme which emerges from Wheelahan's book that is reflected in her references and bibliography. It is the sense that the book is not only the work of a single author located in Queensland, Australia, but is also part of a small but growing international community of scholars in educational studies that is beginning to emerge from the intellectual wastelands left by the post-modernism and social constructivism of the 1980s and 1990s. This community has been located up to now largely in Anglophone countries such as Australia, South Africa and the UK, but is beginning to spread to France, the Nordic countries and through translations to Spanish-, Portuguese- and Greek-speaking researchers and other countries. The label 'social realist' describes the loosely shared set of assumptions of this community, although the term itself is not important. What is important is that it is a sign of an intellectual movement that is an active serious response to the superficiality and rhetoric of so much that is written about education as well as the instrumentalism of educational policies of so many governments and international agencies. As a contribution to that movement, *Why Knowledge Matters in Curriculum* sets high standards of rigour and intellectual commitment.

One of the ironies so well analysed by Leesa Wheelahan in her book is that, just at the time of the emergence of what has become known as the knowledge society, we have seen a displacement of theoretical knowledge, in the disciplinary sense she refers to, in the curriculum and an endorsement of generic outcomes that disavow content. It is not that content itself is important, as in the traditional curriculum, or that we remember much of the content we had to learn in school. The point about access to 'theoretical knowledge' that Wheelahan's book makes is the extent to which disciplinary or domain-based contents are bearers of concepts. It is after all concepts that are the tools we have for thinking about and changing the world and engaging in 'society's conversations'.

The priority that her book gives to discipline-based 'theoretical knowledge' as the core of any curriculum will not be universally popular, either on the Right or the Left and sometimes it may recruit politically unlikely supporters. That is why her critical realist argument that brings together the objectivity and fallibility of knowledge is so important. On a more policy-related issue, the book is also a powerful challenge to the growing obsession among governments and international agencies with qualifications rather than with the knowledge for which qualifications are a proxy. Not only do qualifications often not 'qualify' the holder for anything, their focus on pre-specified written outcomes rather than knowledge means they provide less and less evidence of what someone knows about the world – something that they used to do in the past – at least for the few that were fortunate to obtain them. *Try asking someone with a level 2 school leaving certificate in science what viruses are and why they are important in treating and preventing HIV/AIDS.*

Michael Young
Emeritus Professor of Education
Institute of Education
University of London

1 Introduction

What should we teach?

Introduction

What should we teach? What knowledge is important and why is it important? These are key questions for education because 'what we *know* affects *who* we are (or are perceived to be)' (Moore 2007b: 3). The central argument in this book is that access to abstract theoretical knowledge is an issue of distributional justice. It is part of the emerging 'social realist' school of educational theorists who argue that the principal goal of education should be to provide students with access to knowledge. It critiques theories of curriculum that argue that learning should be contextual and situated because this leads to the displacement of theoretical knowledge from the centre of curriculum and in so doing denies students access to the knowledge they need to participate in society's debates and controversies. In other words, unless students have access to theoretical knowledge they are denied the necessary means to participate in 'society's conversation'.

This introduction first considers why access to abstract theoretical knowledge is essential for democracy and why access to it is an issue of distributional justice. The next section discusses the paradox that arises because knowledge is highly valued in the knowledge society, yet it has been displaced from the centre of curriculum by an emphasis on the vocational purposes of education. The third section discusses the crisis of curriculum that has arisen because of the failure of the three dominant approaches to curriculum, which are constructivism, technical-instrumentalism and conservatism, to consider the importance of knowledge in its own right because each, in its own way, subordinates knowledge to other curricular objectives. The fourth section discusses the emerging social realist alternative within the sociology of education and it outlines the main social realist arguments about the place of knowledge in curriculum. This is followed by a section that explores the theories that social realism is drawing on and the way in which theorizing is being extended through collegiate discussion and debate. The penultimate section of the chapter discusses the specific contribution this book seeks to make to social realism by using the sociology of Basil Bernstein and the philosophy of critical realism as complementary modes of analysis. Taken together, these two approaches establish the objectivity and truthfulness of knowledge as the basis for curriculum as the means through which students are provided with access to knowledge about the natural and social worlds. The final section outlines the approach taken in the book and the focus of each chapter.

Knowledge and democracy

The late British sociologist Basil Bernstein (2000) argued that access to abstract theoretical knowledge is a precondition for an effective democracy. He argued that this is because theoretical knowledge is the means that society uses to think the 'not-yet-thought and unthinkable' and to imagine alternative futures. Michael Young (2008a: 41–42), who is a leading sociologist of education in England, explains that theoretical knowledge is the means that society uses 'to "*make connections*" between objects and events that are not obviously related', and 'to "*project beyond the present*" to a future or alternative world'. Theoretical knowledge, which has traditionally been organized as academic disciplinary knowledge, constitutes the means society uses to transcend the limits of individual experience to see beyond appearances to the nature of relations in the natural and social world. All societies need to connect the material and immaterial, the known and the unknown, the thinkable and the unthinkable, the here and the not here, the specific and the general and the past, present and future. The capacity to do so is a precondition for the existence of society.

This is why theoretical knowledge is socially powerful knowledge. Access to theoretical knowledge is important because it provides access to society's conversation about itself. This conversation includes debates about how society should respond to perceived threats such as global warming, but also debates about society's values, norms and mores and questions such as whether banks need more regulation, whether the nation should participate in war, or how refugees should be treated when they land on foreign shores seeking asylum.

Students need access to knowledge if they are to participate in this conversation. This does not mean that they all need to understand the complexities of physics or English literature. Rather, they need access to 'disciplinarity' or disciplinary styles of reasoning so that they understand how knowledge is used and the broad criteria that need to be applied in evaluating the validity of arguments. For example, a capacity to use knowledge from the humanities and social sciences provides students with a way of assessing arguments in politics and evaluating competing policy proposals, while a broad understanding of the scientific method provides at least some access to debates about how humankind should shape its relationship with the natural world, as exemplified by debates about global warming.

Students also need access to knowledge because the increasing complexity of technology, work and society means that the knowledge demands of most occupations is increasing. Young (2006a: 115) argues that, while all jobs require context-specific knowledge, 'many jobs also require knowledge involving *theoretical* ideas shared by a community of specialists' located within the academic disciplines. Workers need to be able to use theoretical knowledge in different ways and in different contexts as their work grows in complexity and difficulty. They need to be able to access decontextualized disciplinary systems of meaning if they are to select and apply contextually specific applications of that knowledge. For example, electricians, mechanics and engineers need to understand mathematics if they are to select an appropriate formula and apply it correctly. Child-care workers and teachers need to know about theories of child development if they are to identify problems in a child's development. They also need sociological insights to understand how relations between educational institutions and families may be mediated by social class or ethnic background in ways that make it easier for some families, but more difficult for others, to be effective advocates for their children. Access or lack of access to such knowledge leads to real consequences. Continuing this example, a lack of sociological insight may result in unequal outcomes of education being explained as deficits of those who are disadvantaged, rather than the outcome of socially differentiated access to knowledge and education in which middle-class students are privileged because of the congruence between their home and school environments. Moreover, all workers need access to the theoretical knowledge that underpins their occupational field of practice if they are to participate in the debates and controversies within their field. These examples illustrate the way in which occupational progression is strongly related to educational progression because education is the main way in which most people are provided with access to theoretical, disciplinary knowledge. Consequently, all qualifications should provide students with the disciplinary knowledge they need to study at a higher level within their field in addition to immediate occupational outcomes.

The retreat from knowledge in curriculum

The paradox is that while education is supposed to prepare students for the knowledge society, the modern curriculum places less emphasis on knowledge, particularly theoretical, disciplinary knowledge. The essence of the argument justifying the retreat from knowledge in curriculum is that the knowledge society has transformed the nature of knowledge so that the tacit, contextual and immediately applicable is more productive than the disciplinary and codified, resulting in an emphasis on contextualized and situated knowledge on the one hand, and 'generic' skills and capacities on the other (Chappell 2004).

This applies to all sectors of education and training, but particularly to post-compulsory education and training which includes the senior years of school, vocational education and training (VET) and higher education. Learning outcomes have been redefined so that they are increasingly tied to the workplace, and the curricular emphasis is on ensuring that students are 'work-ready' as a consequence of putatively authentic and relevant learning experiences. This is reflected in many countries in government reforms of qualifications so that they are more firmly based on generic skills or employability skills (Young 2007b).

The emphasis on the contextual and specific is a move away from the traditional concern of curriculum which has been to provide some students with access to decontextualized knowledge organized relationally through disciplinary systems of meanings. The process of vocationalization has, as would be expected, had the greatest impact on vocationally oriented programs in both VET and higher education, but it also has had an impact on traditional academic programs. Academic pathways differ from pathways designed to prepare students for the professions or vocational occupations because the purpose of academic qualifications is to induct students into 'classified' disciplinary knowledge. In contrast, the purpose of vocational and professional qualifications is to induct students into a field of practice and the theoretical knowledge that underpins practice as the basis for integrating and synthesizing each (Bernstein 2000). There is thus continuity between vocational and professional education, and both are distinguished from academic qualifications. Academic qualifications face 'one-way' to the disciplinary field of knowledge, whereas vocational and professional qualifications must face 'both-ways': to the field of practice and to the disciplinary knowledge that underpins practice (Barnett 2006). Academic qualifications emphasize the traditional, 'pure' academic disciplines, whereas vocational and professional qualifications emphasize applied disciplinary knowledge as these are the disciplinary tools that underpin practice (Barnett 2006; Young 2006c). However, while academic and vocational/professional education have different purposes, both have traditionally sought to provide students with the capacity to *recognize* different types of knowledge so that they can distinguish between everyday knowledge and theoretical knowledge, and between different fields of theoretical knowledge, for example, between physics and chemistry or sociology and psychology.

These boundaries are rendered less visible by the current emphasis on the contextual. Generalist and liberal arts qualifications are affected by the displacement of knowledge from curriculum, partly by the emphasis on generic skills and generic attributes, but also by 'smorgasbord' programs that emphasize transdisciplinarity that take as the object of study a feature of the world rather than the structures of knowledge. This is expressed, for example, in the use of 'problem-based learning' as a key principle for organizing curriculum so that students focus on a particular problem and use different disciplinary insights to understand that problem. It is in contrast to organizing the curriculum around disciplines and engaging with problems through explicit negotiation of disciplinary boundaries, which includes the criteria used by the disciplines to evaluate knowledge. The place of disciplinary knowledge is also weakened in academic programs that emphasize student choice across a range of disciplines as the principle of curricular coherence, in contrast to a curricular principle designed to induct students into the boundaries that define and insulate different disciplines, the structures of knowledge within disciplines and the sequencing of knowledge that such induction entails (Muller 2006a).

All of these trends are also reflected in curriculum for vocational and professional qualifications, but the displacement of theoretical knowledge from curriculum is driven further in these qualifications because of their focus on preparing students for a field of practice. Learning in 'realistic settings' is emphasized, particularly workplace learning (see Boud 2006). Knowledge is most marginalized in VET qualifications that are based on competency-based training such as National Vocational Qualifications in England and the similarly structured Training Packages in Australia, because all outcomes are tied to specific workplace roles and tasks.

The crisis of curriculum theory

Debates about the changing nature of knowledge in the knowledge society have led to theorizing about the curriculum and new understandings of the purpose of education and the nature of pedagogy. Cullen *et al.* (2002: 68) exemplify this when they explain that, while understandings of pedagogy and ensuing methods and practices vary between the sectors of post-compulsory education and training, nonetheless 'A "new pedagogy" is emerging, drawing on constructivist theory and practice as its main source of understanding.' They explain that:

> Context has become an immensely significant element of the new pedagogy: both the context (changing environment, proximal forces) of the whole education enterprise itself but also the significance which context has acquired within the pedagogy, and in the making and remaking of the curriculum. The very nature of knowledge is perceived differently. The curriculum, in term [sic] of both content and process, reflects this through a move away from propositional knowledge to knowledge as contextualized and contingent, as well as, often, more immediately applicable.
>
> (Cullen *et al.* 2002: 68–69)

The emphasis on context is shared by two major approaches to curriculum – social constructivism and technical-instrumentalism – while the third major approach to curriculum, conservatism, continues to eschew the contextual in favour of tradition. While there are differences between different social constructivist theories, there is, as Chappell (2004: 4) explains, 'general agreement that learning involves the active construction of meaning by learners, which is context dependent, socially mediated and situated in the "real-world" of the learner'. This focus on the tacit, contextual and applied is at the expense of disciplinary knowledge. The focus on the contextual arises in instrumentalism because it is concerned primarily with producing knowledge and skills needed in the economy and the broader purposes of education are subordinated to this goal.

Even though instrumentalist and constructivist curriculum theorists have different philosophical premises and theorize the nature of contexts differently, they share a common concern with context and both emphasize the contextual, situated and problem-oriented nature of knowledge creation and learning. Both sacrifice the complexity and depth of knowledge in curriculum in favour of 'authentic' learning in the workplace. Consequently, both support the notion of a 'hybrid' curriculum by emphasizing, as Muller (2000: 57) explains in his critique of hybrid curriculum, 'the permeability of classificatory boundaries and the promiscuity of cultural meanings and domains'. Young (2008a: 37) also critiques hybrid curriculum, and explains that supporters of the hybrid curriculum 'reject any claims that the boundaries and classifications of the curriculum reflect features of knowledge itself and are anything more than a product of history'.

In contrast to hybrid curriculum, 'insular' curriculum emphasizes traditional disciplinary boundaries for constructing curriculum. Muller (2000) explains that debates about the hybrid curriculum and the insular curriculum are cast in terms of progressive/conservative polarities. He explains that 'progressive' curriculum theory aims above all to cross cultural boundaries, because boundaries are seen to constrain and limit freedom:

> To live a life beyond bounds and without boundaries is the dominant ethical ideal ... to enquire into facts and meanings that exceed epistemological boundaries is the primary research ideal ... to teach children to cross boundaries wherever they may find them is the ideal of pedagogy ... to treat the world as a continuous network of interlinked intensities and flows beyond all divides and divisions is all there should be ...
>
> (Muller 2000: 75)

An example of this approach is provided by Thomson Klein (2004) who argues that 'Transdisciplinary vision, which replaces reduction with a new principle of relativity, is transcultural, transnational and encompasses ethics, spirituality and creativity.'

Transgressing disciplinary boundaries appeals to radicals (who are usually constructivists) and instrumental neo-liberals (in contrast to conservatives) even though the borderless social reality they envisage is constituted differently. Young (2008a: 37) explains that the negation of boundaries is attractive to many radicals because it exposes the way in which boundaries are imposed by the powerful in their own interests and then universalized and naturalized as the ideal that pertains to the whole society. For many radicals, particularly post-modernists, the academic disciplines and the structures of knowledge represent the world outlook of those who have dominated education and are the means through which the voices of the dominated are delegitimized, devalued and excluded from 'what counts'.

Neo-liberalism, on the other hand, regards the market as the ultimate mechanism for the free flow of knowledge, products and people and boundaries are a problem because they constrain this movement. Government policy makers favour the hybrid curriculum because it questions the authority and autonomy of specialist knowledge producers and renders the latter's work more open to accountability measures (Young 2008a: 37). Consequently, identifying hybrid curriculum as intrinsically progressive is selective, because neo-liberal instrumentalists can use it as a tool of managerialism. It is the means through which the purpose and role of education is defined (or redefined) through the prism of micro-economic policy, which encompasses and redefines social objectives of increased participation in education and training as necessary for the formation of human capital and less to do with broader social reasons concerning social justice and the nature of civil society. The focus of the curriculum in this instance is on 'relevance' to the workplace measured by the 'impact' of learning on workplace outcomes, which is narrowly defined as relating directly to workplace tasks, roles or problems, rather than equipping students with the knowledge they need to participate in society's conversation more broadly.

Muller (2000: 57) explains that, in contrast to the hybrid curriculum, the 'insular' curriculum emphasizes disciplinary boundaries and 'highlights the integral differences between systems of knowledge and the differences between the forms and standards of judgement proper to them'. Whilst it need not be so, this position is usually associated with conservative models of curriculum that emphasize tradition as the basis of authority and authoritative knowledge, rather than the intrinsic features of knowledge itself (Muller 2000: 57). The main role of education in this perspective is the *transmission* of knowledge and culture as authoritative truths. Its importance lies as a mechanism of social selection and stratification by the way in which access to knowledge is distributed and by outcomes that are examined and ranked with clear winners and losers. Moore and Young (2001: 447) explain that conservatism is less concerned with knowledge and its epistemological status and more concerned with enculturation into traditional values and norms, based on a relationship of deference to traditional bodies of knowledge taught in traditional authoritarian ways that require submission to become 'the kind of person it is supposed to make you'.

Consequently, constructivism, instrumentalism and conservatism each fail to place knowledge at the centre of curriculum because each downplays the significance of knowledge and subordinates it to other curricular goals. This means that, in one way or the other, knowledge is regarded *instrumentally* and not as a causally important objective in its own right because of the access it provides to the nature of the world and to society's conversation. Each treats knowledge as 'equivalent to a representation of social order incorporating principles of inclusion and exclusion, of hierarchy and power' (Moore 2007b: 3). It is just that the normative social order each envisages is different. The consequence is that the failure of the three dominant approaches to curriculum has resulted in a crisis in curriculum theory that has displaced knowledge from the centre of curriculum.

A social realist alternative

In contrast to constructivism, instrumentalism and conservatism, this book argues that the primary purpose of education is the acquisition of knowledge, because, as Young (2008a: 81) explains, it is this that distinguishes education 'whether general, further, vocational or higher, from all other activities'. Educational theorists within social realism argue that students need to be provided with access to theoretical knowledge so that they can navigate the boundaries between theoretical and everyday knowledge and between different kinds of theoretical knowledge. It is this that equips them to participate in society's conversation and in the debates shaping the field of practice for which they are being prepared.

Social realism is *social* in arguing that all knowledge is socially produced by communities of knowledge producers, while it is *realist* in arguing that that knowledge is about an objective world, one that exists independently of our social constructions of it. Social realists argue that boundaries are a condition of intelligibility of the world because they characterize the social and natural worlds and that the academic disciplines are one means that we use to navigate these boundaries. Muller (2000: 76) explains that 'boundaries are the condition both for the constitution of sense and for the transcendence of boundaries'. Social realists draw on the work of Bernstein (2000: xiii) who explains that the tacit metaphor structuring his work is the notion of boundaries and this includes 'inside/outside, intimacy/distance, here/there, near/far, us/them'. He continues:

> The crucial metaphorising is *what the boundary signifies*. Condensing the past but not a relay for it, rather a tension between the past and possible future. The boundary is not etched as in copperplate nor as ephemeral as in quicksand, and is sometimes more enabling than disabling.
>
> (Bernstein 2000: xiii)

However, boundaries can be enabling only if they are recognized and navigated. Students must have access to these boundaries because, as Muller (2000: 71) explains:

> to cross the line without knowing it is to be at the mercy of the power inscribed in the line. The question is *how* to cross, and that means paying detailed attention to the politics of redescription and translation and to the means required for a successful crossing.

Providing students with the capacity to recognize and navigate boundaries allows them to choose how they will engage with them as well as the capacity to maintain or transform them. Social realists argue that a key boundary that students must be equipped to access is that between theoretical and everyday knowledge. This means that the distinction between education and other social domains (such as the workplace) remains important because each provides access to a different type of knowledge, even though the two must be brought into a relationship within vocational and professional curriculum (Barnett 2006). Consequently, the purpose of formal education is, as Young (2008a: 164) explains:

> to enable students to acquire knowledge that: (i) is not accessible to most people in their everyday lives, and (ii) enables those who acquire it to move beyond their experience and gain some understanding of the social and natural worlds of which they are a part.

There are two issues about which social realism and constructivism agree: first, like constructivism, social realism rejects the conservative view that knowledge is timeless, universal and independent of the social context in which it was produced. Second, social realism accepts the constructivist premise that knowledge is socially produced by communities of knowledge producers, and that these communities are characterized by struggles around power and competing interests (Young 2008a: 88–89). However, that is not the end of the matter. The constructivist argument that knowledge is a product of social practices leads to two problematic conclusions, even though different types of constructivism emphasize one or the other. The first is that knowledge is primarily and ultimately about power because it is the product of communities of knowledge producers seeking to maintain their power and privilege and results in the power of the powerful to legitimate and impose their definitions and categories of knowledge on the less powerful. The second is that the distinction between theoretical and everyday knowledge can be collapsed because both are a product of social practices (Young 2008a).

In response to the first argument, Young (2008b: 13–14) distinguishes between *knowledge of the powerful* and *powerful knowledge*. They are related but they are not the same. Knowledge of the powerful is shaped and distinguished by unequal social access to knowledge production, acquisition and use. Social elites are over-represented in elite schools that focus on preparing students for the academic disciplines and professions; they are over-represented in the elite universities; and, they are over-represented in the elite professions that are close to social power. Analysis of knowledge of the powerful is concerned with the way in which access to knowledge is mediated and given legitimacy and it is an important aspect of any analysis of knowledge. Young (2008b: 14) explains, however, that characterizing knowledge as high status does not tell us anything about knowledge itself. In distinguishing knowledge of the powerful from powerful knowledge, Young (2008b: 14) argues that the latter:

> refers to what the knowledge can do or what intellectual power it gives to those who have access to it. *Powerful knowledge* provides more reliable explanations and new ways of thinking about the world and acquiring it and can provide learners with a language for engaging in political, moral and other kinds of debates.

Arguments about distributional justice and access to knowledge are premised on the distinction between knowledge of the powerful and powerful knowledge. The privileged access of the powerful to theoretical abstract knowledge provides them with the ability to mobilize knowledge to think the unthinkable and the not-yet-thought. Powerful knowledge is powerful because of the access it provides to the natural and social world and to society's conversation about what it should be like. Knowledge will inevitably bear the marks of its production because it is socially produced, reworked and modified by communities of knowledge producers, and the state of our knowledge must at any time be regarded as a work-in-progress. However, while knowledge will bear the marks of power and privilege that is not *all* that it does. Arguments about distributional justice are concerned with ensuring equitable access to knowledge as a work-in-progress so that the less powerful can contribute to the shape and nature of knowledge and this includes participating in defining what is important within knowledge fields.

Arguments that reduce knowledge to power contribute to the exclusion of the less powerful from access to powerful knowledge because knowledge is not treated as real in its own right and access to it is not problematized.

Social realism also rejects the second constructivist argument that knowledge can be defined as '*just another set of social practices*', which is an argument that renders theoretical and everyday knowledge commensurable (Young 2008a: 89, emphasis in original). However context may be theorized within different socio-cultural or constructivist approaches, this argument assumes that knowledge does not have features that are independent of these social practices. In focussing on social practices, it denies that there are epistemic relations of knowledge that must be considered in their own right and judged by the extent to which they provide access to the social and natural world. Moreover, this argument can result in privileging some forms of social practices as superior to others, for example in privileging the workplace as a site of learning over the educational institution because the former is more 'authentic'. It fails to understand the importance of maintaining the boundary between educational institutions and the workplace precisely because of the access each provides to different kinds of knowledge. This distinction is particularly important for vocational and professional curriculum, because curriculum must provide access to the theoretical knowledge that underpins practice on the one hand, and the tacit and contextual knowledge of the workplace on the other (Barnett 2006). Attempts to collapse the distinction between both types of knowledge impoverish both.

Social realism differs from the dominant approaches to curriculum because it treats knowledge as causally important in its own right. It argues that knowledge has transcendent properties beyond the specific conditions under which it was produced precisely because it provides access to the natural and social worlds, even though our knowledge is never perfect and always a work-in-progress. This entails a twofold commitment to objectivity: first, it entails a commitment to the notion that the natural and social worlds exist independently of what we may think about them. Many will perhaps accept that the natural world exists independently of our conceptions, but find the premise that the social world is similarly independent somewhat difficult. The argument here is that the social world exists independently of our conceptions even though they are an important part of it, particularly in shaping social relations. However, the social world is a product of the interplay of social relations *and* historical, natural, material and economic relations. The second commitment to objectivity is premised on the first: if the world exists objectively and is not a construct of our minds or discourse, then the purpose of knowledge is to understand that objective reality, even if our knowledge is always partial, socially mediated and marked by the social conditions under which it was produced, and is fallible as a consequence. The first commitment is to the existence of an objective reality and the second is to objective knowledge as the basis for the curriculum. Both types of commitment to objectivity mean that the normative goal of curriculum should be to provide students with access to the truth, even though we understand that our knowledge is always a work-in-progress towards the truth, and that it is fallible and revisable in the light of new evidence (Young and Muller 2007).

Theorizing the curriculum

Young (2008a: 112–13) explains that the purpose of the sociology of education is not only to theorize the *context* of education but also its *content* and the relationship between the two. Consequently, social realism needs to understand both the social basis of knowledge and the nature of knowledge itself. It needs to do so if it is theoretically to ground the commitment to objectivity and to the pursuit of truthfulness as the basis for structuring knowledge in curriculum. This requires an analysis of the nature of knowledge, the way it is related to the objects that it is about, the way it is produced, the structures of different kinds of knowledge, the different social relations that underpin abstract theoretical knowledge and everyday knowledge respectively, and the implications of all this for the way knowledge is reproduced in curriculum and acquired by students. This is because the nature and structure of knowledge and the way it is produced has curricular implications for the way it is classified, sequenced, paced and evaluated in curriculum (Bernstein 2000; Muller 2006a). It is necessary to identify the social conditions of knowledge production and acquisition, if curriculum is to be structured to distribute access to it equitably. This is why social realists do not take knowledge as a given and/or limit their focus solely to its reproduction in curriculum.

Social realism is a developing perspective within the sociology of education that is heavily indebted to the late nineteenth century sociology of Emile Durkheim and the complementary late twentieth century sociology of Basil Bernstein. While both have their limitations, they provide important theoretical tools to analyse and differentiate between different kinds of knowledge by distinguishing between abstract and everyday knowledge, the role each plays in society and the social relations on which each rests. However, it is because both have their limitations that continued theorizing about the nature of knowledge is important.

Social realism takes seriously the view that knowledge is a work-in-progress developed by social processes of production, and that this occurs primarily by engaging in collective work and collegiate discussion and debate. As a consequence, theorizing is open-ended and developing, and this is expressed in the different ways in which the objectivity of knowledge is understood within social realism. Young and Muller (2007: 177) differentiate between two realist approaches. The first is a 'formalist' kind of realism that bases its model of objectivity in the structures of knowledge itself, so that these structures assume considerable importance. The second is a 'naturalistic' kind that focuses on the relationship between knowledge and the objects of that knowledge, and consequently argues that there are important affinities between the natural and social sciences because both seek objective knowledge about their particular objects, even though they may differ in methods they use in doing so (Moore 2007b). Young and Muller provide the philosophy of Cassirer as an example of the formalist approach, while an example of the naturalistic approach is an anti-positivist philosophy such as critical realism. However, rather than seeing this as a point of division, it is instead the basis of dialogue and discussion. They explain that it is not necessary to choose one or the other because 'The primary choice ... is between objectivity and anti-objectivity' (Young and Muller 2007: 177). Moreover, the two approaches are not necessarily mutually exclusive and each can inform the other. This provides the basis for fruitful dialogue that can enrich social realist understandings and expand shared theorizing around the pivotal contribution of Bernstein and his Durkheimian analysis.

This book contributes to social realist theorizing of knowledge and the curriculum by drawing on the sociology of Basil Bernstein and the philosophy of critical realism to develop conceptual tools to theorize the nature of knowledge and the way it should be structured in curriculum. It is able to draw on both for two reasons: first, because there is an interdependent relationship between philosophy and sociology and each brings different insights and addresses different issues; and second, because of the complementary nature of critical realist philosophy and Bernsteinian sociology. The book draws on philosophy and sociology because theorizing the place of knowledge in curriculum requires a philosophical analysis of the nature of knowledge and the relationship between knowledge and its referents, and it requires a sociological analysis of the social conditions of knowledge production and acquisition. While there are overlaps between philosophy and sociology, broadly speaking, philosophy explores the epistemic relations between knowledge and the object that that knowledge is about as well as the conditions under which we gain access to, and the limits of, knowledge. It is the basis upon which the objectivity and pursuit of the truthfulness of knowledge are established. Sociology explores the social relations of knowledge which focuses on the relationship between knowers and knowledge and the social practices used to produce knowledge. It is the basis upon which the social conditions necessary to produce objective knowledge is established as well as the necessary social conditions for its acquisition. Furthermore, each informs the other because there are sociological preconditions for philosophy as its existence presupposes specialized social practices and communities of knowledge producers, and there are philosophical preconditions for sociology in setting ontological and epistemological boundaries to theory development (Bhaskar 1998d).

The book draws on Bernsteinian sociology and critical realist philosophy respectively because each provides insights into the nature of knowledge, while each is insufficient on its own to theorize curriculum. Bernstein's strength is his analysis of the social relations of knowledge, whereas critical realism's strength is its analysis of the epistemic relations of knowledge. Bernstein provides an analysis of the social structuring of knowledge, the social relations that underpin theoretical and everyday knowledge and the way social relations mediate and distribute access to knowledge in ways that provide access to some and not to others. However, while this is an essential aspect of the analysis of knowledge and the way it should be structured in curriculum, we must also understand the epistemic relations of knowledge because, arguably, students must have epistemic access to knowledge if they are to have social access to it. In other words, to access knowledge students must first understand it, and analysing the epistemic relations of knowledge is important in considering the way it should be structured in curriculum. Drawing from each allows us to see that knowledge is *co-determined* by social relations and epistemic relations (Moore 2004; Maton 2006) and to explore more thoroughly the nature of these relations than would be possible by relying exclusively on either approach.

There are important differences between Bernstein and critical realism as well as important commonalities. Bernstein emphasizes the *structures* of knowledge and the way these structures are implicated in different kinds of social relations and social practices. He argues that the structure of the academic disciplines and the divisions between them have causal properties that shape the way knowledge is produced and acquired. Critical realism emphasizes the *aboutness* of knowledge or the relationship between knowledge and its object, because knowledge is causally related to, although not identical with, the object that the knowledge is about. Bernstein emphasizes the structuring role of knowledge in society and the distinction between esoteric (theoretical) and mundane (everyday) knowledge as the basis for social practice, while critical realism emphasizes practice in the external social and natural world as the basis of knowledge. Bernstein's ontological premise about the nature of the world, what it is like and how it is structured, is largely Durkheimian and idealist, while critical realism's is largely materialist.

However, there are also important commonalities that make it possible to develop conceptual tools that can be used to theorize curriculum by drawing on each. Both see society as consisting of objective structures (such as social class) that constrain and enable differently positioned agents by the social distribution of access to power, and in this sense both can be characterized as social realism. Both also agree on the *sui generis* reality of knowledge and its independence from those who produced it and the context in which it was produced. They agree that while knowledge is socially and historically constructed it is not reducible to that context, and that it is necessary to go beyond sense data to understand the real (Johnson *et al.* 1984). So, while knowledge is marked by the conditions of its production, and in this sense is historically and socially situated, it also has transcendent properties that endow it with its *sui generis* reality, independence and the capacity to transcend particular contexts so that it can be used to think the unthinkable and the not-yet-thought. Both use similar modes of analysis theoretically to identify causal mechanisms or principles that contribute to the social structuring of society. It is this that enables Moore (2006b: 43, fn 6) to say that even though Bernstein was dismissive of 'epistemological botany' and attempts to categorize him as one thing or the other, that nonetheless 'Bernstein's theory is best understood as a form of critical realism'.

Approach taken in this book

The approach taken in this book is to first identify the nature of knowledge and how it is produced as the basis for theorizing the way in which it should be structured in curriculum. It considers what theoretical knowledge must be like if it is to provide the basis for society's conversation and what is needed if students are to have access to it. This is the process through which the conceptual tools used in this book are developed arising from an analysis of Bernstein and critical realism. These conceptual tools are then used in later chapters to analyse why we have a crisis of curriculum theory and to critique conservatism, instrumentalism and constructivism. Bernsteinian theory and critical realism are also used to explore the changes in society that contributed to the displacement of knowledge in curriculum and to consider why the dominant theories of curriculum are valorized and persist even though they cannot consider knowledge in its own right and thus provide the grounds for knowledge in curriculum.

Chapter 2 briefly outlines the Durkheimian origins of Bernstein's approach before exploring Bernstein's account of the structures of knowledge, the way it is produced and the way it is reproduced in curriculum. As outlined above, Bernstein's analysis provides insights into the way in which the structures of knowledge are implicated in the social relations of knowledge, but also the way in which such knowledge is distributed, and the relations between knowledge and power. He demonstrates the causal and emergent properties of the structures of knowledge and their implications for the way in which knowledge is transmitted and acquired. He provides the basis for structuring knowledge in curriculum so that students 'recognize' different types of knowledge and consequently demonstrate that they can do so through producing or 'realizing' the required outcomes of learning. Chapter 3 evaluates and critiques Bernstein's analysis of the structures of knowledge and the way knowledge is produced. It draws on critical realism to argue that Bernstein's contribution needs to be supplemented to consider the epistemic relations of knowledge, because students' social access to theoretical knowledge is mediated by their epistemic access.

Chapter 4 uses critical realism to develop a realist basis for curriculum. It asks the critical realist question, 'what must the world be like if we are to have knowledge of it' (Bhaskar 2008). It outlines the critical realist argument that we need to go beyond underlying appearances or events to understand the interplay between generative mechanisms and their causal powers and structures that produce the reality that we experience (Sayer 2000). This is because the world is complex and stratified and characterized by ontological depth. Critical realists argue that the outcomes we experience are always the product of co-determination of the causal properties of different generative mechanisms (like social class) that interact in open systems and that we need to understand the way this happens if we are to understand the events that occur in the world and our experience of them (Bhaskar 1998d). It argues that students need access to this complexity to understand the world they live in. This chapter lays the basis for a critique of instrumentalist and constructivist theories of curriculum in subsequent chapters because both are premised on a 'flat' ontology as a consequence of their emphasis on the experiential. Chapter 5 uses critical realism to argue that the academic disciplines provide access to the natural and social worlds, even if the knowledge they generate is fallible and revisable. It builds on Bernstein's analysis of the social relations of knowledge and extends this through an analysis of its epistemic relations. It considers the way in which critical realism and Bernsteinian theory can be brought together to inform curriculum.

Chapter 6 presents a sociological analysis of the changes in society that have led to the relativizing of knowledge in curriculum. It focuses on Anglophone countries and argues that the social transformations associated with globalization and changes to the nature of work, particularly in the relationship between labour and capital, have transformed the relationship between knowledge and society and contributed to the displacement of knowledge from the centre of curriculum. These social processes contributed to and were reinforced by changes in the disciplines that inform curriculum such as linguistics, psychology, social anthropology, sociology and sociolinguistics (Bernstein 2000: 42). The rise of post-modernism in these disciplines and associated changed conceptions of the human actor meant that knowledge was relativized and subordinated to the development of intrinsic human capacities so that the focus was on knowers rather than knowledge. The result was a crisis in curriculum theory in which there was no effective challenge to the vocationalization of education, a process that further contributed to the displacement of knowledge from curriculum (Young 2003b: 554).

Chapter 7 argues that the crisis of curriculum arises because the dominant models of curriculum have displaced knowledge from the centre of curriculum as a consequence of the way they downplay the significance of knowledge and subordinate it to other curricular goals. It analyses conservatism, instrumentalism and constructivism and the way each 'precludes a debate about knowledge in its own right' (Moore and Young 2001: 446). It uses a Bernsteinian analysis to argue that each of these approaches exists in relationships of affinity and opposition with the others, resulting in a 'pedagogic pallet' (Bernstein 2000). It extends this Bernsteinian framework to argue that these relationships are shaped by the dominance of instrumentalism which selectively appropriates from conservatism and constructivism.

Chapter 8 considers the special case of competency-based training because of its popularity with policy makers in many countries as the solution to skilling the workforce to create internationally competitive national economies. Competency-based training is hegemonic in Australia, where it is the mandated model of curriculum for all VET qualifications, and it has substantial influence in other countries such as Britain, South Africa and New Zealand. The arguments the chapter develops can be used also to critique other outcomes-based approaches to curriculum. It extends the analysis in the previous chapter, and argues that while constructivism and instrumentalism are distinct theoretical approaches to curriculum, the relationship between the two structured the development of competency-based training so that constructivists must be implicated in its dominance in policy. The chapter presents a theoretical argument to demonstrate that this is a consequence of a focus on *contexts*, and that instrumentalism and constructivism are inconsistent with the possibility of objective knowledge as a result and thus cannot provide the grounds for curriculum. It uses Australia as a case-study to illustrate this, while the arguments are relevant to other countries with similar systems.

The conclusion outlines the social realist alternative model of curriculum and argues that the disciplinary basis of academic and vocational/professional qualifications needs to be restored and made explicit. It argues that vocational and professional qualifications should include two outcomes: the first is to prepare students for a field of practice; the second is to provide students with the basis for *educational progression* within their field to underpin occupational progression (Lolwana 2005; Allais 2006). These dual outcomes provide students with the capacity to contribute to debates shaping their field of practice *and* to contribute to society's conversation more broadly.

Conclusion

Educational theories are always underpinned by theories of society and theories of knowledge, even if they are not always made explicit (Young and Muller 2007: 175). This book seeks to make clear the theories of society and knowledge of the dominant models of curriculum, while at the same time proposing an alternative. Conservatism, technical-instrumentalism and constructivism are explicit in their theories of society while their theories of knowledge are more opaque as a consequence of the instrumental way they treat knowledge. Conservatism subordinates knowledge to tradition, constructivism to power and social practices and technical-instrumentalism to relevance. The features of knowledge are less important than the purpose it is designed to serve.

Social realism is also underpinned by theories of society and knowledge. However, in this case, rather than subordinating knowledge to a particular social purpose, knowledge is the means by which that social purpose is realized and consequently it must be treated as causally important in its own right. It is intrinsic to a theory of society because access to knowledge is the means through which individuals are able to participate in society's conversation. The point of education is to provide students with that access so that they can participate in this conversation, and this is why access to knowledge is an issue of distributional justice and why fair access to it is necessary for a democracy.

This is why educational theory matters. It has practical implications for the way knowledge is structured in curriculum and the way access to it is socially distributed. The advent of universal systems of schooling and tertiary education in wealthy countries has not resulted in greater social equality even though the percentage of the population completing school and participating in tertiary education is far greater than in years past (Centre for the Study of Higher Education 2008). In Australia, as in many other wealthy Western countries, social elites continue to have privileged access to the elite universities and professions. The role that access to knowledge in school plays in this process is not often theorized.[1] In Australia, 'stronger' students are more likely to undertake the academic disciplines as part of their senior school certificates, while 'weaker' students are more likely to undertake vocationally oriented subjects, particularly VET subjects using competency-based training curriculum. Who are the stronger and weaker students? Stronger students are more likely to come from high socio-economic backgrounds and weaker students from low socio-economic backgrounds. Teese *et al.* (2006a: 18) explain, that 'achievement differences are the means through which social disadvantage is relayed'. The apparently meritocratic basis of schooling masks the social and economic roots of underachievement (Young 2006c: 59). This in turn mediates access to pathways to tertiary education so that VET in Australia (and in similar countries) is over-represented with students from low socio-economic backgrounds, while higher education is over-represented with students from high socio-economic backgrounds, with this being most pronounced at the elite universities (Foley 2007; Centre for the Study of Higher Education 2008; Santiago *et al.* 2008b).

Social inclusion policies in countries such as Britain and Australia emphasize school retention and participation in post-school education. These are important goals in their own right because the evidence suggests that students who do not finish school are most at risk of social exclusion based on a contingent relationship with the labour market. However, while social inclusion is important, it is not the same as social justice. The emphasis in social justice is on distributive justice and the different outcomes that arise from the structuring of relations of privilege and disadvantage. In contrast, the emphasis in social inclusion is on exclusion and on the deficits of those who are excluded with fewer questions asked about the distributive mechanisms that produce advantage and privilege as well as disadvantage. An emphasis on social inclusion is not enough because it does not allow attention to be focused on the mechanisms *internal* to education that result in unequal outcomes (Bernstein 2000). As part of the goal of achieving higher school retention rates, senior school certificates are being reconstructed in many countries to make them more relevant by tying learning to direct vocational outcomes and by emphasizing student choice. This is problematic because, as Young (2008b: 10) explains, 'Without an explicit concept of knowledge acquisition, policies that give priority to widening participation and student choice could well be the basis for new, albeit less visible, inequalities'.

The working class needs access to powerful knowledge if it is to participate in society's conversation. Theorizing the nature of knowledge is thus a key task of the sociology of education, because this provides an understanding of the way it should be structured in curriculum so that there is equitable access to it. This book is a contribution to that task.

2 A Bernsteinian analysis of knowledge and the implications for curriculum

Introduction

This chapter outlines Bernstein's analysis of the nature of knowledge and the relationship between knowledge and power. It explains the way in which abstract knowledge is the site for society's conversation about the unthinkable and the not-yet-thought and why access to such knowledge is an issue of distributional justice. It establishes the importance of theoretical knowledge in curriculum and the argument that students must have access to knowledge if they are to participate in this conversation. However, Bernstein's contribution extends beyond establishing the centrality of knowledge in curriculum; his analysis demonstrates that the way knowledge is structured has implications for the processes used to produce knowledge and then to reproduce it in curriculum. His analysis of the 'pedagogic device' reveals how the structure of pedagogic discourse and the rules shaping the way it is distributed, recontextualized and evaluated is a mechanism for relaying power relations in society in ways that include and exclude.

The first section of the chapter explains Bernstein's debt to Durkheim in distinguishing between esoteric and mundane knowledge as the basis for understanding the distinction between theoretical and everyday knowledge, the relationship between them, and the role each plays in society. This is followed by an explanation of Bernstein's analysis of theoretical and everyday knowledge as systems of meaning that are structured as vertical and horizontal discourses respectively and the implications for curriculum. The next section outlines Bernstein's distinction between singulars, regions and generic modes of organizing knowledge. Broadly speaking, singulars refer to the academic disciplines and regions refer to applied disciplinary knowledge. In contrast, generic modes of knowledge refer to 'genericism' expressed as generic skills or attributes that underpin the vocationalization of knowledge in curriculum. The penultimate section discusses Bernstein's theory of the pedagogic device which is an analysis of the way knowledge is relocated from the field in which it was produced to be reproduced in curriculum. It is focussed on the way in which pedagogic practices mediate access to knowledge. The final section discusses the implications that arise from this analysis for curriculum.

The role of sacred and profane knowledge in society

Bernstein's work is fundamentally Durkheimian because of his analysis of the nature of knowledge and the role that different forms of knowledge play in mediating social relations and structuring society (Moore 2004: 120). Durkheim argues that all societies distinguish between sacred or esoteric knowledge on the one hand, and profane or mundane knowledge on the other. Esoteric knowledge is theoretical and conceptual knowledge, while mundane knowledge is everyday knowledge (Bernstein 2000: 157).

Esoteric and mundane knowledge are necessary for society's existence – each plays an indispensable role. Knowledge of, and life in, the mundane, everyday world is necessary for society to reproduce itself materially. Esoteric knowledge performs two functions. First, esoteric knowledge consists of socially produced 'collective representations' of a society that allow it to transcend the limits of individual experience to see beyond appearances to the real nature of relations in the (natural and social) world. Collective representations allow society to make, classify and systematize connections and inner relations between things, and to connect the past, present and future by connecting the material and immaterial worlds (Muller 2000: 78; Young 2008a: 41–42). They are the means society uses to conduct a conversation with itself about alternative futures by permitting discussions about what society *should* be like. Collective representations also play a second, normative role (Muller 2000: 78). They provide the moral 'glue' that holds society together by establishing society's values, norms and mores, and in so doing, connect the individual to the collective (Durkheim 1960: 336). This too is a condition for the existence of society. Students need access to these collective representations if they are to participate in society's conversation.

Durkheim argued that religion was historically the paradigmatic form of theoretical and abstract knowledge and this is why it was sacred knowledge. In contrast, mundane knowledge was profane knowledge because its concerns were the concerns of the profane, everyday world. Religion provided the moral code and integrative basis necessary for society to exist and was the framework through which society's collective representations were first developed. Religions are in essence the collective representations of societies and reflect societies back to themselves. They express the general social relations of particular societies and this is why religions differ between societies and epochs (Durkheim 1967: 29–30). Religion was paradigmatic for theoretical, abstract knowledge which was later expressed as specialized forms of knowledge most associated with academic disciplines because of the way in which religion negotiated the boundaries between the material and immaterial worlds, but also because religion, philosophy and science share the same concerns: 'they are nature, man, society' (Durkheim 1967: 476). In emphasizing the continuity of religious and scientific knowledge, both Durkheim and Bernstein emphasize the discontinuity between esoteric knowledge and mundane knowledge, or knowledge of the every day.

Vertical and horizontal discourses

Bernstein elaborates Durkheim's concepts of esoteric/sacred and mundane/profane knowledge to analyse the structures of each and the social relations of knowledge creation and reproduction that underpin each. Bernstein saw his work in evolutionary terms. He explains that his work until the 1980s resulted in 'a theory of the construction of pedagogic discourse, its distributive, recontextualising and evaluative rules, and their social basis' (Bernstein 1999: 157). His prior work had not interrogated the forms or structures of discourse, with the consequence that 'the internal principles of their construction and their social base, were taken for granted and not analysed' (Bernstein 1999: 157). He turned his attention to this task towards the end of his life with his analysis of vertical and horizontal discourses.

Bernstein says that esoteric knowledge – or conceptual, abstract knowledge – is a form of vertical discourse, whereas mundane knowledge or everyday knowledge is a form of horizontal discourse. Each discourse has its own grammar (or rules) by which it is structured which in turn shapes the further development of knowledge within that discourse and the social relations upon which it is based (Bernstein 2000: 156). Distinguishing between vertical and horizontal discourses was necessary to overcome the homogenizing of each, resulting in stereotypical characterizations in which 'one form [is] … romanticised as a medium celebrating what the other form has lost' (Bernstein 1999: 158).

Mundane knowledge is tied to specific contexts and events so that the meaning of mundane knowledge is understandable only within that specific context and the material base it rests upon (Bernstein 2000: 30). It is particularized knowledge, because its selection and usefulness is determined by the extent to which it is relevant in a particular context (Gamble 2006b). Because meaning is context specific, it is 'consumed' by that context and cannot easily be applied elsewhere. This is why it is difficult for mundane knowledge to be a driver of change beyond the context in which it is enacted. The structure of mundane knowledge or horizontal discourse is *segmented* by the specific context in which it is realized (for example, the workplace, home or local sporting club). This gives rise to segmental knowledges which are not necessarily transferable to other contexts except where features of the context and social relations are similar. Bernstein (2000: 157) says that horizontal discourse is 'likely to be oral, local, context dependent and specific, tacit, multilayered and contradictory across but not within contexts'. The principle by which knowledge is selected and applied is relevance to the local context, and the local context is usually the site in which learning that knowledge (and how to apply it) takes place. This means that meanings, knowledge and competences acquired in one context (or segment) do not necessarily have meaning or relevance in another (Bernstein 2000: 159).

Bernstein (2000: 30) argues that esoteric knowledge is potentially powerful knowledge because it is the site of the 'unthinkable' and the 'yet-to-be-thought'. Esoteric knowledge has the potential to challenge the social distribution of power because of its capacity to transform knowledge and how that knowledge is used, even if this capacity is not always realized. Such knowledge is indirectly related to a material base because it is decontextualized or generalized knowledge, and this means that there is a potential for a gap to arise between that knowledge and its material base, which Bernstein (2000: 30) refers to as the '*potential discursive gap*'. Bernstein (2000: 30) argues that this gap can 'become (not always) a site for alternative possibilities, for alternative realisations between the material and immaterial' and can 'change the relations between the material and immaterial'. This is the site of the 'unthinkable', the 'impossible' and the 'not-yet-thought', and this is why esoteric knowledge has power and status, and why access to it is always regulated by a division of labour and by distributive rules that provide access to some, but not others (Bernstein 2000: 31).

Esoteric or conceptual knowledge is structured as a vertical discourse because, unlike horizontal discourse, knowledge is not segmented by and integrated through the specific context in which it is realized. Rather, vertical discourses consist of 'specialised symbolic structures of explicit knowledge' in which the integration of knowledge occurs by the integration of meanings and not by relevance to specific contexts (Bernstein 2000: 160). Bernstein (2000: 160) says that 'The procedures of *Vertical discourse* are then linked, not by contexts, horizontally, but the procedures are linked to other procedures hierarchically'. The acquisition of vertical discourse requires the development of the capacity to integrate meanings so that these meanings 'are not consumed at the point of its contextual delivery' (Bernstein 2000: 160). Learning contextually specific applications of knowledge rather than the disciplinary system of meaning in which it is embedded ties that knowledge to that context. It does not leave students with the conceptual tools they need in other contexts, or to select different contextually specific applications of knowledge in the same context. Students thus need access to the system of meaning, although this occurs in different ways depending on the nature of the discipline.

The structuring of different kinds of vertical discourses

There are two main kinds of vertical discourse. The first form of vertical discourse 'takes the form of a coherent, explicit and systematically principled structure, [and is] hierarchically organised, as in the sciences' (Bernstein 2000: 157). Bernstein (2000: 160) calls this a vertical discourse with a hierarchical knowledge structure. The knowledge base is shared by practitioners of the discipline, and knowledge is developed by integrating propositions at increasing levels of abstraction (Muller 2006a). Physics is often used as an exemplar of a vertical discourse with a hierarchical knowledge structure. Knowledge thus develops (is produced) by generating *new* meanings and integrating them within existing frameworks or revising those frameworks. However, the way knowledge is produced also has implications for the way in which it is reproduced in curriculum at all levels of education. Induction into these disciplines consists of induction into the hierarchical knowledge structure, and progression within the discipline depends on the capacity to integrate meanings at different levels. Students need to understand basic principles before moving on to more complex ones; learning and hence the curriculum is sequential. Students have to understand what comes before to understand what comes after (Muller 2006a, 2006b).

A second kind of vertical discourse 'takes the form of specialised languages with specialised modes of interrogation and specialised criteria for the production and circulation of texts, as in the social sciences and humanities' (Bernstein 2000: 157). Bernstein defines these as vertical discourses with a horizontal knowledge structure. This is not the same as a horizontal *discourse* which defines knowledge by and integrates knowledge within the social or cultural context or segment. Instead, vertical discourses with horizontal knowledge *structures* segment knowledge (and to this extent they are similar to horizontal discourses) by different languages within each discipline, each of which has different (and often opposing) ontological and epistemological assumptions. For example, conflict and functionalist sociological theories construe their object of study (society) differently, ask different questions and may have different methods of investigation. Knowledge is developed by the development of new languages with their own designated speakers and rules that define the language, distinguish it from the others within the discipline, and generate canonical texts and names. Induction into these disciplines (such as sociology) involves learning to 'manage names and languages together with their criticisms' (Bernstein 2000: 164). This induction depends on the capacity to recognize and keep distinct different (and putatively incommensurable) meanings, while being able to integrate meanings with the language adopted as one's own. Students in these disciplines thus need to adopt a stance, a theoretical framework, or language that they use to 'gaze' upon the world (Bernstein 2000: 164).

Bernstein makes further distinctions within horizontal knowledge structures. Some of these languages have 'strong' grammars which define the object of knowledge and generate empirical descriptions of it, as in, for example, many theoretical frameworks in economics. Speakers of one language can often talk to speakers of other languages within the discipline and can, at least some of the time, agree on how to define the object of study and what counts as evidence in research. In contrast, this is more difficult in those disciplines that consist of a series of languages that have weak grammars or shared rules. In these disciplines (such as sociology) it is difficult to generate empirical descriptions because the different languages cannot agree on how to define the object of knowledge and the way it should be researched. For example, functionalist and conflict sociology would define, explain and research the nature of social inequality in society in ways that are quite different – their premises are completely different. Each of the languages has different epistemological and ontological assumptions. These languages are (to greater or lesser degrees) incommensurable and speakers of one cannot engage with speakers of the other (Bernstein 2000: 163–66).

Moore and Maton (2001) ask: why do some disciplines have languages with a strong grammar, while others have languages with a weak grammar?

Their response has been to develop and extend Bernstein's analysis with their concept of the epistemic device. They explain that Bernstein's analysis of the structures of knowledge focusses on the social relations of knowledge (how communities of knowledge producers produce knowledge, the 'rules' they use, canonical texts, etc) and not on the epistemic relation of knowledge. A focus on the epistemic relation means that a prior question has to be asked: how are truth claims generated and judged within the discipline? In other words, what is the key legitimating principle of the development of knowledge in the discipline? They distinguish between disciplines in which the key legitimating principle is the epistemic relation between knowledge and its object, and those in which the key legitimating principle is the social relation between knowers and knowledge. Disciplines that focus on the epistemic relation orient towards the *non-arbitrary* or objective features of knowledge, whereas those that focus on the social relation orient towards the *arbitrary* features of knowledge.

The non-arbitrary features of knowledge refer to the relationship between knowledge of the object (for example, knowledge of the periodic table in chemistry) and the object that the knowledge is about (the chemical elements to which the periodic table refers). It is the *aboutness* of the knowledge that makes it non-arbitrary because if the knowledge were about something else, it would be different. Hierarchical knowledge structures (such as chemistry) and horizontal knowledge structures with a strong grammar (such as economics) focus on the non-arbitrary features of knowledge. At its most extreme, this approach generates positivist accounts that deny the involvement of social relations in the production of knowledge (Moore and Maton 2001). Knowledge becomes an unmediated, direct account of its object rather than an account which is socially mediated and produced and thus always fallible and revisable in light of new evidence.

Horizontal knowledge structures with weak grammars in contrast ask about the situated perspective of the person who is 'gazing' upon the object of exploration and the concepts and theories they are using to examine it. The emphasis moves to the way in which the socially situated observer or knower *construes* the object because, it is argued, different observers construe the object differently. At the most extreme, this approach denies the involvement of an objective reality because all reality is socially constructed and therefore there is no object that is independent of the social constructions or discourses that generated it. This approach draws on the social relations or arbitrary features of knowledge. It is arbitrary because the content of knowledge changes depending on *who* is generating it. There is no real object that can be defined independently of who is gazing upon it (Moore and Maton 2001).

Moore and Maton argue that all academic disciplines have an epistemic (non-arbitrary) and social (arbitrary) dimension, but that different aspects of this relation are emphasized depending on the nature of the discourse. The principle of legitimation is the means by which different disciplines establish the basis for knowledge claims, and is the basis 'whereby the knowledge structures and grammars of intellectual fields are maintained, reproduced, transformed and changed' (Moore and Maton 2001: 161). It is the principle of legitimation that generates strong grammars and weak grammars. This provides helpful insights into why vertical discourses are structured differently.

Singulars, regions and generic modes of knowledge

Bernstein's analysis of knowledge as horizontal and vertical discourses, and as different types of vertical discourses, is further developed by his analysis of the different modes of organizing knowledge within the academy and its recontextualization within curriculum in all educational sectors. The growing complexity of the social division of labour is reflected in the growing complexity of knowledge. He distinguishes between singulars, regions and the generic as different modes of organizing knowledge. Singulars refer to singular bodies of knowledge, and most of the academic disciplines fit into this category. He associates the growth of singulars in the second half of the nineteenth and first half of the twentieth century with the exigencies of managing a growing British Empire, which required the development of a more differentiated division of labour underpinned by specialized knowledge structures (Bernstein 2000: 54).[1]

Regions are at the interface between academic disciplines (singulars) and the field of practice for which students are being prepared (for example, medicine) (Bernstein 2000: 52). They refer to the *applied* disciplinary knowledge that underpins professional and vocational practice (Young 2006c: 55). Regions draw on, integrate and recontextualize knowledge from singulars as the theoretical basis of practice in occupations and professions, and the growth of the regions is associated with the growth of the professions (both old and new), particularly since the second half of the twentieth century. Bernstein adds a third principle for distinguishing and organizing knowledge in the late twentieth century, which he describes as the generic mode. This relies less on the academic disciplines or applied academic disciplines for its knowledge base, and more on the principle of market relevance as the principle for selecting knowledge for fields of practice (Bernstein 2000: 53). The generic mode is elaborated below.

Singulars and the inner/outer distinction

The way in which knowledge is organized has implications for identities. Academic disciplines are strongly *classified* bodies of knowledge because they have strongly insulated boundaries between them. Each has a unique name (for example, physics or sociology), with specialized languages and rules that stipulate what is included as knowledge and how knowledge is to be created, specialized texts, rules of entry and rewards and punishments (Bernstein 2000: 52). Bernstein (2000: 52) says that: 'Singulars are, on the whole, narcissistic, oriented to their own development, protected by strong boundaries and hierarchies.' He argues that socialization (and hence personal identity) is expressed by loyalty to the academic discipline, which is a commitment to its 'otherness': 'The sacred face sets them apart, legitimises their otherness and creates dedicated identities with no reference other than to their calling' (Bernstein 2000: 54). Identities in singulars are formed by an inner orientation to knowledge, or an inner relation of meanings. This inner orientation becomes the basis for orienting practice in the outside world.

Bernstein (2000: 82) argues that the inner/outer distinction has its origins in religion, specifically Christianity, and that it is a 'doxic principle of European consciousness'. It was historically based on a dislocation between the inner (self) and (one's) outer (practice), in which an inner commitment to Christ was a precondition for living in the outside world. He says:

> Christianity drives a wedge between inner self and outer practice. It creates a gap which becomes the site for new awareness. To think and feel outside your culture and practice is intrinsically an abstract orientation.
>
> (Bernstein 2000: 83)[2]

Bernstein (2000: 82) argues that the inner/outer distinction was historically important in structuring singulars in the medieval university, so that the development of singulars that explored *the Word* ('grammar, logic and rhetoric') preceded those that explored *the World* ('arithmetic, astronomy, geometry and music'). The inner/outer distinction is also the basis upon which access to knowledge and different identities is distributed in society more broadly. Bernstein's (2003: 13) point is that class relations 'generate, distribute, reproduce and legitimate distinctive forms of communication, which transmit dominant and dominated codes, [so] ... that subjects are differentially positioned by these codes in the process of acquiring them'. Those who are inducted into singulars have a particular orientation to meanings and knowledge that is a consequence of the social division of labour – they are inducted into the 'otherness' of knowledge, while this access to the sacred is denied to others.

However, Bernstein (2000: 54) argues that singulars are 'like a coin with two faces, so that only one face can be seen at a time', because they are linked to the profane world. This must be so, because singulars must exist within the profane world, and rely on relations in the profane world for their existence. Beck (2002: 619) argues that Bernstein provides insights into the way in which an 'authentic inner dedication could co-exist (and had co-existed) with a finely honed capacity to protect self-interest where necessary' and 'that this did not *ipso facto* compromise the legitimacy of intellectuals of certain kinds seeing themselves as guardians of intrinsic educational values – rather, the reverse' (Beck 2002: 619). Beck and Young (2005: 186) argue that the sacred face of inner dedication is just as real as the profane face, with the latter often (although not exclusively) expressed as self interest, or more broadly, with 'mundane issues of economic existence and power struggles'. This means that practitioners of singulars can still have a real commitment to knowledge that is not reducible to their social interests or stakes in the struggle in the field.

Regions and the inner/outer distinction

The co-existence of the sacred and profane within the same modality of identity is useful for exploring identities within regions of knowledge. The classification of knowledge within regions is weaker, because the principle used to select and translate knowledge is the requirements of the field of practice and not the structure of knowledge itself (and its disciplinary classification). Beck and Young (2005: 187) explain that Bernstein did not specifically discuss the way the regionalization of knowledge impacted on identity formation in the 'traditional' professions. However, they use Bernstein's broader analysis to posit an 'inner/outer' relationship intrinsic to the formation of professional identities which is similar to practitioners of singulars (Beck and Young 2005: 187–88). They argue that in the traditional professions (for example, medicine and engineering) strong forms of inner dedication in professional identity arose because of the historical links between the professions and their knowledge bases (the singulars), their emphasis on collegiate autonomy, and collegiate control over training and admission to the profession. In this way they were able to define the boundaries of their knowledge base, the development and enforcement of codes of conduct and socialization within the profession. The result was '*the creation of a professional habitus*' (Beck and Young 2005: 188).

Grubb (2005: 4–5) provides insights into the relationship between the professions and their knowledge bases in explaining the rise of professional education in the United States. He explains that many professions did not require professional front-end qualifications until the end of the nineteenth century, and that previously professional education was acquired in multiple ways, including on-the-job training interspersed with continuing education. The growing authority of science accompanied the movement of the professions into university education, and 'Every profession created a liturgy about the importance of specialized knowledge. In turn, scientific knowledge brought with it the ability to benefit society and to serve one's clients better' (Grubb 2005: 5). Grubb says that these claims could and do seem self-serving in retrospect, but they also had substance because professionals were increasingly required to draw on abstract, theoretical bodies of knowledge that could not be acquired on the job or through daily practice (Grubb 2005: 5). So in some senses, the proliferation of singulars was directly related to the development of regions and both were based on an inner commitment to knowledge, although the nature of that commitment differed.

Genericism and the inner/outer distinction

Generic modes of knowledge differ. In Australia as in England, the origins of the generic mode lie in the human capital driven educational reforms in the 1980s. The first expression of the generic mode in these countries was the introduction of competency-based training models of curriculum in the further education sector in England (Jones and Moore 1995) and in the vocational education and training (VET) sector in Australia (Goozee 2001), but this is only one aspect of genericism. Genericism is a means of organizing and constituting curriculum and for establishing relations between various components. The purpose of genericism is oriented towards work, and the principle used to select knowledge is 'relevance' as defined by work. Genericism underpins the vocationalization of curriculum in all sectors of education, and is reflected in the emphasis on generic skills or attributes.

Genericism is based on a new concept of work and life in which every area of life is perpetually transformed, and the concept of trainability is now the key principle governing the construction of curriculum and pedagogy (Bernstein 2000: 59). Bernstein (2000: 50) explains that the process of perpetual re-formation 'Is based on the acquisition of generic modes which it is hoped will realise a flexible transferable potential rather than specific performances.' He argues, however, that generic capacities to be taught and 'trained' cannot be considered independently of the vocation or occupation for which individuals are preparing, because it is this that provides individuals with their identity and the context they need to make sense of these 'meta-thinking' and 'meta-learning' strategies (Bernstein 2000: 59). He explains that 'this identity arises out of a particular social order, through relations which the identity enters into with other identities of reciprocal recognition, support, mutual legitimisation and finally through a negotiated collective purpose' (Bernstein 2000: 59). Because the concept of 'trainability' is devoid of social content and divorced from vocations which are the basis of identity, there is now no framework in which actors can recognize themselves except through the:

> materialities of consumption, by its distributions, by its absences. Here the products of the market relay the signifiers whereby temporary stabilities, orientations, relations and evaluations are constructed.
>
> (Bernstein 2000: 59)

Bernstein (2000: 85–86) argues that the basis of knowledge creation for the last 1,000 years was a humanizing principle based on inner commitments to knowledge, first expressed as religious knowledge and replaced over time with secular knowledge. It has now been replaced by a new dehumanizing principle which is not inner commitments to fields of knowledge or fields of practice, but market utility. The principle used to select knowledge is its relevance as determined by the market, with knowledge valued insofar as it is valued by the market (Bernstein 2000: 55). Bernstein (2000: 86) argues that 'Knowledge, after nearly a thousand years, is divorced from inwardness and literally dehumanised.' This leads to the divorce of knowledge from knowers, and affects the way in which knowledge is produced and classified into different knowledge fields. Bernstein (2000: 86) argues that the commodification of knowledge which results from subordinating knowledge to markets 'disconnects inner from outer, as a precondition for constituting the outer and its practice, according to the market principles of the New Right'. Arguably, this commitment to markets is not unique to the New Right, as it characterizes human capital theories more broadly and is championed by labour governments as well as conservative governments in countries such as Australia, England and other Anglophone countries. It would perhaps be more correct to argue that the market principle does not so much sever the inner from the outer, as reverse the hierarchy so that the outer is now the principle of selection for the construction of the inner, a process that must lead to profound reshaping of the conditions of knowledge creation and the formation of identities.

The restructuring of the relationship between regions and singulars through the prism of the generic will potentially change the nature of both because genericism increasingly provides the context in which both must operate. Inner commitment is increasingly replaced by external accountabilities and audit and the development of subjectivities in which, as Ball (2003: 217) explains, individuals 'calculate about themselves, "add value" to themselves, improve their productivity, strive for excellence and live an existence of calculation'. The singulars will be weakened because their continued presence (particularly in the 'new' and less prestigious universities) will be determined by the call for relevance (defined as market relevance) and their unity will be fragmented (Beck and Young 2005: 189). This has had and will continue to have implications for pedagogic practice in all sectors of education by shaping the principles used to select and recontextualize knowledge for curriculum and consequently for the nature of the pedagogic device.

The structure of pedagogic discourse and power

Bernstein's key insight was that the structure of pedagogic discourse and the nature of pedagogic practices carry the message of power, as much as the content of pedagogic discourse. He criticized social reproduction theorists (such as Bourdieu and Bowles and Gintis) for focussing on the content of pedagogic discourse and not its structure. Such approaches reduce education to 'a carrier of power relations external to education' rather than exploring the way in which the structure of pedagogic discourse and practice are the mechanism 'whereby external power relations can be carried by it' (Bernstein 2000: 4). If the content of education is the message that is *relayed*, then the structure of pedagogic discourse is the *relay*. The pedagogic code refers to the way knowledge is classified and framed, while the pedagogic device refers to the distributive, recontextualizing and evaluative rules that mediate access to the pedagogic code. Bernstein (2000: 27) says that 'This device has internal rules which regulate the pedagogic communication which the device makes possible.'

The pedagogic code: the classification and framing of knowledge

Pedagogic discourses carry the message of power in the way knowledge is 'classified' and 'framed'. The relationship between the two can vary and in the process establish different relations of power and control. The classification of knowledge is concerned with the 'what' of knowledge, and it is an expression of relations of power because it is associated with the power to define 'what counts' and how it is to be differentiated. For this reason, Bernstein called the classification of knowledge the *voice* of power. Boundaries refer to the way in which contexts are defined, differentiated and insulated from each other. Power is thus concerned with the relations *between* boundaries (Bernstein 2000: 5). Moreover, relations within boundaries are also defined by determining knowledge that is included and excluded. Academic disciplines are strongly classified bodies of knowledge because they have strongly insulated boundaries between them.

Framing regulates forms of interaction and the locus of control over who can speak, and the pace, sequence and form of this interaction. The way in which knowledge is framed is structured by social relations of control. It is the 'how' of knowledge, and 'it establishes legitimate forms of communication appropriate to the different categories. Control carries the boundary relations of power and socialises individuals into these boundaries' (Bernstein 2000: 5). The way knowledge is framed shapes the way the voice of power is expressed. It shapes the form the voice takes and way the 'message' of power is realized. For this reason, Bernstein refers to the framing of knowledge as the *message* of power.

Bernstein distinguishes between relations of power (the classification of knowledge) and relations of control (the framing of knowledge) even though in practice the latter is always the means through which the former is realized (Bernstein 2003: 23). This is because classification determines *what* can be expressed, but framing determines *how* it is expressed. However, it is necessary to distinguish between the two because 'the what' can be classified (insulated) more or less strongly and 'the how' can be framed (expressed) more or less strongly. Different relations between classification and framing are therefore possible. This is important because in speaking in different ways, the message has the potential to transform the voice. This means that 'Voice sets limits to message but ... message becomes a means of change of voice' (Bernstein 2003: 23). In other words, whilst relations of power are established through the classification of boundaries, the way in which social practices operate within these boundaries has the potential to alter the relations of power. Thus, while power and control are analytically distinct, each is embedded in the other and requires the other for its realization (Bernstein 2000: 5). The 'elaborated pedagogic code' refers to the strength of the internal and external relations of classification and framing and 'variation in the strength of classification and framing values generates different modalities of pedagogic practice' (Bernstein 2000: 100).

Knowledge can be externally and internally strongly or weakly classified and externally and internally strongly or weakly framed. Strongly classified knowledge means that knowledge learnt within the educational institution is strongly distinguished from knowledge of the everyday world, and knowledge is presented in disciplinary frameworks that are distinguished from each other. Bernstein (2003) explains that early schooling often classifies knowledge weakly, but this becomes progressively stronger throughout secondary school, particularly in senior secondary school. This refers to the external relations of classification. Knowledge is also internally classified within categories: 'We could talk about the relation between objects, between tasks and between persons within a classroom ... In this way power relations give rise to boundary rules and so to classificatory principles' (Bernstein 2000: 99).

Strong internal framing vests control in the teacher, whereas strong external framing sharply distinguishes between the pedagogic context and activities and the external context, so that the family, community, or workplace does not overlap with the educational institution (Bernstein 2000: 99). Strongly framed pedagogic practice locates the locus of control over the pacing, sequencing and evaluation of knowledge with the teacher, whereas weakly framed practice provides students with more *apparent* control. Different aspects of pedagogic practice can be strongly or weakly framed; for example, pacing and sequencing may be weakly framed giving students more control over the learning process, while evaluation may be strongly framed (Morais and Neves 2001).

The classification and structuring of knowledge in curriculum is an important focus of analysis because it has an inner logic and emergent properties that are implicated in power, particularly through the access curriculum provides to 'orientations to meanings'. The orientations to meanings that are associated with power are the capacity to use abstract, decontextualized knowledge, rather than specific knowledge content that is a product of disciplinary knowledge. This means that altering the content of the curriculum so it is more 'progressive' does not necessarily alter the principles of classification and framing, and thereby the relations of power. Arnot and Reay (2006: 92) explain that: 'The tragedy of democratically inspired pedagogies is likely to be their lack of consequence in being able to challenge classification structures'. Apparently progressive pedagogies that *appear* to weaken the relations of classification and framing by blurring the boundaries between home and the educational institution do not necessarily alter the relations of power either, because they render the boundaries between different kinds of knowledge (and contexts) opaque, in ways that make it more difficult for working-class students to recognize (Bernstein 2000, 2003). This point is further elaborated below.

The pedagogic device and the construction of pedagogic discourses

Bernstein (2000: 202) says that the pedagogic device is 'the condition for the construction of pedagogic discourses'. The pedagogic device reproduces or transforms power relations in education by mediating the way knowledge is distributed, recontextualized and evaluated in curriculum. Bernstein (2000: 202) refers to the ensemble of distributive, recontextualizing and evaluative rules as the pedagogic device. This ensemble generates pedagogic discourses, codes and practices (Singh 2002). Singh (2002: 572) explains that Bernstein's notion of the pedagogic device can be used to analyse 'the processes by which discipline-specific or domain-specific expert knowledge is converted or pedagogised to constitute school knowledge'.

The distributive, recontextualizing and evaluative rules of the pedagogic device relate to three respective arenas or fields (Bernstein 2000: 202). The first field is the field of knowledge production which usually (but not exclusively) takes place in universities and other private and public research institutions. The second field is the recontextualizing field which consists of two components. The first is the 'official' recontextualizing field (ORF) comprising government education departments 'created and dominated by the state for the construction and surveillance of state pedagogic discourse' (Bernstein 2000: 115). The ORF is, to a greater or lesser extent, in conflict with the 'pedagogic' recontextualizing field (PRF) which consists of university-based teacher education departments, curriculum writers, educational journals and papers and their readerships, and others outside the official recontextualizing field who are implicated in the construction of pedagogic discourses (Bernstein 2000: 115). The third field is the field of reproduction which refers to the reproduction of knowledge in curriculum in educational institutions. Knowledge that is reproduced in curriculum undergoes another process of recontextualization as it is 'appropriated by teachers and converted into modes of common or shared classroom knowledge in interactions with students' (Singh 2002: 577). The field of knowledge production consequently creates discourses, the recontextualizing field transmits them, and the reproduction field is concerned with their acquisition (Bernstein 2000: 37). Bernstein (2000: 202–3) explains that the rules of the pedagogic device are not the same as the pedagogic code (relations of classification and framing): 'rules are not codes but [are] the *resources* for codes, differently resourced by different groups realizing different distributions of power and principles of control'.

The pedagogic device: distributive rules

Distributive rules provide different levels of access to abstract and decontextualized meanings to students depending on their social background. They do this in two ways. The first is by providing a school environment that is culturally congruent with the home environment of middle-class students where children are inducted into abstract decontextualized language and meanings from an early age (Hasan 2001). Arnot and Reay (2004: 149) explain that the curriculum cannot be wholly acquired at school and that 'Middle-class homes tend to provide an effective second site of acquisition with effective official pedagogic context and support'. Second, Bernstein (2003: 77) argues that schools with high proportions of working-class students are more likely to 'stress operations, local skills rather than the exploration of principles and general skills, and the pacing is likely to be weakened'. Alternatively, a variety of stratifying measures are used in areas where the social catchment is mixed. Bourne (2003) illustrates the way in which apparently 'student-centred' approaches exclude some students from such access by deeming some students to be 'ready' to engage in abstract and decontextualized meanings while others are deemed not ready. She says that students' attainment is 'biologised' in this way (Bourne 2003, 2004).

Teese (2000: 178) illustrates the way in which these stratifying processes interact with social backgrounds to result in different orientations to abstract knowledge (in this case mathematics) and a different positioning of the self in relation to this knowledge. While Teese did not explicitly invoke Bernstein in this example, it is nonetheless an implicit Bernsteinian analysis and illustrates the way in which Bernstein's conceptual language is capable of 'translation' into a language of description that explains different outcomes in education.[3] Teese found different orientations to mathematical knowledge within and between groups of students undertaking the three mathematics subjects in the Victorian Certificate of Education (the senior school certificate) in Australia. These subjects are hierarchically organized from the 'least' to the 'most' difficult mathematics. Those students who were doing well within each subject were more likely to agree with the proposition that mathematics is a scientific discipline compared to those who were not doing well, and with the metaphor that the mathematics classroom is a laboratory where students learn to use tools. The proportion within each group who agreed with this proposition was highest in the most difficult mathematics subject, and it was lowest in the least difficult mathematics group. Teese says that the highest overall proportion agreeing with this statement were students taking the two most difficult mathematics subjects together as part of their senior school certificate, and would have been higher still had it not been for:

> the behaviour of the elite male students in this stream. For 13 per cent of them deserted the laboratory in favour of a truly aristocratic image. Their mathematics classroom was a 'studio in which you learn to be an artist'.
>
> (Teese 2000: 178)

In contrast, those who were not doing well within each group were more likely to agree with metaphors that conveyed empty purpose and authoritarian social relations: 'No research setting, the mathematics classroom was to many a place of work where repetitive operations were performed on instruction from superiors' (Teese 2000: 178). The proportion within each group who agreed with this proposition and in so doing 'declare themselves office workers or factory hands' was highest with the group undertaking the least difficult mathematics and lowest in the group undertaking the most difficult mathematics (Teese 2000: 180). Teese (2000: 180) explains that students agreeing with this imagery 'had not succeeded in taking possession of mathematics at its interior. Like consumers, they could only handle the products of mathematical thought – the algorithms – not drive the processes.'

Those undertaking the least difficult mathematics were more likely than students in the other two groups to report that the pace of instruction was too fast and that they couldn't understand what was asked of them, demonstrating that the way in which mathematics was framed excluded them. This was so even though there had been reductions in content and difficulty in the mathematics they were asked to do compared to the other two groups (Teese 2000: 181). Achievement in mathematics was stratified by social background with those in the lowest socio-economic groups most likely to drop mathematics, to undertake the least difficult mathematics subjects, and to achieve the lowest results in each mathematics group (Teese 2000: 184). Teese (2000: 184) explains that:

> It is a measure of the implicit cultural homogeneity of the mathematics curriculum as a whole – based on sequenced and overlapping content and a shared conceptual emphasis – that the average social level of students rose at each level of performance, not only in the one preparatory subject, but in each mathematics subject.

The pedagogic device: recontextualizing rules

Recontextualization rules regulate the work of those constructing pedagogic discourses, and in so doing underpin the construction of the 'what' and 'how' of pedagogic discourse (relations of classification and framing) (Bernstein 2000: 115). Recontextualization rules determine what knowledge is to be selected from the field in which it was produced and translated to pedagogic knowledge and practice. They give rise to a recontextualizing principle which is the principle used to *delocate* knowledge from the field in which it was produced and practised to *relocate* it in curriculum (Bernstein 2000: 113–14). When knowledge is selected and reshaped through curriculum it is always with principles that differ from the way in which it was produced. For example, the entire field of physics cannot be reproduced within the physics curriculum; there must be principles used to select knowledge and relocate it in curriculum.

The recontextualizing principle mediates the way knowledge is classified by disciplinary or non-disciplinary frameworks and the way in which it is framed by competing perspectives about human nature and the purpose of education. Bernstein (2000: 33) explains that 'Pedagogic discourse is constructed by a recontextualizing principle which selectively appropriates, relocates, refocuses and relates other discourses to constitute its own order.'

The principles used to construct the curriculum are the instructional discourse. It is the principle used to decide 'what matters' in curriculum. However, 'what matters' is always tied to 'why it matters', and this is tied to the type of person envisaged by pedagogic discourse. The 'why it matters' is underpinned by rules of social order which Bernstein (2000: 13) refers to as the regulative discourse. He argues that the instructional discourse is thus embedded within the regulative discourse. The instructional discourse will generate rules around the selection, sequencing, pacing and evaluation of knowledge (the way knowledge is framed), but this will be according to principles of the social order (the regulative discourse).

Dewey provides a good example of this when he explains that educational theory historically has been marked by the opposition between those who believe education is developmental by helping individuals to realize their inherent capacities on the one hand, and on the other, beliefs that individuals must be changed from without by 'overcoming natural inclination and substituting in its place habits acquired under external pressure' (Dewey 1938: 17). Each frames knowledge differently depending on their underlying assumptions about human beings. The former is less concerned with comparisons and more focussed on individual development, while the latter is more concerned with selection, ranking and comparison against external benchmarks. When he was the Australian conservative Federal Minister for Education from 2001 until the end of 2005, Dr Brendan Nelson provided a very good example of the way instructional discourses are embedded within the regulative discourse with his insistence that schools grade students against national criteria which included failing grades (so that some students must fail). He insisted that students be ranked by quartiles both within their class and within their state. He explained in a radio interview that: 'The nature of life itself is that all of us are being compared to one another' (Nelson 2005). He went on to say that parents are looking to schools to foster discipline and to explicitly teach values – that is, discipline and values external to students.

Instructional and regulative discourses can vary in the strength of their framing so that there may be 'weak framing of regulative discourse and strong framing of instructional discourse' (Bernstein 2000: 13). Bernstein says, though, that where there is weak framing of instructional discourses, there is always weak framing of regulative discourses, and that such relations are most likely to result in an 'invisible' pedagogy, based on implicit and opaque rules (Bernstein 2000: 13–14). This is because weak framing of instructional discourses results in apparent greater control by students and this does not align with regulative discourses that seek to shape students by external and authoritarian means.

The pedagogic device: evaluative rules

Evaluative rules are used to evaluate students. Bernstein (2000: 115) explains that the evaluative rules regulate 'pedagogic practice at the classroom level, for they define the standards which must be reached'. Students must demonstrate they can produce the required 'text' called for by the implementation of the pedagogic code (that is, students implicitly understand the assessment process and how to produce the 'right' outcome). The extent to which they can do so depends on the extent to which they have the necessary 'recognition and realization rules'. Students need to *recognize* the *type* of knowledge they are dealing with. They need to know, for example, that they are now speaking psychology and not sociology, or chemistry and not biology. This is not just a question of identifying and understanding specialized knowledge, but also of understanding knowledge as contextualized within its disciplinary system of meaning and decoding it.

Bernstein argues that the capacity to 'recognize' the nature of knowledge being studied is associated with a student's experience *beyond* education, and the extent to which the underlying principles of knowledge selection, conceptualization and abstraction are part of a student's repertoire. Moreover, students may be able to recognize the appropriate form of knowledge, but may be unable to *realize* or produce the required assessment. For example, a student may be able to recognize when they are 'speaking' physics or mathematics, but may not have internalized the rules they need to 'realize' the required assessment outcome. They may not understand the implicit rules they must obey when they are to be assessed. The operation of recognition and realization rules is at the level of the acquirer and students are evaluated on the extent to which they have successfully internalized them. The struggle between the official recontextualizing field and the pedagogic recontextualizing field is, ultimately, over the evaluation rules because, as Bernstein (2000: 36) explains 'This is what the device is about. Evaluation condenses the meaning of the whole device ... The purpose of the device is to provide a symbolic ruler for consciousness.'

Implications for curriculum

The implications for curriculum arising from Bernstein's analysis are that students need access to disciplinary knowledge as the means by which they are provided with access to powerful knowledge. Curriculum must be premised on helping students to acquire the capacity to recognize the boundaries between different kinds of knowledge, and to use (realize) disciplinary meanings appropriately as they progress from school to tertiary education. Social access to abstract, decontextualized language and concepts is mediated by epistemic access, but in turn epistemic access is mediated in different ways depending on the way the discourse is structured in curriculum. Hierarchical and horizontal knowledge structures must be differentiated in curriculum and pedagogic practice, because as Muller (2006a: 72) explains 'different knowledge structures have different curricular specificatory requirements'.

Similarly in discussing teaching in universities, Neumann *et al.* (2002) argue that the disciplines differ in their teaching and learning processes. They say that 'pure' and 'applied' and 'hard' and 'soft' disciplines are distinguished (broadly speaking) by the social purpose of the discipline, the structure of knowledge, the cognitive demands made on students, the kinds of outcomes that are expected and associated teaching, learning and assessment practices. They argue that ignoring these differences between the disciplines by trying to fit them all into one mould by, for example, stipulating the same approaches to assessment or course design may undermine learning rather than enhance it (Neumann *et al.* 2002: 414).

Knowledge that is strongly classified and framed provides signals to students that help them to develop the recognition and realization rules they need to navigate the boundaries between different kinds of knowledge effectively. This is the basis of a 'mixed pedagogy', which is, as Muller (2004: 6) explains, an approach that draws together Bernsteinian scholars who emphasize different political concerns. It includes those concerned with the development of the individual and their 'competence' on the one hand, and on the other, those who are theorizing the elements of a 'radical visible pedagogy'. 'Mixed pedagogy' as an approach emphasizes the importance of making the boundaries between different kinds of knowledge clear to students as a condition for equitable access to the specialized identities that schools distribute by the way they mediate access to abstract, decontextualized knowledge. Muller (2004: 6) explains that: 'this mixed form will have crucial dimensions that must be visible; that is, strongly classified or framed (the foremost contender currently being the explicitness of evaluation criteria), as well as crucial ones that are most effective when weakly classified and framed.' Aspects of framing that may be more weakly framed are the sequencing and pacing of knowledge thus giving students more control over processes of learning, and strong framing over assessment to make the assessment tasks and criteria explicit.[4]

Weakly classified knowledge in curriculum at school, VET and higher education potentially disadvantages students from working-class backgrounds because, as discussed earlier, they do not always have the 'recognition and realization' rules they need to distinguish between different kinds of knowledge and the kinds of practices that are required in each. It is true that the boundaries of knowledge can be rendered opaque for all students by the way in which curriculum is structured, particularly if the emphasis is on contextualized learning and/or problem-focussed curricular approaches. But even here middle-class students are advantaged compared to working-class students within such approaches because they are more able to distinguish between abstract, decontextualized language and the context in which it is being applied in curriculum that emphasizes the contextual and situated.

Students are also denied access to the boundaries between different kinds of knowledge and the capacity to navigate them when they are tracked into more vocationally oriented programmes that are based on blurring the distinction between theoretical and everyday knowledge. This is often the case for students who are academically 'weaker' and is based on two assumptions: first, that they will find such programs more relevant to their everyday lives and their aspirations for a job; the second is the belief that such students will be more motivated by a vocational curriculum than an academic one (Young 2006c: 58). But, asks Young (2006c: 59) 'do learners with limited knowledge of language or mathematics in practice find it easier to apply such knowledge than to acquire it in the first place?' He says the evidence is that they do not, and programs that emphasize 'key skills' in contrast to subject knowledge are not a sound basis for progression to higher levels of learning, particularly in progressing to higher education.

In his critique of school curriculum, Freebody (2006: 25) argues that school subjects which use multi-disciplinary or inter-disciplinary approaches do not always have a discernible relationship to the disciplines to which they are related, and consequently cannot provide students with criteria to determine 'instances of good, bad and indifferent' applications of this knowledge. Moreover, he argues that inter-disciplinarity requires of both teachers and students 'an even more sophisticated grasp of disciplinary knowledge (and of disciplinarity as a pragmatic, recruit-able resource) than does "straight-ahead" higher-classified disciplinary teaching and learning' (Freebody 2006: 25). He argues this is an irony because it is precisely these sorts of programs that are offered to academically weaker students, and we know they are more likely to be working-class students.

Conclusion

It is sometimes difficult to distinguish between the *production* and *reproduction* of knowledge in Bernstein's work. The line between the two is distinguishable (as Bernstein demonstrates), but it is iterative, and the way in which knowledge is produced has implications for the way in which it is reproduced in universities, VET and schools. However, such a distinction can be difficult because the concepts of classification and framing are fundamental to exploring both the production and reproduction of disciplinary knowledge, and to the distinction between singular, regional and generic modes of knowledge organization. The way in which disciplines are insulated from each other and the structure of knowledge within each has implications for the way in which knowledge is produced and reproduced, and for the way in which knowledge is recontextualized inwardly (as in the academic disciplines) and outwards to fields of practice. Bernstein (2000: 99) explains that 'Classification holds together, in one concept, horizontal relations and vertical or hierarchical relations.'

The outcomes of this chapter are to demonstrate that abstract knowledge is the site for society's conversation about itself, and therefore that access to such knowledge is a question of distributional justice. Bernstein's analysis of vertical and horizontal discourses helps us to understand that a key purpose of education is to induct students into vertical discourses, because this is the key location in which students are inducted into 'systems of meaning'. His analysis establishes the importance of structuring knowledge in curriculum so that it is accessible to students so they can navigate between different types of knowledge and use them appropriately. The structuring of knowledge in curriculum matters as much as the content of curriculum. The next chapter considers in more depth the implications of Bernstein's analysis for the structure of curriculum. It argues that Bernstein's analysis can be strengthened by exploring the epistemic relations of knowledge, because students' social access to knowledge is mediated by their epistemic access.

3 Evaluation and critique

A modified Bernsteinian basis for curriculum

Introduction

This chapter evaluates and critiques Bernstein's analysis of the structures of knowledge and the way knowledge is produced. It argues that Bernstein's analysis of the social relations of knowledge needs to be extended to include the epistemic relations of knowledge to allow an analysis of the way in which knowledge is co-determined by both. Bernstein's analysis of vertical and horizontal discourses allows him to develop a rich and differentiated account of the social relations of knowledge, but he is less able to distinguish the different ways in which the epistemic relations of vertical discourses may be structured beyond his analysis of hierarchical and horizontal knowledge structures and strong and weak grammars. His relative neglect of the epistemic relations of knowledge leaves him without criteria for judging the epistemic claims of theories, particularly within hierarchical knowledge structures. His analysis needs to be extended because the curriculum has to be underpinned by a theory of epistemology as well as a sociological analysis of the conditions of knowledge, because epistemology provides the basis for considering questions about the objectivity and possibility of truthfulness of knowledge. This is critical realism's contribution and is why critical realism complements Bernstein's approach.

This chapter extends Bernstein's analysis by drawing on critical realism to argue that the epistemic relations of vertical discourses can be differentiated by the extent to which they objectively orient towards their object of study, even though the resulting knowledge is fallible. The first section demonstrates that Bernstein's relative neglect of the epistemic relations of knowledge is as a consequence of his rationalist ontological premise. It results in overly homogenized accounts of knowledge structures, particularly hierarchical knowledge structures, while his analysis of horizontal knowledge structures is more nuanced. It argues that we need to distinguish approaches within disciplines as well as between disciplines and Moore and Maton's (2001) notion of the epistemic device is one way we can do this. The second section illustrates the way in which the epistemic relations of knowledge within hierarchical knowledge structures can and should be differentiated by drawing on Moore's (2004) analysis of normative and naturalized epistemologies. This section also uses Collier's (2003) critical realist analysis to ground the objectivity of knowledge. The final section argues that an integrated analysis of the way knowledge is co-determined by its social and epistemic relations provides more robust grounds for critiquing curriculum and for analysing the boundaries between the sacred and profane and their relationship within curriculum.

The need for a focus on the epistemic

A commitment to the objectivity and truthfulness of knowledge as the basis for curriculum is fundamental if students are to be provided with the knowledge they need to engage with the natural and social worlds, and to participate in debates and controversies within their intended field of practice and in society's conversation more broadly. Moore (2004: 147) explains that 'a curriculum is an organization of knowledge involving the selection of content and *also* the structuring of the relationships within the content'. He argues we must also be concerned with the way knowledge is produced as well as the way in which it is reproduced in curriculum because the two are related (Moore 2004: 148). Relationships between different elements of curriculum are structured (implicitly or explicitly) by a theory of knowledge or epistemology. Epistemology is concerned with the possibility of the truth of knowledge claims, even if these claims are revisable in the light of new evidence. Judgements are based on epistemological claims because 'Epistemology is concerned to establish how we can come to hold beliefs that (a) are believed to be true, (b) are in fact true and (c) can be demonstrated to be true' (Moore 2004: 157). Curriculum needs to provide students with access to these three criteria so they develop the capacity to judge the objectivity of knowledge. This is in contrast to traditional conservatism in which the purpose is to transmit knowledge as unquestioned universal truths. Providing students with the capacity to apply these criteria helps them to develop a critical approach to knowledge so that they may test and demonstrate the objectivity and truthfulness of knowledge.

Bernstein's analysis needs to be extended to include the epistemic relations of knowledge to permit a focus on the *aboutness* of knowledge – the relationship between knowledge and the object that that knowledge is about. While Bernstein turned his attention to knowledge structures towards the end of his life, his emphasis was still on the social relations of knowledge rather than the aboutness of knowledge. This is because he was using the sociology of knowledge as his lens, and this necessarily focusses on the social conditions of knowledge rather than its epistemic conditions. Moore and Maton (2001: 154) explain that 'studying the *production* of knowledge brings to light a new issue: the basis of knowledge claims'. They argue that the trajectory of Bernstein's work was leading in this direction.

Critical realism and Bernstein can inform each other because each focusses on a different aspect of knowledge. Bernstein's analysis of the structures of knowledge focusses on an aspect of knowledge that is not sufficiently acknowledged by critical realism, which is the way in which these structures are related to socially powerful knowledge and the way access to such knowledge is distributed. In illustrating the causal and emergent properties of knowledge structures, Bernstein introduces a novel argument that could enrich critical realist arguments about knowledge. Critical realists mostly focus on the emergent properties of the *content* of knowledge or the relationship between particular concepts within a theory.[1] Fairclough *et al.* (2002: 9) are an exception to this when they say that 'critical realism has tended to operate with an insufficiently concrete and complex analysis of semiosis. It has tended to take symbol systems, language, orders of discourse and so on for granted, thereby excluding central features of the social world from its analysis.'

Beck and Young (2005: 185) explain that Bernstein was less concerned with the internal content of disciplinary knowledge, and that he was agnostic about their epistemological standing. Moore (2004: 142) argues that Bernstein's insistence that theories generate languages of description about their objects of study 'in such a way that the theory is independently tested against reality and open to modification in light of that testing' means that Bernstein was insisting on 'an external *ontological* imperative'. Moore's argument is convincing, but this is an area where Bernstein's argument was implicit and underdeveloped, because his focus was on the structures of knowledge that he considered to be independent of the content of knowledge.

Arguably, Bernstein's focus on the structures of knowledge arises from the rationalist premise he shares with Durkheim.[2] Both find the distinctiveness of theoretical knowledge in the universal distinction between sacred and profane forms of knowledge and systems of meaning characteristic of all human societies (Durkheim 1967; Bernstein 2000; Young 2008a, 2008b).[3] The nature of this distinction provides sacred knowledge with its context-independent properties. This means that the *objects* of sacred or esoteric knowledge recede in importance relative to the *structures* of knowledge. The structures of knowledge have a *sui generis* independence from the objects of knowledge; it is the structures of knowledge that are real and it is these that are the generative mechanism for the production of new knowledge. The content of knowledge becomes arbitrary. Bernstein (2000: 29) illustrates this when he says that the 'line between these two classes of knowledge is relative to any given period' with the consequence that 'the content of these classes varies historically and culturally'. He argues 'that these two classes of knowledge are intrinsic to language itself; it is the very nature of language that makes these classes possible' (Bernstein 2000: 28–29). Bernstein locates the historic origin of the codes structuring each class of knowledge and the relations of classification and framing intrinsic to them in the fields of symbolic control which were the kinship and religious systems. This is so even though 'the *location* of codes lie in the class regulation of forms of social relationships *and* distribution of activities' (Bernstein 2000: 176). This establishes 'the word' as the basis for 'the world', but it also provides the 'space' for the world to change the word, as illustrated in the previous chapter that discussed the relationship between relations of power (relations of classification) and relations of control (relations of framing).

The epistemic relations of knowledge raise important problems for curriculum about the basis for knowledge claims and the way in which knowledge should be structured. Along with Durkheim, Bernstein's emphasis on the structures of knowledge treats current disciplinary divisions as a given, and as a consequence this must constrain the development of knowledge if the current boundaries set the possible degrees of freedom. Young (2008a: Chapter 3) explains that while Durkheim has made a fundamental contribution to understanding the nature of knowledge, Durkheim (and arguably Bernstein) is not able to explain the way in which (or why) knowledge changed from religious to scientific knowledge, how knowledge became increasingly differentiated, and why abstract thought and scientific knowledge expanded dramatically from The Enlightenment. Neither Durkheim nor Bernstein are able to provide criteria for determining changes that should be supported and changes that should be opposed to the development of knowledge and its structures and neither can they if the content of sacred and profane knowledge is arbitrary. This is because their main emphasis is on the way social relations are implicated in structuring knowledge and less on the aboutness of knowledge or the relationship between knowledge and its object. A focus on the aboutness of knowledge provides some basis for exploring changes within and between disciplinary boundaries as our knowledge of the world changes.

Bernstein presents a comprehensive analysis of the different ways in which the social relations of knowledge can be constituted, but he does not offer a similar analysis of the different ways the epistemic relations of knowledge can be constituted. For example, as discussed in the previous chapter, Bernstein demonstrates that there are epistemic consequences that arise from the social structuring of knowledge in his analysis of vertical and horizontal discourses because each is accessed and acquired in different ways. Similarly, an exploration of the epistemic relations of knowledge reveals that there are implications for the social relations of knowledge. This is because, as critical realists argue, the nature of the object determines the methods that we use to explore it, and this rules some knowledge producing social practices in and others out; it is not a case of 'anything goes' (Bhaskar 1998d). For example, Groff (2008: 4) argues that a commitment to the realist ontological premise that the world exists objectively independently of our thoughts of it – that is, it is not 'construed' by the way we understand it – precludes relativism about knowledge, for if the world is as it is 'then all competing claims about it cannot be equally sound'. An analysis of the epistemic relations allows a more nuanced understanding of the social relations of knowledge production by revealing that, while the structures of knowledge are an important causal mechanism, so too are the specific social practices used to produce and access that knowledge. This allows these specific social practices to be evaluated according to the epistemic access they provide to the objects of their knowledge. It asks questions about the extent to which those practices produce knowledge that is objective and true, as far as we know.

Bernstein's focus on the structures of knowledge means that he restricts his critique to relativist disciplines with weak grammars. He has no grounds for critiquing knowledge structures with strong grammars or for evaluating the knowledge claims they make. Bernstein (2000: 166) foregrounds the structures of knowledge at the expense of the objects of knowledge and the methods used to access that knowledge when he cites Popper to argue that there 'are no differences between the Social and Natural sciences'. As a consequence, the phenomena being studied (that the natural and social sciences research) is 'irrelevant to the question of the status of knowledge'. He argues that while the natural and social sciences have, for the most part, similar methods, the social sciences have in common with the humanities a similar organization of knowledge because they are constituted as serial languages (Bernstein 2000: 166). Bernstein has here posited equivalences of method between the natural and social sciences (including those with weak grammars) by a sleight of hand. He assumes that the methods of the social sciences and the natural sciences are the same and then dismisses this as an issue (or a source of differentiation).

This does not logically flow from his broader analysis in which he argues that a problem with disciplines with weak grammars is their incommensurable ontological and epistemological assumptions, and this means that the *methods* they use are also in contention. Acquiring the capacity to distinguish between serial languages within a discipline through the prism of the 'gaze' one has adopted as one's own (Bernstein 2000: 164) also entails the capacity to distinguish between the different methods of exploration each uses. While sociology may be one of the more extreme examples of disciplines with weak grammars, sociology students are inducted early on into debates about whether sociology is a science (Giddens 1993: 20) and ensuing debates about quantitative and qualitative research methods. For example, Spratt (2003: 236) informs students in an introductory chapter on social research methods that 'Understanding research methods also involves understanding theories of knowledge and philosophical standpoints.'

Asserting the commensurability of methods between the natural and social sciences provides Bernstein with the basis for arguing that the differences between hierarchical and horizontal knowledge structures must arise from the different structures of knowledge and grammars associated with each, because that is the key way in which they can be differentiated. This approach tends to produce over-homogenized accounts of disciplines with strong grammars as well as those with weak grammars, and in particular, his account of hierarchical knowledge structures (such as physics) seems to be over-homogenized.[4] We need to account for the paradigm shifts in the natural sciences as well as the incremental growth of knowledge in these fields through processes of incorporation, integration and abstraction (Chalmers 1999).

We also need to account for variation within knowledge structures with weak grammars. For example, in contrast to the pervasiveness of relativism within sociology in countries such as England, Australia and Continental Europe, Porpora (2008) argues that sociology in the United States is still (mostly) deeply empiricist and based on positivist notions of causality. Moore and Muller (2002: 630) say that Bernstein's rather pessimistic account of the discipline of sociology is 'on the face of it, quite unable to account both for the originality of Bernstein's own corpus or for the way in which it has developed and become modified over time'. They argue that embedded in Bernstein's account 'is a normative model for transition to a strong grammar' and that 'sociology will only survive if it makes this transition' (Moore and Muller 2002: 631). Bernstein's approach may be a distinct language within the sociology of education, but it is a language with a strong grammar and so differs from relativist approaches. It also provides a good example of the way sociology can be structured, but this argument will not be won unless it can be demonstrated that such approaches provide superior epistemic access to their objects of study.

The need to distinguish between disciplines and within disciplines

A mechanism is therefore needed to distinguish between disciplines and to distinguish between different approaches within disciplines, recognizing that these are different levels of analysis. This provides us with the basis for critiquing the way knowledge is produced and subsequently recontextualized in curriculum and for developing criteria to support change. Moore and Maton's (2001) notion of the epistemic device is one way we can do so. It is helpful to use their notion of the epistemic device to characterize the principle of knowledge legitimation as a *tendency* that operates at the level of the discipline rather than a law that governs everything that happens within disciplines. It is also helpful to think of Bernstein's characterization of the processes (social relations) that contribute to structuring hierarchical and horizontal knowledge structures (and those with strong and weak grammars) as tendencies. So too are the existing structures of knowledge – hierarchical knowledge structures provide the conditions by which new knowledge is produced and the structure it will take, and horizontal knowledge structures do likewise. This is not tautological – we would need to analyse what it is about these structures that contribute to producing new knowledge in its own likeness – its rules, methods of knowledge production and so forth. So the principle of knowledge legitimation and the processes that contribute to the structuring of knowledge produce tendencies – at the level of the discipline – that account for whether it is structured as hierarchical or horizontal knowledge, and in the case of the latter, whether it is constructed as serial language with a strong or weak grammar. A discipline therefore can be characterized by a weak grammar overall, but particular approaches within the discipline can still be characterized by strong grammars. This means that while the principle of knowledge legitimation and the structure, grammar and social relations of knowledge contribute to the structuring and organization of knowledge within a discipline, they do not determine all approaches within that discipline. This is able to account for Bernstein's strong language of description and strong grammar within a discipline that is structured through serial, largely incommensurable, languages and weak grammars.

To put this in the language of critical realism; Bernstein has identified generative mechanisms and their causal properties that (in part) shape the creation of new knowledge which is the structure and grammar of the discourse, and this has been further developed by Moore and Maton (2001) with their analysis of the epistemic device that governs the principle of knowledge legitimation. However, these generative mechanisms and their causal properties interact in necessary and contingent ways with other generative mechanisms in open social systems so that their effect is always moderated. One such mechanism (amongst others) is the existence of knowledge structures with strong grammars that act as exemplars to practitioners in disciplines with weak grammars. This is because (in this example) generative mechanisms are mediated by agency. Another is interdisciplinary cooperation as the complex objects or phenomena they study necessitates multiple disciplinary insights (Bhaskar and Danermark 2006). While disciplines are bounded, they are not hermetically sealed. As is explained in the next two chapters, critical realists seek to identify generative mechanisms and their causal powers and the *tendencies* they produce when actualized, rather than rigid laws of development that predict outcomes (Sayer 1992, 2000; Bhaskar 1998d). To describe the structures of knowledge, their grammars and their underpinning legitimating principles as causal mechanisms that produce tendencies when actualized in no way diminishes their importance. Rather, it extends the reach of these concepts by allowing us to account for instances where different outcomes result because of the interplay of a variety of causal mechanisms.

Young and Muller (2007: 189) also propose a method of distinguishing between and within disciplines. They explain that the principle of verticality is a categorical one that can be used to consign 'knowledge structures to either a theory-integrating or a theory-proliferating category. On the other hand, grammaticality is an ordinal principle, constructing a continuum of grammaticality within each category, or perhaps across the entire spectrum' (Young and Muller 2007: 189). So disciplines are categorized by whether they are a theory-integrating discipline (a vertical discourse with a hierarchical structure), or by whether they are a theory-proliferating discipline (a vertical discourse with a horizontal knowledge structure which is structured as serial languages). The strength or weakness of the grammar within each discipline can vary within and between disciplines, and so it can differ in degree – and thus be counted as an ordinal principle. This is able to explain the existence of Bernstein's own approach within the discipline of sociology. However, they explain that this does not solve all the problems with Bernstein's approach and they propose a model drawn from Cassirer who 'classifies different types of objectivity, according to the relationship that the concepts of knowledge form have to their object' rather than classifying knowledge structures (Young and Muller 2007: 196). The next section explores the objectivity of knowledge, and argues that Bernstein's analysis could be extended by incorporating critical realist notions of the objectivity of knowledge.

The objectivity of knowledge

The objectivity of knowledge is a key question for curriculum because it concerns the extent to which knowledge provides students with access to the objects that

that knowledge is about. Objective knowledge is objective precisely because it reveals properties of the object that it is about (Collier 2003). Criteria are needed for evaluating the objectivity of knowledge as the basis for developing curriculum and for providing students with the tools they need to evaluate knowledge.

Moore provides an excellent example of the way in which the epistemic relations of knowledge can be distinguished within hierarchical knowledge structures and horizontal knowledge structures with strong grammars, thereby allowing a more nuanced analysis than that which is derived from an exclusive focus on the grammar of a language structure. Moore (2004: 157) does so by distinguishing between disciplines with 'normative' epistemologies and those with 'naturalized' epistemologies. Both seek an objective basis for knowledge. He explains that normative epistemologies seek to identify the '*formal* conditions for holding certain beliefs as true (with the a priori form of logical justification)' (Moore 2004: 157). The truth or otherwise of a statement is determined by the extent to which it satisfies these formal conditions. Normative epistemologies can be further divided into those that are based on 'coherentism' (which means that beliefs must support each other coherently as the basis of justification) and 'foundationalism'. Foundational beliefs can be derived from divine revelation, rational deductive propositions, or empirical observations (Moore 2004: 158).

The use of empirical observations to ground foundational beliefs is most associated with positivism and is premised on assumptions that the world consists of discrete objects that are not related in causal ways, and that knowledge can be gained by observations of constant conjunctions of events. It is perhaps more precise to say that positivism assumes we can never *determine* causality because we only see the *effects* of causation because many different causes can produce the one result that we see, with the result that 'every effect is a distinct event from its cause' (Hume 1921 [1777]: 27). Therefore, all that we can say with any certainty is that conjunctions of events arise, but without distinguishing between necessary and contingent relations (Sayer 1992). Positivism assumes that knowledge can be gained from careful operationalization of our concepts that are then verified (or falsified) by empirical observations. Moore (2004: 159) explains that: 'The critique of positivism centres on the possibility of such a non-mediated, presuppositionless language of perception and its associated methodology.' He explains that positivism failed because it was demonstrated that such a language was impossible, and this is because our observations are always conceptually mediated (though not conceptually determined) (see Sayer 1992, 1998, 2000).

Popper (1962) tried to overcome the problem of the impossibility of developing a neutral language of description by using deductive reasoning in his hypothetico-deductive approach. He argued that theories can generate testable hypotheses by deductive logical reasoning, and while a theory could not be proved, it could be falsified and in this way bring us to a closer approximation to the truth: '*Only the falsity of the theory can be inferred from empirical evidence, and this inference is a purely deductive one*' (Popper 1962: 55, emphasis in original). However, this can still be characterized as a normative and not a naturalized epistemology because in using deductive logic to generate testable hypotheses, Popper substitutes the 'logic of things' with the 'relations of logic' (Bourdieu and Wacquant 1992: 123). In other words, he substitutes the relations between things in the natural and social world with the laws of deductive logic and the laws of probability. Niiniluoto (1999: 6) argues that this means that the Popperian approach puts together statements like '"God exists", "Electrons exist", and "Stones exist" into the same class of metaphysics'.[5]

Naturalized epistemologies share with normative approaches the view that we need to understand 'how knowledge should be produced in order that we might produce better knowledge' (Moore 2004: 157). However, in contrast to normative epistemologies, naturalized approaches recognize the social origins of all knowledge and are concerned 'with the *social conditions* under which true beliefs come to be produced and accepted as such' (Moore 2004: 157). Recognizing the social origins of knowledge also means that knowledge is revisable and we cannot produce knowledge that is beyond doubt (Moore 2004: 164). Knowledge is thus fallible. Communities of knowledge producers engage in debate and discussion to determine the best ways of producing valid and reliable knowledge, and the methods and approaches that are shared and agreed over time in part constitute the basis for objective knowledge. Moore and Young (2001: 456) illustrate this when they argue that:

> the objectivity of knowledge is in part located in the social networks, institutions and codes of practice built up by knowledge producers over time. It is these networks of social relations that, in crucial ways, guarantee truth claims and give the knowledge that is produced its emergent powers.

This *is* an important and indispensable aspect of the objectivity of knowledge; however it needs to be extended because it is a necessary but not sufficient condition for grounding the objectivity of knowledge. Bernstein presents an essentially 'conventionalist' approach to knowledge, in which the objectivity of knowledge lies in the shared social practices of knowledge producers and in the structures of knowledge, rather than in the relationship between knowledge and the referents of that knowledge. But what if, as in the case in many natural sciences (and some social sciences), these conventions are based on normative and not naturalized epistemologies? Or even on relativist epistemologies as in many of the social sciences? We need a basis for critiquing these conventions.

So how should we ground the objectivity of knowledge? Andrew Collier, a leading critical realist, argues that the objectivity of knowledge can be understood in three ways. Collier (2003: 134) says that 'The first and central use of the word "objectivity" is to refer to what is true independently of any subject judging it to be true.' It was an objective truth that the earth revolved around the sun before Copernicus and Galileo proclaimed it so. Something may be objectively true even if no-one believes it to be true. The second meaning of objectivity concerns the objectivity of human judgements. Knowledge is objective (but still fallible) if it is *caused* by its object, and 'not by some feature of its subject other than that subject's openness to the effects of the object' (Collier 2003: 135). Such knowledge is objective because it is *about* something. However, knowledge and the object that the knowledge is about are not identical because knowledge is not a direct correspondence or translation of the object, and so an objective judgement can be more or less fallible (this is discussed in more depth in the next two chapters on critical realism). The third meaning of objectivity concerns objectivity as a human attitude, and this is closest to Bernstein's approach. Collier (2003: 137) says that:

> This is an attitude of trying to make one's judgements objective in the second sense; trying to make one's beliefs and values conditional upon what is objectively true and valuable – objective in the first sense … Objectivity as an attitude means openness to refutation by data derived from the real objects with which we are concerned; the alternative is to be shut up in one's own subjectivity.

All three senses are needed to ground the objectivity of knowledge. It is apparent that normative approaches do not do so because they seek a priori conditions that must be met in establishing knowledge which are not necessarily related to the objects of knowledge. This means that the object that the knowledge is about recedes in importance.

Bringing the social and epistemic together: implications for curriculum

The implications of the preceding analysis are that the social and epistemic relations of knowledge have repercussions for each other, and consequently for the way knowledge is structured in curriculum. A focus on the epistemic is required because there is no social access to knowledge without epistemic access; students need to understand knowledge if they are to have social access to it and use it productively. However, the need for a focus on the epistemic extends beyond this. Without explicit inclusion of the epistemic we are left with only the structures of knowledge and the epistemic consequences that ensue from these structures. While a key principle for the structuring of knowledge in curriculum, this does not exhaust the epistemic relations of knowledge or determine the objectivity of knowledge. A focus on the epistemic is needed if we are to pursue truthfulness in which knowledge can be demonstrated to be true based on the available evidence that we have, even if new evidence leads to its revision. Bringing the social and epistemic together provides the basis for critiquing curriculum so that knowledge is judged by the extent to which it provides access to its objects, as well as the extent to which curriculum provides students with access to the structures of knowledge and systems of meaning. Students must be provided with grounds for critiquing and evaluating knowledge.

A focus on both allows us to theorize the boundaries between the sacred and profane to explore the way in which they are related *at work* and *in curriculum*.

This is a key question for the senior years of schooling and for tertiary education (which in Australia includes vocational education and training and higher education) because the emphasis moves increasingly to prepare students for a field of practice – to prepare them for work. We need to start exploring the way in which the sacred is embedded in the profane, particularly as work changes and higher levels of knowledge are needed in response to technological change and new patterns of work organization (Young 2006a). While the purpose of academic qualifications is to induct students into fields of disciplinary knowledge, there is also a greater emphasis on the knowledge base of vocational and professional curriculum as a consequence of changes to work and society, which is, as Young (2006c: 57) explains, summed up in the notion of the knowledge society.[6] This leads Daniels (2006: 172) to argue that we need to theorize the *relationship* between scientific and everyday knowledge and he cites Vygotsky to demonstrate the way in which scientific concepts become gradually embedded in the everyday. Muller (2000: 82) explains that 'No one lives only in the sacred or only in the profane. The problem also runs deeper: neither the everyday world nor the world of science is epistemologically homogenous.'

A focus on the objectivity of knowledge as a key dimension of the epistemic relations of knowledge allows us to see that scientific and everyday knowledge cannot be distinguished on the basis that the former is objective whereas the latter is not. This is because everyday knowledge can be objective knowledge in the three senses used above: knowledge can be objectively true; knowledge about the object can be caused by the subject's openness to the object; and subjects can seek objective knowledge about objects as a human attitude. Indeed, Gellner (1982), Horton (1982), Sayer (1992, 2000) and many others argue that the irrationality of relativism within disciplines in the social sciences can be contrasted to the 'objective' knowledge of the everyday. This is because in having to live in the world, we must engage with objects, events and people in it and we cannot 'construct' beliefs about them in any way we choose. The development of some level of objective knowledge about the environment in which we live is a condition for living in the world.

While both the theoretical and everyday can be objective knowledge, theorizing the relationship between them reveals that we need to differentiate between the *process of acquiring* conceptual, theoretical knowledge and *the context in which it is applied* in the workplace.[7] While everyday knowledge arises from everyday interactions, the key lesson from Durkheim and Bernstein is that abstract, theoretical knowledge is acquired as systems of meaning which are 'general, explicit and coherent', in which the integration of knowledge occurs by the integration of meanings and not by relevance to specific contexts. Workplace learning may provide students with access to objective knowledge, but this is not the same as providing them with access to objective knowledge that is structured as general, principled knowledge. This is the basis for negotiating the relationship between theoretical knowledge and the workplace in curriculum. In other words, the process of creating, acquiring and using theoretical knowledge may not occur at the same time, and acquiring theoretical knowledge as a system of meaning is necessary if it is to be mobilized to understand the particular. It is the basis upon which students are provided with the capacity to identify, select and apply contextually specific applications at work. The process of applying knowledge in new contexts also has implications for the system of meaning because in applying knowledge we gain a better understanding of the object, and the shortcomings of our knowledge in relation to the object. This contributes to processes of disciplinary change – not just in the applied disciplines, but also in the 'pure' disciplines (Young 2006c). The difference between producing, acquiring and using knowledge are discussed in more depth in the next two chapters on critical realism and in Chapter 8, on competency-based training and the appropriation of constructivism by instrumentalism.

Conclusion

This is a modified Bernsteinian analysis because it builds on Bernstein's analysis by drawing on the work of Bernsteinian theorists and by drawing on critical realism. It extends his analysis of the social relations of knowledge by incorporating the epistemic relations of knowledge thereby commencing the exploration of the way they co-determine knowledge. The epistemic relations of knowledge can be differentiated by focusing one level of analysis at the discipline and another within the discipline. This allows for a more nuanced analysis and avoids the over-homogenization of different types of knowledge, particularly in the natural sciences and in social sciences with strong grammars. It also used Moore's distinction between normative and naturalized epistemologies to differentiate within hierarchical knowledge structures and horizontal knowledge structures with strong grammars to analyse the extent to which they provide access to the objects of their knowledge. It drew on critical realism to establish grounds for the objectivity of knowledge and demonstrated that while both theoretical and everyday knowledge can be objective, the former is accessed as a system of meaning while the latter is accessed contextually.

A focus on the epistemic also enables an analysis of the relationship between the sacred and profane, and the way each is implicated in the other in work and in curriculum. Using both the social and epistemic relations of knowledge provides the basis for critiquing the production of knowledge and its reproduction in curriculum. It is the basis upon which conservative, instrumentalist and constructivist approaches are critiqued in later chapters. The analysis of the epistemic relations of knowledge is further developed in the next two chapters on critical realism.

4 What does commitment to realism mean for curriculum?

Introduction

The exposition, analysis and critique of critical realism and its implications for curriculum are considered in this chapter and the next. This chapter establishes the basis for knowledge, while the next considers the relationship between knowledge and the objects that the knowledge is about, how knowledge changes, the relationship between the disciplines and how students are inducted into the disciplinary structures of knowledge. Thus, the focus of this chapter is ontological because it is concerned with the nature of what exists. It asks the critical realist question: what must the world be like if we are to have knowledge of it? The focus of the next chapter is epistemological because it asks: given that the world is real and exists independently of our conceptions of it, how do we gain knowledge of it? The way we understand the world to be structured and constituted (the ontological) consequently sets boundaries around the way we gain knowledge of it (the epistemological).

The key argument underpinning both chapters is that our knowledge *of* the world arises from our practice *in* the world, and as our practice leads to better understandings of the objects we are researching, it also contributes to changes in the classification and structure of knowledge and their disciplinary boundaries. This demonstrates that knowledge is not identical with the objects that it is about and it is therefore fallible. Indeed, knowledge must be fallible or it would never change. Knowledge changes and the structure and content of the disciplines change as a consequence of the interplay between our practice, social relations and insights from already existing knowledge within the discipline and in other disciplines.

The first section of this chapter outlines the metaphysical premise underpinning critical realism. The second section explains critical realist ontological arguments about the nature of the world and causation. This is followed by a discussion that explains and distinguishes between the real, the actual and the empirical as different domains of the real. Examples of all these concepts are provided. The penultimate section discusses and evaluates critical realist arguments about the differences and similarities between the natural and social sciences. The chapter concludes by considering the implications for curriculum and argues that access to disciplinary knowledge is the means by which students are provided with access to the complexity of the world.

The metaphysical premise

All philosophies and theories are premised on metaphysical assumptions and critical realism is no exception. Sayer (1992: 286, fn. 3) explains that:

> Metaphysics concerns the meaning of the most basic categories in which we think, such as time, space, matter or relation. Despite its pejorative connotations in some circles, no system of thought can escape some or other metaphysical commitments.

These assumptions or commitments are the necessary starting point for enquiring into the nature of the world. Another way of putting this is to say that all philosophies and social theories are realist about something (Bricmont 2001: 106). This includes relativist theories of society and knowledge that insist that both are social constructions created by discourse which (in stronger versions) are ultimately incommensurable because knowledge is and can only be the situated perspective of actors. Such approaches make non-relativist assumptions about society and knowledge as their starting point as they must (the social is constituted by the discursive), even if these non-relativist assumptions contradict their tenet that all knowledge is relative.

Collier (1994: 6) explains that 'stronger' realist theories such as critical realism are premised on objectivity, fallibility, transphenomenality and counter-phenomenality. Something is objectively true regardless of whether we know of its existence and may be true without appearing directly in events or in our experiences. Knowledge is fallible because the events that happen, our experiences and the knowledge that we derive from these events and experiences are only a part of the world – there is a lot that we don't know or haven't yet experienced. This means our knowledge claims may be revised or refuted by new evidence (the fallibility of knowledge is discussed in more detail later in this chapter). Transphenomenality tries to grasp the underlying reality of structures and mechanisms that generate events and experiences: 'We may have knowledge, not just of actions but of characters; not just of historical events but of social systems; not just of family likenesses but of the molecular structure of DNA' (Collier 1994: 6). Counter-phenomenality refers to instances where the deep structure of generative mechanisms contradicts appearances. The example often given to illustrate this is Marx's analysis of commodity fetishism, in which the social relations of exploitation intrinsic to capitalism seems to be the impersonal working of commodity exchange within a free market (Bhaskar 1998d: 52). Vygotsky (1978: 63) explains that:

> If every object was phenotypically and genotypically equivalent (that is, if the true principles of its construction and operation were expressed by its

outer manifestation), then everyday experience would fully suffice to replace scientific analysis. Everything we saw would be the subject of our scientific knowledge.

Roy Bhaskar (1998c: 19) is most associated with the development of the philosophy of critical realism, and he explains that critical realism developed in response to both positivist and idealist theories of science. He explains that critical realism (or any philosophy) can theorize only about the *possibility* of different sciences, rather than determine the outcomes (and contents) of these sciences (Bhaskar 1998d: 3). Philosophy can 'specify the (ontological) conditions ... and the (epistemological) conditions that must be satisfied' to theorize the conditions for the existence of the natural and social sciences and the relationship between them, but the realization of this project is 'the substantive task, and contingent outcome, of the practice of science itself' (Bhaskar 1998d: 3).

In a similar vein, Sayer (2000: 78) explains that the main focus of critical realist philosophy is ontology and rather than epistemology. However, Sayer explains that critical realism *underlabours* the social sciences by providing a realist framework for complementary social theories that explore society.[1] Outhwaite (1998: 283) argues that critical realism is a philosophical ontology and not a scientific ontology because it does not identify the structures and causal mechanisms that each of the sciences or social sciences explores – only the individual sciences can do this. Bhaskar (1998d: 5) agrees, arguing that philosophy can tell us that the world is stratified, and that such stratification is a necessary condition for the possibility of scientific activities, but 'it cannot tell us *what* structures the world contains or *how* they differ'.

Critical realist philosophy 'underlabours' and makes a contribution to the natural sciences and social sciences by the use of transcendental arguments. A transcendental argument is used to determine if a particular account of something is possible. Collier (1994: 20) explains that a transcendental argument commences with the question: what must be true in order for *x* to be possible, hence the critical realist question: what must the world be like if we are to have knowledge of it? The same question can be used to critique relativist and positivist conceptions of the nature of the world. It would do so by demonstrating what the world would need to look like if the relativist or positivist approach were to be possible, and then demonstrate that the world does not look like this. A transcendental argument is a key part of a transcendental critique which is used to show that something is impossible in its own terms (Bhaskar 1998d: 120). Theories are not always consistent with their underlying philosophical premises and this is why it is important to identify continuity between the underlying philosophical premise of theories and the foundational statements they make about the nature of reality. For example, Polanyi (1983 [1966]: 70) argues that modern science fails to recognize the implicit metaphysics upon which it is based. The search for the *hidden* is the *raison d'être* of science, but:

> Modern science arose claiming to be grounded in experience and not on a metaphysics derived from first principles. My assertion that science can

have discipline and originality only if it believes that the facts and values of science bear on a still unrevealed reality, stands in opposition to the current philosophic conception of scientific knowledge.

(Polanyi 1983 [1966]: 70)

Critical realism is therefore a philosophy that has implications for social sciences and other academic disciplines because, as Archer (1995: 22) puts it, ontology 'acts as both gatekeeper and bouncer for methodology'. This is because the way we theorize the nature of the world has implications for the methods we use to explore it. However, our ontological conceptions are also challenged by our explanatory methodology. If we find as a result of our explorations that social reality is different from the way we theorized it, then this should modify our ontological conceptions (Archer 1995: 23).

Bhaskar (1998a: x–xi) explains that critical realism is premised on 'a clear concept of the continued independent *reality* of being ... the *relativity* of our *knowledge*' and '*judgemental rationality*'. The reality of being means that the existence of the natural and social worlds is a condition for our knowledge of them and that they are not constructions of our minds. However, our knowledge will always be fallible because knowledge of the natural and social worlds is not identical to those worlds; concepts have different properties to the objects they describe (Bhaskar 1998d: 142).[2] Judgemental rationality is the basis upon which we judge some theories to be better than others. Even though knowledge is fallible, there are grounds for choosing some accounts over others, and indeed this is a condition for the growth of knowledge and science (Norris 2008).

Critical realists start from the assumption that the *world* is structured in a particular way, and that it is the structures of the world rather than the structures of our mind that make our knowledge of the world possible. Collier (1994: 27) explains that the conditions for knowledge include that 'the world must be ordered in space and time, behave in a regular manner, consist of things and their properties, which can be measured and which only change in accordance with causal laws'. He says that, on the face of it, this list is very similar to Kantian idealism and Kant's list of conditions for the possibility of knowledge. However, the difference arises because Kant derived his list from the *structures of the mind* and the capacity of our minds to impose the categories on phenomena we experience, whereas Bhaskar derives his list from the structures of the world. For Kant, the structures of the mind are universal and knowledge that is derived from these structures is infallible because it has been deduced through the use of pure reason. In contrast, for Bhaskar knowledge is fallible because the conditions for knowledge are to be found in the structures of the world, and the extent to which we have access to these structures is a contingent question and shaped by the particular social practices societies use to develop knowledge.

What must the world be like?

What is the nature of the natural and social worlds if they are not constructs of our imaginations or discourse? Bhaskar (1998c: 37) says that 'the world consists of things, not events'. He says that most things are complex and internally differentiated and 'possess an ensemble of tendencies, liabilities and powers' (Bhaskar 1998c: 37). This is in contrast to David Hume, one of the founders of British empiricism, who argued that the world consists of independent objects that are not causally related. Hume (1921 [1777]: 27) explains that: 'Motion in the second Billiard-ball is a quite distinct event from motion in the first; nor is there anything in the one to suggest the smallest hint of the other'. All that we can know is that something happened, and we are limited to counting the number of times it happened. In this way, the real is understood as the constant conjunction of events and the purpose of science is to predict that these conjunctions of events will occur.

Rather than Hume's billiard balls hitting against each other in contingent ways, critical realists argue that the world comprises objects that are necessarily related and contingently related. If objects are necessarily related this means they must be related for the objects to be as they are. If objects are contingently related, this means that objects may be related, but it is not essential to the object that they are related, but nor is it impossible for them to be related. New outcomes emerge as a consequence of objects relating to and acting upon each other (Sayer 1992). These objects have propensities to act in particular ways given their composition, and they may or may not act in these ways when they interact with other objects in open systems because each may affect the way the other acts. Critical realism seeks to identify the underpinning generative (and relational) mechanisms that give rise to events in the world and our experience of them. There are also many things which *do not* happen but *could* happen as a consequence of being nullified or modified by other objects (Sayer 2000: 12). Bhaskar (2008: 51–52) explains that:

> There is nothing esoteric or mysterious about the concept of the generative mechanisms of nature, which provide the real basis of causal laws. For a generative mechanism is nothing other than a way of acting of a thing. It endures, and under appropriate circumstances is exercised, as long as the properties that account for it persist. Laws then are neither empirical statements (statements about experiences) nor statements about events. Rather they are statements about the ways of acting of independently existing and transfactually active things.

Critical realists argue that the (natural and social) world is complex and stratified. As an illustration, Collier (1998b: 263) explains everything is governed by the law of physics; some, but not all things are governed by the laws of biology; and more recently, some but not all things are governed by the law of capitalist economics. These different strata (and others not identified here) interact to make factory production possible. We need to understand the relations between mechanisms of different strata to understand the pluralistic and stratified outcomes that we observe. Collier (1998b: 263) gives as an example: 'The factory will work when the laws of physics and economics permit, but either a mechanical breakdown or a recession will stop it'.

The process of *emergence* describes what happens when different structures, objects, mechanisms interact in a world characterized by complexity and ontological depth. The interplay between these different elements produces something new which cannot be reduced to its constituent components, even though these constituent components are necessary for their existence (Sayer 2000: 12). Polanyi (1983 [1966]: 34) explains that higher-level strata emerge from lower-level strata, and the upper relies on the lower and on the laws that govern the lower, but the upper cannot be explained exclusively in terms of the lower.[3] For example, the laws of chemistry are necessary for biology to exist, but it is the action of biological elements that explains biology (Collier 1998b). The purpose and workings of machines cannot be explained by physics or chemistry even though both need to be invoked to make machines work and to fix them when they break; we have, instead, to understand the operational principles of machines (Polanyi 1983 [1966]: 38–39). Polanyi (1983 [1966]: 41) explains that speech depends on voice production, but voice production does not explain the combination of sounds into words, whereas vocabulary does; vocabulary does not explain how words are formed into sentences, whereas grammar does and so it goes.

Stratification and emergence also apply to the social world (and therefore the social sciences). For example, while they are intrinsically related, individuals, groups and society are three different kinds of 'objects' with different properties, none of which is reducible to the other. While groups and societies would not exist unless individuals existed and both emerge from social relations between agents occupying social positions, it is not possible to add up all the individuals in society or a group to arrive at either (as with nominalism or methodological individualism). Individuals have capacities that organizations or groups do not have and vice versa. Individuals have capacities for cognition, perception and consciousness, whereas groups can have a flat or hierarchical organizational structure, and a society can have an old or young demographic structure, and can be more or less class differentiated and so on (Archer 1995, 2000). So even though society and groups depend upon the activity of individuals, each has different properties. Bhaskar explains that people in their conscious activity often unconsciously reproduce (and less often transform) the social institutions that govern their activities:

> Thus people do not marry to reproduce the nuclear family or work to sustain the capitalist economy. Yet it is nevertheless the unintended consequence (and inexorable result) of, as it is also a necessary condition for, their activity.
> (Bhaskar 1998d: 35)

The example of society demonstrates the way in which higher-level strata can act reflexively to affect its lower level constituent components. The demographic profile of a society, its class structure and the distribution of social roles will shape the system of opportunity available to different groups and individuals (Archer 1995, 2000). Moreover, because we are embodied beings, we cannot understand the social without also exploring the relationship between the social and the biological (and material) to understand the iterative relationship between higher- and lower-level strata, and between different kinds of strata in open systems (Sayer 2000: 13). Sayer (2000: 13) illustrates this argument about the way in which strata interact and react by explaining that we cannot ignore, among other things, 'contraception, medicine, agriculture and pollution' in explaining society.

The real, the actual and the empirical

Critical realism argues that it is necessary to identify *three* levels of reality in the social and natural worlds. The three levels are the real, actual and empirical. This is illustrated in Table 4.1

The domain of the real consists of structures and their generative mechanisms. Structures and mechanisms are *real*, they are not 'theoretical entities' or 'logical constructs' (Collier 1994: 44; Bhaskar 2008: 47). They generate the events that happen, and the things we experience. An example of a (complex) structure with generative mechanisms that interact with other social structures and mechanisms in the social world is social class, while gravity is an example in the natural world. Nor are objects and structures fixed in time. Changes to an object will also result in changes to causal powers: 'engines lose their power as they wear out, a child's cognitive powers increase as it grows' (Sayer 1992: 105).

There is debate amongst critical realists over whether underlying generative mechanisms can be observable. Bhaskar (1998c: 42) argues that the exercise of generative mechanisms, the events they produce and our perception of them are not normally in phase, except when the 'social activity of science … makes them so'. This means that, as a general rule, generative mechanisms cannot be observable. However, while generative mechanisms may not be observable directly, we may nonetheless be *aware* of the exercise of causal powers and of their sequences because of their effect (Bhaskar 1998b: 89). Sayer (1992: 280) disagrees, arguing that the extent to which causal mechanisms are visible or not is an empirical question: 'Clockwork, the ways of producing commodities, electing MPs, etc., involve mechanisms which are no less observable than the effects they produce'. However, all agree that observability is not a necessary condition for the existence of generative mechanisms and events, even though observation may make us more confident that a mechanism or object exists (Sayer 2000: 12). For example, gravity exists despite not being directly observable. Consequently, critical realists invoke a *causal* criterion for making claims about what exists,

Table 4.1 The domains of the real, actual and empirical

	Domain of real	Domain of actual	Domain of empirical
Mechanisms	✓		
Events	✓	✓	
Experiences	✓	✓	✓

which is by virtue of the effect of the exercise of powers inherent in generative mechanisms (Bhaskar 1998b; Sayer 1992).

Bhaskar (1998d: 170) differentiates between structures and generative mechanisms with the former consisting of internally related objects or practices, whereas generative mechanisms refer 'only to the causal powers of ways of acting of structured things'.[4] Structures 'just *are*' or 'more normally *possess* their causal powers' (Bhaskar 1998d: 179). Structures may consist of internally related objects so that their generative mechanisms or powers emerge from this combination and cannot be reduced to its individual components (Sayer 2000: 14). The example used in the previous section of society as emergent from individuals also illustrates this point. Generative mechanisms and their causal powers are intrinsic to objects and structures; they are 'that aspect of the structure of a thing by virtue of which it has a certain power' (Collier 1994: 62). Collier gives these examples of generative mechanisms and their powers:

> that aspect of the structure of an oxygen atom by virtue of which it can combine with two hydrogen atoms to form a molecule of water; that aspect of a DNA molecule by virtue of which it can replicate itself; that aspect of a market economy by virtue of which it can go into an overproduction crisis; that aspect of a person's brain-structure by virtue of which he or she can acquire a language.
>
> (Collier 1994: 62)

This distinction between objects/structures on the one hand, and generative mechanisms/causal powers on the other, makes it possible to identify the different outcomes that are possible from the interaction of multiple structures and multiple generative mechanisms. Events are multiply determined by the interaction of different mechanisms, and this means that the same mechanism (and its underlying structure) can produce different results, and different mechanisms the same result (Sayer 1992: 108). For example, markets may sustain or undermine a range of different structures (Bhaskar 1998d: 170). Markets have different consequences when they manage relations of exchange between those producing, buying and selling manufactured goods compared to the effect they have when they are used as the method for allocating public funding to, and structuring relations between, educational institutions. There may be a point to the former, but the latter often results in greater hierarchical stratification between educational institutions and more unequal outcomes for disadvantaged students because they must compete in an unlevel playing field for access to educational institutions (particularly universities) (Marginson 1997b). Policy decisions made by the state (the state as a structured entity and the capacity to make policy decisions as one aspect of its causal powers) may interact with the labour market in different ways to encourage women to have more or fewer children. This may reinforce or undermine the nuclear family. The nuclear family may be supported or undermined by different mechanisms, through, for example, the level of public support available to single parents, the social infrastructure that is available (like childcare and public transport), the migration of labour in response to economic boom or recession, or war which results in destruction and high numbers of refugees and family dislocation.

Structures and their generative mechanisms operate *transfactually*. Transfactuality means that, all other things being equal, mechanisms will persist and act in accordance with their properties and structures (Bhaskar 1998a: xii). However, because structures and their generative mechanisms interact in open systems, some cancel each other out or change the way in which they act. All this means is that 'A generative mechanism will operate when suitably triggered' (Collier 1994: 62). Bhaskar (1998a: xi–xii) explains that the powers inherent in a generative mechanism may 'be possessed unexercised, exercised unactualized, or actualized undetected or unperceived'. The causal powers and mechanisms of an object or structure may be 'possessed unexercised' when it is prevented from acting because of the effect of other objects and their mechanisms and powers. For example, women can get pregnant, but not all do for a variety of reasons. They may choose not to, or they may be prevented from doing so for biological or social reasons (or both). This is an example where the powers inherent in a biological mechanism are unexercised. The powers inherent in an object or structure may be exercised unactualized as in the example of a bureaucracy that implements a course of action that is not realized because of other factors. As an illustration, the Reserve Bank of Australia lowered the official interest rate to stimulate economic activity in response to the depressed economy, but the major banks chose not to pass on the entire cut to borrowers.

The powers of objects or structures are exercised but unperceived when we cannot perceive the process or outcome directly. For example, Onyx and Bullen (2000) conclude from their research that government is not related to social capital because individuals who answered their survey about social capital did not perceive the role of government. Other research demonstrates the fundamental importance of government in building positive social capital and argues that government plays a crucial role in building civil society (Cox and Caldwell 2000). It does not mean that government plays no role in building (or limiting) social capital because we cannot *see* what government does or perceive its effects. In this case, the powers inherent in the generative mechanisms of the state acting as a social structure are 'actualized undetected or unperceived' (Bhaskar 1998a: xii).

Consequently, the aim of (natural and social) science is not to identify *immutable laws* but *tendencies* of things to act in particular ways (Collier 1994: 62–63; Bhaskar 2008: 52). Causal laws exist, but they are best understood as tendencies and not as inexorable processes that result in constant conjunctions of events. Causation is not determined by the number of times things happen. All Humean science or social science can tell us is the number of times the billiard balls hit each other. Our purpose should be to try to identify the way in which causal mechanisms or powers act in ways that are internally related because they are intrinsically related to their object, or in ways that are contingently related (that is, neither necessary nor impossible) (Sayer 2000: 11). Consequently, the aim of natural and social science should not be *prediction*, but *explanation*.

It may be possible in closed systems (as in some but not all natural sciences) to manipulate all variables and determine causation by causing something to happen a number of times. But even here, what is being identified is the causal mechanism and the effect is the number of times something happens in a closed system (Bhaskar 1998d). The natural world is not a closed system so the findings in a closed system or controlled experiment apply in limited and qualified ways in the natural world – they describe causal mechanisms in isolation from their interaction with other mechanisms. The social world is by definition an open system as are many natural sciences and the search for constant conjunctions of events, or the requirement that such conjunctions be present as proof of the existence of an object or relationship, is misguided because 'at best these might suggest where to look for candidates for causal mechanisms' (Sayer 2000: 14). This last point is elaborated by Lawson (1998: 149) who argues that (in the social sciences) *partial* regularities occur, and he refers to these as demi-regularities, and this '*prima facie* indicates the occasional, but less than universal, actualization of a mechanism or tendency, over a definite region of time-space'. However, the identification of demi-regularities is only a starting point and is not an explanation, and nor is it a way of using inferential statistics to attribute weightings to factors to 'explain' or 'account for' outcomes (Carter and New 2004: 9).[5]

The interaction of generative mechanisms and their causal powers gives rise to *events*, which Bhaskar (1998c: 41) describes as the domain of the actual, where things actually happen. Collier (1994: 9) explains that 'No event or action exists before it occurs or is done, but its agent and/or patient always does. A battle does not first exist and then be fought, but the armies do first exist and then fight.' The reason why outcomes cannot be fully predicted in advance is that events are always co-determined by the interaction of multiple, stratified objects and their generative mechanisms (Collier 1998b: 263). Some events can be perceived while others cannot. The tree does indeed make a sound when it falls in the forest, even if there is no-one there to hear it. The extent to which we perceive events is an empirical question and one that is continually reshaped by science as we discover new ways to observe events empirically that previously were discernible only through their effects.

Unless we acknowledge a 'depth' ontology in this way, we are left with 'actualist' accounts of causation that restrict the real to events ('every time A happens, B happens') (Collier 1994: 7), and this denies the existence of underlying structures and objects. It assumes that what happens is all that could happen and denies the possibility that things may be otherwise. Or, when applied to the social world, it can result in voluntarism so that all that is necessary for change is for agents to do otherwise, thus ignoring the way agents' actions are limited (but not determined) by the social, material and natural worlds in which they live.

The third domain is the domain of the empirical, which 'is comprised only of experiences' (Collier 1994: 45). The condition of our experience of the effects of generative mechanisms or events is that the event producing our experience must have been generated in the domain of the real and taken place in the domain of the actual. Bhaskar (1998c: 41) explains that empirical realism collapses the domains of the real, actual and empirical into one domain – the empirical – which restricts the real to that which we can experience. Instrumentalist and constructivist theories of curriculum are both guilty of this in different ways as will be demonstrated in Chapter 8. A focus on the 'empirical world' results in the 'epistemic fallacy' because it reduces the ontological question of what exists to an epistemological question of what we know or can experience, so that the limits of the world are coterminous with our knowledge of it (Sayer 1998: 133). It also results in anthropocentrism because 'The world is what men can experience' (Bhaskar 1998c: 42).

Even if the boundaries of the world are expanded to include events that are unobservable as well as those that are observable, unless underlying objects or structures are also posited there can be no explanation that distinguishes between necessary and contingent relations producing these events. Moreover, *absences* cannot be explained (Archer 1995); for example, why women are still under-represented in senior management in universities, or the relative absence of 'interest groups' of the most disadvantaged sections of the population as a significant force in political life compared to other social groups and vested interests. This leads to a 'reliance on a "purely positive", complementing a "purely actual", notion of reality' (Bhaskar and Norrie 1998: 562). Why things *do not* happen cannot be explained.[6] Bhaskar (1998c: 43) explains that he is not arguing that 'experiences are *less* real than events, or events less real than structures'. His point is that events and experiences do not *exhaust* the real and that events and our experience of them depend for their existence on the interplay of different objects, structures, mechanisms and powers in the domain of the real.

The natural and social worlds – the natural and social sciences

Bhaskar (1998d: 20–21) argues that while social objects and phenomena cannot be studied in the same way as natural objects and phenomena, 'they can still be studied "scientifically".' He argues that the principles used to produce explanations in the natural and social sciences are substantially the same, because in both cases explanation seeks to establish relationships between the real, actual and empirical. However, while the stratification of the real and processes of emergence apply to the social as well as the natural world, it does not therefore mean that the methods of the natural sciences can be unproblematically applied to the social sciences. This is because the nature of the object that we are investigating determines what we can know about it and the processes we use for finding out about it (that is, the practices we use). This is why it is not possible to have a universal method to account for objects that do not have universal properties. For example, Bhaskar (1998d: 25) says that:

> it is the nature of objects that determines their cognitive possibilities for us; that, in nature, it is humanity that is contingent and knowledge, so to speak, accidental. Thus it is because sticks and stones are solid that they can be

picked up and thrown, not because they can be picked up and thrown that they are solid (though that they can be handled in this sort of way may be a contingently necessary condition for our *knowledge* of their solidity).

There are important differences between the natural and social sciences that are a consequence of the ontological differences in the nature of structures and objects in the natural and social worlds. Bhaskar identifies three ontological limits that differentiate the natural sciences from the social sciences, one epistemological limit and one relational limit. However, as explained below, these distinctions are controversial among critical realists (Benton and Craib 2001: 133). Bhaskar (1998d:38) explains that the three ontological limits arise because of the differences between the social and natural worlds. Society is real in its particular way and the differences between the social and natural worlds arise from the emergent social properties of society. The first ontological limit is that social structures are activity dependent; the second is that social structures are concept dependent; and the third is that social structures are only relatively enduring, unlike the more enduring structures in the natural world. The epistemological limit refers to the impossibility of creating closed systems in the social sciences, whereas this is possible in (at least some) natural sciences (but not in astronomy, for example). The relational difference arises as a result of the different relationship the social sciences have with society compared to the natural sciences and nature.

The three ontological limits that distinguish the natural and social sciences

The first ontological limit – that social structures are activity dependent – arises because social structures are maintained by the activities of agents and so do not exist independently of these activities, whereas this is not generally true of structures in nature (Bhaskar 1998d: 38). A capitalist economy reproduces the means of subsistence based on determinate social relations and the extent that it does so depends on the activity of those engaged in those social relations and productive activities, whereas oxygen does not exist to keep humankind alive, even though that is a necessary condition for our existence. Oxygen exists independently of the activities it governs (our capacity to breathe), although oxygen does not exist independently of its component structures and their activities.

The second ontological limit – that social structures are concept-dependent – arises because social structures are produced by actors who act on their beliefs and reasons. Again, this is different to the natural world. Individuals may marry or partner for many reasons. Some may even do so because they love each other! However, romantic love does not (and historically has not) exhaust the reasons why people partner and form families (Giddens *et al.* 2006). This means that the natural and social worlds are distinguished because the social world is in part constituted by *meanings* and the conceptions agents have of their activity as well as the material dimensions of their activity. Sayer (2000: 17) explains that because meaning is not only externally descriptive of social phenomena but also partly constitutive of that phenomena, that 'Meaning has to be understood, it cannot be measured or counted, and hence there is always an interpretive or hermeneutic element in social science.' He says that while critical realism draws from causal explanations in 'naturalist' accounts of the real, actual and empirical, it also must use '*verstehen*' or interpretative understanding as part of that explanation.

Interpretative understanding is also important because the *reasons* people have for what they do can also be a cause and this is an important part of social science research, as are the ideas and beliefs that underpin the reasons why people act. As Bourdieu (1988: xiv, 16, 27) explains, agents' representations (situated perspectives and understandings) are an integral part of the object we wish to study because these representations are part of objective reality. This is different to positivist social research that eschews interpretative understanding in favour of behaviours, processes and people's views that can be measured and subject to statistical interpretation. That which can be measured is (often without any real basis), while that which cannot be measured isn't. There is debate over the extent to which reasons *can* be causes because we need to distinguish between justifications and reasons, or between reasons explicitly known to the actor versus reasons known only at the level of the unconscious (Carter and New 2004: 12–13). However, these debates do not detract from the general point, which is that *why* people do things is important, and that in some circumstances reasons can be causes because they explain why people act in a particular way (Sayer 2000: 18). Sayer (2000: 18) argues that critical realism 'poses a wider conception of causation than is customary, in that it does not assume that all causes must be physical'.

Moreover, the everyday conceptions people have for acting in the way they do may be true, false, or contradictory, but all are important for the social science researcher because such conceptions may be important in explaining the phenomenon, and because these conceptions inform what people do (Danermark *et al.* 2002: 36–37). Sometimes social science contradicts prevailing social views about particular issues or problems, and this is why critique is an important part of social science. For example, 'school drop-outs' in wealthy countries where most young people finish school are often considered to be lazy, lacking in motivation and from families that don't value education. In other words, students and their parents are blamed and often penalised by insisting that young people who receive welfare benefits return to study or 'training' even though their experiences of education were primarily ones of humiliation, failure and alienation. Social science offers competing accounts to explain the problem of early school leaving. One account offered by Bernstein (among others) locates the problem in the way in which schools distribute access to knowledge to some and not to others, and in the vastly different level of resources available to students from wealthier backgrounds. In contrast, 'There can be no equivalent of this in the natural sciences. Black holes may be unpleasant things to contemplate, but that is no criticism of them. They exist – or don't – and there's an end of it' (Collier 1998a: 446). The social scientist will want to criticize and explain the reasons why people hold a false belief.

The third ontological limit – the relatively enduring nature of structures in the social world compared to the more enduring structures in the natural world – arises because unlike structures in the natural world, social structures and their causal mechanisms and powers change and so they therefore 'may not be universal in the sense of space-time variant' (Bhaskar 1998d: 38). The social structures that humankind has used to reproduce itself and to produce the material conditions necessary for its continued existence have changed throughout epochs. Gravity has not (although our knowledge of it has changed over time) (Bhaskar 2008: 85–86).

The epistemological and relational limits that distinguish the natural and social sciences

The epistemological limit – the impossibility of creating closed systems in the social sciences – arises because the social world can *only* consist of open systems. This is unlike some aspects of the natural world where closure is possible. Closure makes experimental science possible as prediction can be based only on experiments conducted in closed systems (Bhaskar 1998d: 45). The conclusion that Bhaskar (1998d: 45–46) draws from this is that 'criteria for the rational development and replacement of theories in social science must be *explanatory and non-predictive*'. However, Bhaskar explains that this difference has no ontological significance in itself, because 'laws' in both the natural and social sciences must be analysed as tendencies and not as constant conjunctions of events. Rather, the difference arises in the way we access knowledge about them. The social world can consist only of open systems because human beings are by nature purposeful, reflexive and active beings who constantly monitor and interact with their surroundings and decide to act in particular ways. Even if strictly 'experimental' conditions were established (as for example, adherents of different theories of psychology try to achieve), this is still not a closed system because of the nature of human beings, their reflexivity and their capacity to alter the conditions in which they are placed (within limits) (Archer 2000).

The relational difference – the different relationship the social sciences have with society compared to the natural sciences' relation with nature – arises because the social sciences are part of their own subject matter or field of inquiry and this means they 'are *internal* with respect to their subject-matter in a way in which the natural sciences are not' (Bhaskar 1998d: 47). The concepts and theories that the social sciences use to explain the social world can also be turned on the social sciences themselves, and there is an iterative relationship between the social sciences and society. This means that in the social sciences 'the process of knowledge-production may be causally, and internally, related to the process of production of the objects concerned' (Bhaskar 1998d: 47). The social relations and social practices of natural scientists and social scientists thus differ because:

> While natural scientists necessarily have to enter the hermeneutic circle of their scientific community, social scientists also have to enter that of those whom they study. In other words, natural science operates in a single hermeneutic while social science operates in a double hermeneutic.[7]
>
> (Sayer 2000: 17)

Sayer (2000: 44) explains that unlike the natural sciences, the findings of social science can change social practices because they provide actors with a different understanding of their social world and what they need to do as a consequence. In explaining the nature of the double hermeneutic, Giddens (1987: 20) says that philosophers and social sciences have often considered the way in which 'lay' concepts become part of the conceptual structure of the social sciences, but few have considered the way in which the social sciences contribute to (and in his view, help to constitute) the social world (Giddens 1987: 20).

Critique – are the natural and social sciences so different?

Collier (1994) and Benton and Craib (2001) do not dispute Bhaskar's notions of ontological depth (the real, actual and empirical), stratification, emergence, processes of co-determination and causal powers, but they do criticize Bhaskar for overplaying the distinction between the natural and social worlds and thus between the natural and social sciences. Collier (1994: 238) argues convincingly that in bending the stick against positivism Bhaskar has gone too far in the direction of relativism, whereas the stick that needs to be straightened is the relativist stick because no-one believes in positivist notions of absolute and final truth any longer.

Benton and Craib (2001: 134) draw from Benton's earlier work to argue that Bhaskar's insistence on the activity dependence of social structures 'comes close to undermining his [Bhaskar's] own ontological distinction between structure and agency'. For example, Bhaskar (1998d: 37) says that while society is only present in human action, that human action and society cannot be 'identified with, reduced to, explained in terms of, or reconstructed from the other'. This is because each has different properties: agents do not *create* society, 'they *reproduce* or *transform* it' by drawing on available ideational, social, economic and material resources within existing objective social structures (Bhaskar 1998d: 34). The distinction between human beings and society is important and failure to make this distinction results in voluntarist idealism in the case of those who privilege agency (agents could act otherwise if they so chose), or mechanistic and over-socialized accounts of agency in the case of those who privilege structure (structure determines agency) (Archer 2000). This is why Bhaskar (1998d: 33) argues that 'People and society are not ... related "dialectically". They do not constitute two moments of the same process. Rather they refer to radically different kinds of thing.'

In insisting on the activity dependence of social structures Bhaskar runs the risk of denying the existence of unactualized powers at the social level. This is because structures exist only by virtue of the activities they govern, and if there is no activity there is no structure (Collier 1994: 245). But (as Bhaskar demonstrates) social structures have powers that can be exercised unactualized, or actualized unperceived. For example, Benton and Craib (2001: 134) explain that modern nation states do not (mostly) exercise the vast destructive powers inherent in their armies and weaponry. Collier (1994: 246) says in this case that 'One might even say paradoxically that the power [of the state] is realized though unexercised.'

Similarly, Bhaskar's argument for the concept dependence of social structures is overplayed. Bhaskar (1998d: 35) demonstrates this quite effectively himself in the examples given earlier in this chapter where he explains that people do not marry to reproduce the nuclear family or go to work to reproduce the capitalist economy, although this is what happens when they engage in these activities. So while individuals do have concepts and ideas about their activities these are not generally related to the social structures of which they are a part. That is, they do not wake up today and consider how they will contribute to reproducing capitalist social relations and sustain (or undermine) capitalist relations of exploitation in their workplace (although some may). To suggest otherwise is to suggest that social structures are homologous to and the direct consequence of agents' conceptions as with many relativist accounts. This reduces the task of analysis only to understanding how people create inter-subjective meaning because it is this that constitutes social relations. However, this conflates agents' conceptions and social structures when they have different properties *including* different ideational bases. This is illustrated by Bhaskar (1998d: 36) who explains that the rubbish collector's reasons for collecting the rubbish are different to the reasons why rubbish is collected although each depends on the other. The rubbish collector may or may not derive some meaning from collecting rubbish but this does not exhaust her reasons for doing so. Insisting on the activity-dependent and concept-dependent nature of society may end up with the conclusion that Bhaskar (1998d: 39) argues against, which is that: 'Society exists only in virtue of human activity. Human activity is conscious. Therefore consciousness brings about change.' This results in voluntarism.

Moreover, as Benton and Craib (2001: 134) explain, much social life 'is habitual and routine, involving bodily activity rather than conscious thought or symbolic meaning'. They argue that social structures are not *just* affected or structured by the activities of agents or the conceptions they hold, but also by their engagement in the material and natural world in which they are embedded. This provides important sociological insights that explain for example, the link between social class and occupation and illness. So while understanding meaning is an important part of analysis, agents' conceptions are only one element of a complex social ontology, which must also incorporate analysis of social structures (and social roles and positions) and the way in which humankind engages with the natural, material and social worlds to reproduce and sustain itself.

Benton and Craib (2001: 134) and Collier (1994: 244–45) also argue that Bhaskar's insistence on the relatively enduring nature of social structures compared to the time–space invariant structures of nature is also misleading, because there are many natural sciences in which structures change. Hence, the difference between the natural and social worlds (and therefore natural and social sciences) is only a matter of degree, not one of principle. Benton and Craib (2001: 134) argue that this aspect of Bhaskar's argument arises because he takes sciences such as physics and chemistry as his paradigm for natural science, and this ignores sciences such as meteorology, evolutionary biology and developmental biology. It also ignores the way in which some of the social sciences draw on the natural sciences as in psychology or disciplines such as medicine which traverse the two.

Collier (1994: 243) argues that the natural and social sciences are distinguished because everything to do with humans is differentiated by the fact that human beings are what they are: they possess language, consciousness, engage in intentional activity, can theorize and conceptualize and so forth. He says however, that:

> while the human/natural divide is unique in these respects, it is not unique in this uniqueness: the divide between living and inorganic matter has probably as many and as important features unique to it.
>
> (Collier 1994: 243)

So there are important differences within the natural and social sciences as well as between them. It is the difference in the objects that each science studies that make them 'the possible object of a separate science' (Collier 1994: 243).

Over-extending the three ontological limits that differentiate the natural and social worlds also has implications for the remaining relational and epistemological differences Bhaskar posits. Whilst insights from the social sciences enter into the constitution of their object (society and social practices) so too do the natural sciences, particularly those that have emerged as a consequence of our engagement with the natural world. Collier (1994: 247) argues that our capacity to act arising from the fact of our embodiment and our need to live in the natural world has entered into the constitution of some natural sciences. He argues that the natural sciences have provided the raw materials for scientific knowledge *and* for the way we live in since the beginning of agriculture, stockbreeding, manufacture, navigation and building. Global warming is an example of the way in which humankind has altered the natural world. Benton and Craib (2001: 134) argue that a strongly anti-naturalistic social ontology is a serious obstacle to collaborative research that can address the relationship between different social practices and socio-economic processes and ecological change.

Benton and Craib explain that even though the social sciences are partly constituted by the object they are studying (that is, they are constituted by society to examine society), it is still possible to differentiate between what is studied and the processes used to study it. Otherwise, it would not have been possible for social sciences to determine that the concepts agents have of their activities are not identical to the social structures of which they are part (even though this is a contested proposition by relativist approaches). Moreover, there are social sciences that seek to study different *aspects* of the social (Benton and Craib 2001: 135).

There is, as discussed above, an important epistemological distinction between the natural and social sciences, which is that it is not possible to establish closure in the social world and thereby to conduct experiments. However, there are many natural sciences such as astronomy in which closure is not possible. Collier argues that the difference between the natural and social sciences is that the natural sciences can provide us with more information because they can (in some disciplines) conduct experiments, even if the knowledge so gained is fallible and revisable. He argues that:

> The hermeneutic moment is so prominent in the human sciences not because it is a more essential stage or a more reliable or informative source than in the natural sciences, but because, in the absence of experiments, we have so little else. As a result, we are also much more likely to get things wrong and much less likely to correct them in the human than in the experimental natural sciences. The plurality of theories in the field at any time in the human sciences is partly due to this.
>
> (Collier 1994: 248)

This leaves Collier somewhat pessimistic about the possibility of knowledge in the human sciences compared to the natural sciences, but he does not draw the conclusion that knowledge cannot be gained. He argues that the differences mean that the methods associated with experiments cannot be unproblematically applied to the human sciences (such as the inappropriate application of inferential statistics), but that other approaches such as careful abstraction and the use of transcendental arguments take on greater importance. And as with the natural sciences, our goal should be to seek to understand structured entities, their properties and powers, the way they interact within open systems, the extent to which their powers are unexercised, exercised but unrealized, realized but unperceived, or realized and perceived and the consequences for the events that happen and our experiences of those events.

Conclusion: implications for curriculum

Knowledge can potentially provide humankind with greater understanding of the world and enrich our capacity to live equitably, sustainably, purposively and creatively in that world. Seeking knowledge of the world assumes that the world exists independently of our knowledge of it, otherwise we would be free to construct whatever version we pleased. This presupposes an ontological commitment that underpins curriculum which is that curriculum must, to the extent that it is possible, represent our best understanding of what the world is like. So while knowledge is the means we use to think the unthinkable and the not-yet-thought, this depends on a capacity to relate the present to the future and to alternative futures (Bernstein 2000; Young 2008a). Some alternative futures may not be possible because of the way the world is, while other alternative futures may be possible only if we change what we currently do (as with climate change). This suggests a normative proposition which is developed in more depth in the next chapter, which is that a goal for curriculum should be the pursuit of *truth*, truth (however imperfect it may be) about the world that is accessed through the knowledge we create.

Critical realism has implications for the way curriculum is structured because it demonstrates that we must go beyond experiences and events to understand the real, the way the real is structured and stratified by different objects and structures, the causal powers intrinsic to these objects and structures, and the processes of emergence that result when they interact in open systems. While still fallible, theoretical knowledge allows us to develop an understanding of these processes and in so doing to transcend the experiences resulting from our immediate practice. Students need access to the disciplines so they can abstract from events and experiences to understand different structured entities and the emergent properties that result as a consequence of their interaction. This provides them with access to understanding what happens, what does not happen and what potentially could happen. Consequently, as well as the pursuit of truth as a curricular goal, curriculum should also aim to induct students into the social and epistemic relations of knowledge as the basis for their participation in society's conversation about the unthinkable and the not-yet-thought.

The analysis outlined in this chapter also provides the basis for critiquing the academic disciplines by evaluating the extent to which they provide students with access to the real, actual and empirical. Moreover, the analysis of ontological depth and relations of co-determination provide a basis for theorizing interdisciplinarity in curriculum, particularly in vocationally oriented qualifications which draw on disciplinary knowledge to solve complex problems in practice. For example, while sociology and psychology both develop knowledge about human beings they do so at different levels, and both are fundamental to understanding the way in which human beings develop, interact, develop aspirations and pursue intentional action. Together sociology and psychology help to explore the interaction of the individual and social, while individually they help us to understand aspects of complex and stratified human and social ontology.

This analysis means that while approaches such as problem-based learning are an important element of curriculum, they should not be made the key structuring principle of curriculum. Such approaches are important because they provide students with the experience they need to synthesize and integrate knowledge to understand concrete particulars, and so they have a role in curriculum (Clarke and Winch 2004). However, the integration and appli-cation of knowledge needs to occur by negotiating explicitly the boundaries between different kinds of knowledge. This is because focussing on a problem requires exploration of a co-determined outcome of complex and different causal mechanisms operating at different levels and with different degrees of influence. Part of understanding concrete specifics requires drawing upon systematically organized bodies of knowledge to explain the nature of different aspects of a problem. So while disciplinary knowledge may vary in the degree to which it is systematically organized, conceptually coherent and fallible, it is still a condition for understanding and abstracting different aspects of a stratified world and then for re-uniting them to understand concrete specifics. To understand the latter requires interdisciplinary collaboration by focussing on a particular problem, and problem-based learning approaches allow this to occur. However, interdisciplinarity and multidisciplinarity is here predicated on explicitly negotiating disciplinary boundaries. The next chapter explores these issues from a critical realist perspective.

5 The role of the disciplines in curriculum

A critical realist analysis

Introduction

The purpose of education is to help equip students with the knowledge and capacities they need to make their way in the world. If the world is characterized by complexity, stratification and processes of emergence, then a key role for curriculum is to provide students with access to and the means to navigate this complexity. This is why an ontological commitment to realism has epistemological implications for curriculum. These implications are that curriculum must be founded on a realist theory of ontology, epistemological fallibility and in opposition to judgemental relativity (Bhaskar 1998d). In other words, the guiding insights for curriculum should be that: first, the natural and social worlds exist independently of our conceptions; second, our knowledge about the world will always be fallible; and third, there are few grounds for making judgements and so relativism is avoided. Consequently, while it would be retrograde to teach students one final version of 'truth', they nonetheless need access to the conceptual tools that can help them make these judgements. This chapter develops the argument begun in the previous chapter, which is that the pursuit of truth should be a normative goal of curriculum, recognizing the corrigibility of our knowledge and the need to revise it in light of evidence. Its key argument is that the academic disciplines provide access to the natural and social worlds, even if this access is imperfect.

The first section of this chapter discusses epistemological relativity and presents a realist argument that there are grounds for choosing some theories over others even if all knowledge is fallible. It outlines the epistemological consequences of critical realism's ontological commitments, which were outlined in the previous chapter. The second section distinguishes between disciplinary knowledge and the objects of knowledge by identifying their different properties and the conditions that are necessary for each. The third section discusses the relationship between the disciplines, the nature of disciplinary boundaries and debates between critical realists on these issues, while the concluding section discusses the implications that arise from this analysis for the structure of curriculum.

Knowledge is fallible, but judgements are possible

While our knowledge of the natural and social worlds will never be perfect because there is always a gap between objective truth and the epistemic access we have to the truth, there are still grounds for making judgements between different theories because some are better approximations of the truth than others (Norris 2008). Critical realists can agree with relativists that knowledge is relative, where they differ is that critical realists argue that judgements can be made between different theories because they provide better accounts of the world. In contrast, relativist theories are premised on the notion that 'the real' is socially constructed and so there are no objective grounds for choosing between different accounts. Usher (1996: 19) illustrates this approach when he argues that 'There is no object-in-itself independent of a context of knowing and of the knowing activities of [the] subject.' Differences in knowledge are reduced to 'ways of knowing' so that one form of knowledge cannot be privileged over another, and differences in knowledge are explained as differences between knowers (Maton 2006).

This leads to two types of relativist approach: the first is to argue that systems of knowledge are shared by communities so that they are 'real' for those communities, but are not real for other communities. This is illustrated by Barnes and Bloor (1982: 29) who argue that there are no criteria for judging the rationality or validity of a belief independent of the belief itself and the basis upon which the belief is held to be true. That is, there are no objective grounds for choosing between beliefs separate from the system of belief held by particular cultures.[1] Knowledge is built from inter-subjective meanings arising from shared social practices. This is the premise of constructivist theories in education such as Lave and Wenger's (1991) 'communities of practice' approach in which learning consists of novices moving from the periphery of a community of practice to becoming a recognized and expert member of that community of practice.

The second approach is to reduce knowledge to competing perspectives or 'ways of knowing', with the difference that some groups have the power to impose their perspective as the legitimate and normal perspective. Knowledge (particularly as codified in the academic disciplines) is then construed as social constructions in which truth is validated, power exercised, identities constructed and regulatory regimes extended by defining some knowledge practices as legitimate and others as illegitimate (Edwards and Usher 1994: 93–94; Michelson 2006).[2]

In contrast, ontological realism presupposes epistemological relativity because knowledge is not identical to the world it describes; knowledge and the objects of that knowledge are different and have different properties. This is so for two main reasons: first, as discussed in the previous chapter, we do not have unmediated access to causal mechanisms since we experience only their effects through events that we may or may not perceive directly, and these events and experiences are always multiply determined by the interaction of different mechanisms in open systems. Moreover, our experiences and the events and mechanisms that generate those experiences may not be in phase with one another (Bhaskar 2008: 25).

Second, our knowledge will always be fallible and provisional because there is no direct correspondence between the world and our perceptions of it. Our engagement with the objects of knowledge is always socially and conceptually mediated and this means that our experience of the world is always theory laden (though not theory determined) (Sayer 1992). That is, we do not have 'direct' unmediated perceptual access to the objects of knowledge; we must use existing knowledge and concepts to interpret and understand the natural and social worlds. Our interpretations are often wrong and sometimes this is due to the theories we use when we try to understand the world. However, the fallibility of knowledge supports rather than undermines realism for, as Sayer (1992: 67) explains: 'it is precisely because the world does not yield to just any kind of expectation that we believe it exists independently of us and is not simply a figment of our imagination'. Chalmers (1999: 228) explains that even if we cannot describe the world without using some sort of conceptual framework, we still can test that framework by interacting with the world.[3] We have continually to revise our beliefs and expectations when we try to apply them in the world, particularly when they do not work as we expect due to 'the way the world is' (Benton and Craib 2001: 174).

Admitting the relativity of knowledge does not lead to the slippery slope of relativism or solipsism because we can choose between theories as some explanations provide more 'practically adequate' accounts of the reality they seek to describe. Epistemological relativity *only* makes sense if it is accompanied by the capacity to make judgements about and to choose between different theories, ideas and concepts. Bhaskar (1998d: 58) explains that:

> it is clear that if one is to act at all there must be grounds for preferring one belief (about some domain) to another; and that such activity in particular practices is typically codifiable in the form of system of *rules*, implicitly or explicitly followed.

The existence of different theories to explain the same phenomena also means we must reject the relativist argument that theoretical frameworks are based on different and incommensurable paradigms. Incommensurability arises from descriptions of *different* worlds, whereas *competing* beliefs arise when they are about the *same* world (Bhaskar 1998a: xi). Arguments for incommensurability between theories in a discipline emphasize concepts and ideas that are unique to competing theories at the expense of the many shared (but usually more basic) ideas and concepts. If beliefs are incompatible this can be established only via the shared terms they use to conduct the argument (Sayer 1992: 73). Chalmers (1999: 171) argues that paradigm shifts within particular disciplines are replacements rather than refutations. He says there must be some shared understandings because it is not possible to change the whole web of a particular discipline at once even though particular aspects of it will change and be replaced over time, so that it may look quite different at one point compared to an earlier point. He argues that there are few examples in the natural sciences of paradigms being so different that they shared nothing, and if this were the case, 'it would indeed be impossible to capture an objective sense in which science progresses' (Chalmers 1999: 171). This can, arguably, also apply to the social sciences even though the differences within disciplines in the social sciences may be greater than those in the natural sciences.

Given that competing theories compete because they provide different accounts of the same world, what are the grounds for choosing one over the other? Bhaskar (1998a: xi) explains that:

> if one theory can explain more significant phenomena in terms of its descriptions than the other can in terms of *its*, then there is a rational criterion for theory choice, and *a fortiori* a positive sense to the idea of scientific development over time.

The chosen theory must be able to 'explain' more than its rival or predecessor theory by drawing on the conceptual and methodological tools available within the discipline, even though these tools may change over time (Chalmers 1999). Sayer (1992, 2000) uses the notion of 'practical adequacy' to establish the veracity of the relationship between our theories of the world and the things to which the theories refer. He explains that 'Realists do *not* need to suppose that knowledge mirrors the world; rather it interprets it in such a way that the expectations and practices it informs are intelligible and reliable' (Sayer 2000: 42). His approach emphasizes the way practice mediates the development of knowledge and provides part of the criteria needed to make judgements about competing theories. This means, though, that the explanatory success of knowledge will vary according to the context (Sayer 1992: 69). The differentiated and structured nature of the world accounts for the greater explanatory success of some theories compared to others in the same context, and for the explanatory success of the same theories in different contexts. For example, while behaviourist theories of learning may be able to explain specific changes to behaviour in some circumstances, other theories of learning that emphasize the interplay between the cognitive, the developmental, the individual, the cultural and the social provide more comprehensive accounts. Such theories of learning may provide insights into processes of learning in other social domains and not just those in formal educational institutions (such as the workplace). However, theories of learning may not solve particular skills problems within a workplace if the 'problem' was due to the way work was organized.

The notion of the 'practical adequacy' of knowledge is not to be confused with instrumentalism which evaluates knowledge by the extent to which it works or is useful on the basis that 'all we can say is that things behave *as if* our models of them were true' (Sayer 1992: 71). Sayer explains that instrumentalist standpoints on truth regard knowledge as true if it is useful, whereas realists regard knowledge as useful if it is true. He explains that 'The question is not only what works, but what it is about the world which makes it work' (Sayer 2000: 42). Instrumentalist notions are problematic on two grounds. First, instrumentalism ignores the fact that it is the structures of the world that make our practice possible and not our theories about those structures, so our purpose should be to seek knowledge about those structures (Sayer 2000: 42). Moreover, instrumentalist approaches can be counter-productive and avoid difficult questions on the pragmatic grounds that the existing theory 'works' while still being wrong in important respects (Chalmers 1999: 237). Second, the pragmatic 'it works' argument obscures the difference between theories that abstract aspects of the world by the 'as if' proposition to explain aspects of the world even though we know that it will never be 'as if' (such as economists who posit perfect competition in markets) on the one hand, and on the other, those theories that are imperfectly attempting to grasp the complexity of an aspect of the world, but represent the best we can do at present (Sayer 1992: 71). There is also a normative dimension to theory choice, and this also distinguishes realists from instrumentalists because the point of choosing is to get closer to the truth. This means that 'normative values of truth, rationality, logical warrant, falsifiability under pressure of conflicting evidence, and so forth ... are basic to the very enterprise of science or any other reputable branch of enquiry' (Norris 2008: 100).

The two dimensions of knowledge

There are two dimensions of knowledge. The first is that theoretical knowledge 'is a social product much like any other' because it is produced by historically specific communities of knowledge producers who draw on the conceptual, social and material resources that are available to them when producing new knowledge (Bhaskar 2008: 21). This means the knowledge that is produced 'always consists in historically specific social forms' (Bhaskar 1998d: 11), and one of these forms is the structuring of knowledge into the academic disciplines. The other dimension of knowledge is that it is 'of things' which exist independently of our conceptions, and this means that while knowledge is produced by specific people in specific contexts, the knowledge they produce can't be reduced to this context – it has emergent properties that transcend that context.

Critical realists distinguish between the *intransitive* dimension which refers to the existence of the real (the domains of the real, actual and empirical), and the *transitive* dimension which refers to our knowledge of the real. Collier (1994: 50) says that the intransitive and transitive are the two dimensions of science (broadly defined) that permit a realist ontology and fallibilist epistemology. This is an important distinction because it demonstrates that objects and the knowledge we have of them are not the same. Each has different properties, and while they are related because knowledge is *about* the intransitive object, 'Concept and object ... remain distinct and, in general, dissimilar' (Bhaskar 1998d: 142). The transitive dimension seeks knowledge concerning generative mechanisms in the intransitive dimension, mechanisms that are (more or less) relatively enduring. Collier (1994: 51) explains that 'However much science deepens its knowledge of its *intransitive object*, its product remains a transitive object.' Consequently, processes of change in each may be different. This means that our knowledge may change (the transitive dimension), while the object of our knowledge may remain the same (the intransitive dimension). The reverse is also possible; objects in the intransitive dimension may change resulting in the emergence of a greater 'gap' between knowledge and the object of knowledge which was not there before.

Critical realists argue that knowledge arises from our practice in the world and not from the structures of knowledge. World before word. As our practice leads to better knowledge of the world it also leads to changes in the classification and structures of knowledge. The processes that contribute to structuring the disciplines and to changing disciplinary configurations and the contents of disciplinary knowledge are complex and are the consequence of the interplay between our practice, social relations and the emergent properties of knowledge within disciplines and in other disciplines. This is because the academic disciplines are themselves complex realities; they are partly constituted by social relations because they are social products, but they are also partly constituted by the objects they seek to study.

Theories and knowledge are the raw material of the academic disciplines (rather than the end product) and this raw material is used to deepen knowledge of the intransitive dimension (Collier 1994: 51). Consequently, the practice of creating new knowledge includes using pre-existing knowledge. Existing knowledge is the outcome of *past* agents' practice that we use as a raw material in exploring the world, and in the process we transform that knowledge. Bhaskar (1998d: 34) explains that just as human beings recreate (and sometimes transform) society rather than create it because society pre-exists them, people recreate (and sometimes transform) knowledge rather than create it:

> Thus in science the raw materials used in the construction of new theories include established results and half-forgotten ideas, the stock of available paradigms and models, methods and techniques of inquiry, so that the scientific innovator comes to appear in retrospect as a kind of cognitive *bricoleur*.
>
> (Bhaskar 1998d: 34)

However, once codified, theoretical knowledge has objective properties that cannot be reduced to the conditions of its production. Such knowledge is objective in two senses: first it is objective because it is *about* something and is not reducible to subjective states of knowers. Second, propositions within theories and the way that knowledge is structured have objective properties of their own. Chalmers (1999: 126) argues that theories have properties that are independent of their producers and may even have consequences and implications about which those who created the knowledge are unaware. This contributes to increasing the fertility of a field as others use the ideas and concepts in new and novel ways. However, it may also be that a theory is inconsistent or explains very little (Chalmers 1999: 127). Knowledge does not have to be 'the truth' in either sense of objectivity because each can lead to knowledge that is partially wrong or partially right to a greater or lesser degree.

Codified knowledge also cannot be reduced to what people know; that is, knowledge does not equal knowing. Knowledge has an objective existence independently of knowers, although it could not have been produced without knowledge producers, and the codification of knowledge modifies and contributes to it as a social product so that it takes on a 'layered' structure. Bhaskar (2008: 187) argues that the existence of this stock of knowledge 'is a necessary feature of any human cognitive situation; so knowledge can never be seen as a function of individual sense-experience'. Its production requires specific antecedent conditions (pre-existing knowledge) and specific social practices as a condition of its production.

The production of knowledge

The production of knowledge in the academic disciplines is differentiated from the production of knowledge in everyday life by its purpose. The *raison d'être* of the disciplines is to create knowledge about the objects they study (Bhaskar 1998d: 11–12), whereas everyday knowledge is not gained for its own sake but as part of our 'strategies' in pursuing things that are important to us, in which we are often guided by a 'practical consciousness' (Bourdieu 1990, 1998). The practices of the disciplines are designed to produce knowledge, and 'It seeks and finds only because it seeks' (Collier 1994: 39). While we may have objective knowledge about aspects of the world in the everyday, we tend to 'think *with* our beliefs and concepts but not about them' (Sayer 1992: 25). If we are to develop and extend objective knowledge, we need to think *about* our concepts as well as *with* them and explore the relationship between our concepts and the things to which they refer.

The production of knowledge in the academic disciplines is also distinguished from everyday knowledge by the social practices used to create knowledge. These social practices differ between different disciplines because their objects of knowledge differ and this means they require different methods for exploring their objects. However, methods of inquiry in all disciplines are systematic and consist of (more or less shared) systematic social practices that govern the processes, procedures and rules of investigation and knowledge creation, even though these may change over time. The social sciences and humanities may differ from the natural sciences because, as Bernstein (2000) explains, they consist of serial languages rather than unified hierarchical theoretical frameworks, but *within* each language a shared set of social practices is used to create knowledge. Collier (1994: 56) explains that 'For our reasonable confidence that a science *does* give us genuine knowledge is based precisely on the nature of the mechanisms by which that knowledge was produced.'

The systematic nature of disciplinary practices also demonstrates that knowledge production is *work* and not passive processes of observation or contemplation (although both may be part of the work of knowledge creation) (Collier 1994: 51; Bhaskar 1998d: 13). Knowledge creation is work because its aim is to deepen our knowledge about causal mechanisms and these causal mechanisms are not always immediately identifiable from experience or events. The disciplines create knowledge of objects that are complex and stratified, and in most disciplines the essence of work 'lies in the *movement* at any one level from knowledge of manifest phenomena to knowledge of the structures that generate them' (Bhaskar 1998d: 13).

Relativist arguments that reduce knowledge to power fail to distinguish between the different social practices that the disciplines use to create knowledge and those that they use to ensure their economic survival and to maintain their status, power and exclusivity. Collier (1994: 56) distinguishes between the intrinsic aspects of science which consist of social practices designed to deepen knowledge of its intransitive object, and 'the ideological bias of, and political or economic pressures on, the scientific community' (Collier 1994: 57). These social, political and ideological mechanisms co-determine the production of knowledge. Identifying these 'profane' practices is a necessary part of subjecting knowledge to scrutiny, because, as Collier (1994: 57) explains, 'Would racist theories of "intelligence" ever have been discredited scientifically if it were not for scrutiny motivated by suspicion of their political bias?'

However, identifying and distinguishing between social practices that create knowledge and those that are the marks of power and self-interest is not always straightforward or immediately apparent. Collier (1994: 57) warns that ignoring the 'intrinsic' aspect of knowledge 'simply because their proponents had motives for wanting them to be true' may lead to rejecting knowledge that has some basis. As an illustration, while feminists have justifiably argued that the medical profession has medicalized the social basis of women's unhappiness by labelling it as depression, this does not, nonetheless, discount the reality of depression and the suffering it causes. The medicalization thesis discounts the different contributory factors of depression and the way they interact so that a predisposition towards depression is actualized in one circumstance, but not in another. It discounts the interplay of the biological and social. It also leads to a denial of the reality of the relief women (and men) can sometimes obtain from medication which has been produced by research in medical science. This does not mean that medication is the *only* avenue that should be used to treat depression (or other mental illnesses), but to deny it altogether and deem it to be a mechanism for social control is to subject many to great misery needlessly.

This complexity demonstrates that social relations of power can still mark the production of knowledge, while at the same time providing insights into its intransitive objects. It is true that practitioners in the academic disciplines do not possess a special attitude or superior morality, but this does not mean that their practices do not have a rationality of their own (Bhaskar 2008: 189). Bhaskar (2008: 189) argues that to deny the rationality of scientific (or disciplinary) work is to commit two errors. The first is to suppose that the production of knowledge is not a social activity; we are making the impossible demand that the production of knowledge not be 'marked' by those who produced it. Second, it is also to deny that the systematic production of knowledge is a social activity that is unlike other social activities because its aim is the production of knowledge about the intransitive dimension; it is distinguished by its purpose and practices. It is this that gives knowledge its emergent properties that mean knowledge cannot be reduced to the conditions of its production.

Part of the work of the philosophy and sociology of knowledge is to distinguish between those intrinsic aspects of the production of knowledge and those that arise from relations of power, without reducing the former to the latter. Sayer (1999) addresses this issue through a critique of Bourdieu, in arguing that Bourdieu fails to distinguish between the *use-value* and *exchange-value* of different kinds of capital (economic, social, cultural, etc). He argues that Bourdieu 'excludes evaluations of quality or use-value from his explanation of preferences and actions' (Sayer 1999: 410). In other words, communities of knowledge producers may produce knowledge that has intrinsic merits even if, at the same time, they advance their social position within the field.[4]

Induction into knowledge

Critical realists such as Collier emphasize the importance of induction into the disciplinary structures of knowledge. He explains that experience is not determined 'just by what is there, but what we have already learnt' (Collier 1994: 72). Experience is not, of itself, self-authenticating and self-explanatory. We learn from others how to learn and this includes learning from nature,[5] as well as learning how to become a 'suitably knowing subject' within an academic discipline. There is no universal or abstract 'suitably knowing subject' because each of the disciplines consists of historically specific ideas, concepts, methods and skills (Collier 1994: 54). Induction into the disciplinary structures of knowledge is important even if we wish to overturn elements of those structures, because understanding those structures is a necessary condition for revolutionizing them. This means we need practice in 'thinking other people's thoughts' as a condition for thinking for ourselves (Collier 1994: 71). There is no easy way around this. This is because, as Bernstein (1996: 12) explains 'To know whose voice is speaking is the beginning of one's own voice.' Induction into the disciplines is necessary if students are to recognize different voices and to begin to articulate their own. This is not an argument for induction into the disciplines as timeless truths. The focus is on introducing students to the debates and controversies within disciplines and for creating the conditions for active agency so students can participate in these debates and controversies.

Bhaskar (1998d: 15) says that 'Research and teaching are the two most obvious, yet philosophically under-analysed *tasks* of scientists, just as the laboratory and the classroom are the two most obvious *sites* of knowledge.' This is a valid criticism, particularly of critical realism (Fairclough *et al.* 2002). While this is beginning to change, critical realists have mostly focused on the emergent properties of the content of knowledge in understanding the real or on the relationship between concepts within and between theories and disciplines. Archer (1988) provides an example of this in her analysis of the emergent properties of propositional knowledge *qua* propositional knowledge as distinct from the content of that knowledge. However, arguably, this leads Archer to a reductionist analysis of knowledge because she reduces codified knowledge to propositional knowledge that is subject to the 'law of contradiction', strips it of all other properties and severs it from the broader systems of meaning that provide the context for understanding that knowledge. Collier was not here writing in response to Archer, but his point is relevant nonetheless. He explains that 'the logical necessity of a statement and the causal necessity of what it describes are independent questions' (Collier 1994: 66). Collier (2003: 144) elsewhere explains (again, not in response to Archer) that while there is not a direct correspondence between language and its object, we still need to account for the objects of knowledge. An exclusive focus on comparing ideas means that 'Epistemology loses its reference to what ideas are about and comes to be a matter of coherence between ideas' (Collier 2003: 144).

Bernstein helps us overcome these problems because his analysis identifies the properties of knowledge *qua* knowledge, while his analysis needs to be strengthened to take greater account of the objects of knowledge. His analysis of the structures of knowledge potentially enriches a critical realist analysis of the nature of knowledge and its causal and emergent properties by, in particular, his analysis of the relationship between these structures and related social relations and social practices of knowledge producers. It provides us with greater insights that we can use to distinguish between different social practices of producing knowledge, particularly those social practices that privilege the knower rather than the object of knowledge (Moore and Maton 2001).

Disciplinary divisions, disciplinary change and interdisciplinarity

The division between the disciplines is not *wholly* arbitrary because even though they are in part shaped by complex social relations, they are also shaped by their relationship to their intransitive object (Collier 1997, 1998b). It is true that disciplinary configurations could be organized in different ways and to this extent they are arbitrary, but the nature of the phenomena and objects they observe are much less arbitrary. It is also true that disciplinary boundaries, their knowledge structures, mode of legitimation and methods of research help to construct the object of investigation and render some things visible and other things less visible, but there are limits to this process. The world has a way of impressing itself, and should disciplinary boundaries be constructed in such a way as to exclude key human concerns or key aspects of the world, disciplines would arise to fill this gap. Bhaskar (1998d: 13 emphasis in original) argues that:

> only the concept of ontological depth can reveal the actual historical stratification of the sciences as anything other than an accident. For this can now be seen as grounded in the multi-tiered stratification of that reality, and the consequent logic – of discovery – *that* stratification imposes on science.

The abstract and concrete sciences

Some disciplines, like physics or chemistry, provide insights into *aspects* of the world by identifying their causal mechanisms in isolation of their operation in open systems. Collier refers to these as the abstract disciplines; they are disciplines in which experiments can be used to identify mechanisms and their effects. This is possible in these disciplines because they can artificially construct closed conditions, even if the systems they are based upon are intrinsically open. Designating these disciplines as abstract sciences is not the same as the use of abstract concepts and processes of abstraction, which are common to all disciplines. These disciplines are abstract sciences because (as in the case of physics, chemistry and biology) they abstract *particular* structures and causal mechanisms to demonstrate their actions, '*other things being equal*' (Collier 1997: 22). These disciplines are about aspects of the physical world, but they 'do not predict how anything will behave in the real world where other things are never equal' (Collier 1997: 22). He says that abstract sciences are individuated 'by the kinds of laws that they discover' (Collier 1997: 26).

Collier (1997: 23) contrasts these abstract disciplines with concrete disciplines and he includes in this category all the human sciences and some natural sciences, such as geography, meteorology and medicine. These disciplines are not able to construct experiments in the way of the abstract sciences because their intransitive objects consist of complex objects that are multiply determined. They focus on the emergent outcome of many causal mechanisms operating at different levels in open systems (Collier 1997, 1998b). In contrast to abstract sciences that are individuated by the laws they discover, Collier (1997: 26) says the 'concrete sciences are individuated by their concrete objects'. He also distinguishes the concrete sciences from social practices in referring to the way society uses the insights of the sciences. Social practices are differentiated from concrete sciences by their purpose: the aim of concrete sciences is to explore their intransitive object, whereas the aim of social practices is to use the insights of the concrete sciences. He gives agriculture, health care and war as examples of social practices.[6]

The concrete sciences build knowledge in two ways: first by drawing from the abstract sciences; and second, by trying to explain their own intransitive objects and why things are as they seem to be. The concrete sciences thus build their own stock of abstract concepts which cannot be reduced to or explained entirely in terms of, the abstract sciences. Because the concrete sciences are not able to establish closed systems necessary for experiments, they must use processes that enable them to abstract components of their objects to examine their interrelatedness. However, natural concrete sciences have a greater capacity to borrow from the abstract sciences than the human sciences because of the nature of their objects (Collier 1997: 25).[7]

Collier's distinction between abstract and concrete sciences (and between natural concrete sciences and human sciences) is useful because it allows us to explore the implications for the development of knowledge of a stratified world characterized by ontological depth and emergence. It emphasizes the importance of the concrete sciences, not just by specifying their relation to the abstract sciences, but also in identifying the contribution they make in their own right. In particular, it provides a framework for considering the centrality of applied disciplinary knowledge in curriculum as a precondition for vocational and professional practice. In addition, it provides insights into processes of disciplinary change, as new disciplines are established or old ones reconfigured in response to the development of new objects, changes in existing objects, or an improved understanding of objects.

However, the division of the disciplines in the social sciences is contentious among critical realists with some, such as Sayer (1992: 120), arguing that while the natural sciences reflect different aspects of the natural world, in the social world it is more difficult to establish discrete and bounded objects of study capable of clear disciplinary definitions. He argues that the disciplinary divisions in the social sciences are the outcome of turf wars rather than intrinsic distinctions in their objects of study. Arguably, though, this is not an argument against the social sciences *per se*, because their objects of knowledge still relate to aspects of the world (and their objects), however imperfectly. All it says is that the relationship between them is more permeable than it is in the natural sciences.

Moreover, if the notion of ontological depth applies to the social world as much as to the natural world, disciplinary distinctions must reflect these boundaries even if they are imperfectly drawn. Bhaskar (1998d: 97) argues that the intransitive objects of sociology are different to those in psychology because societies are fundamentally different from, and not reducible to, people, with each possessing different properties. However, the disciplines are related because their intransitive objects are related. The features that characterize us as human beings and then differentiate us as individuals presuppose the existence of the social, while the existence of the social is presupposed by the existence of individuals who act in purposeful, intentional ways and in ways that are guided unconsciously. The disciplines thus must work together and do come together in social psychology, but that does not exhaust the ways in which sociology, and psychology need to work together or can provide insights into each other. Bhaskar (1998d: 35–36) explains that human actions may be explained 'either in terms of the agent's reason for engaging in it or in terms of its social function or role', but the explanation in either case is different because the reasons why individuals engage in an activity may not be (and usually are not) the same as society's reasons for the activity. While this is so, the respective disciplinary insights can have implications for the other in understanding their own intransitive object.

Interdisciplinarity

The disciplines are important because they provide knowledge about aspects of the social and natural worlds, but they do so by abstracting their objects of study from the open systems in which they are situated. This is necessary to identify causal mechanisms and their tendencies to act in particular ways.

However, interdisciplinary research is needed to understand concrete particulars, because the real is always a consequence of co-determination of many different mechanisms. Such interdisciplinary work takes place, however, by explicitly negotiating disciplinary boundaries rather than their negation. This is a different argument to many arguments for interdisciplinarity, most of which are premised on traducing the distinctions between the disciplines.[8] There are gradations of the latter argument which range from multidisciplinarity that does not deny all boundaries, to transcending disciplinary boundaries altogether by creating 'new' spaces for the integration of knowledge, without specifying how that will take place (Moran 2001; Horlick-Jones and Sime 2004).

Interdisciplinary work is necessary because without it one cannot identify, let alone explore, mechanisms of co-determination in open systems. For example, Bhaskar and Danermark (2006) explain that to understand any particular experience of disability, one needs an understanding of sociology, biology and psychology. Individual researchers do not need to be expert in all three areas, but if they are working in an applied area they need to have an understanding of the possible contribution of causal mechanisms in other domains and draw on concepts and knowledge from these areas.[9] Because disciplines are focussed on different aspects of the real, many have the same object of study although they address it at different levels and in different ways, and this provides the basis for methodological pluralism, but not epistemological eclecticism or methodological relativism.

Disciplines are not *just* defined by their object of study; they are also relationally defined by the way in which they relate to or differ from other disciplines and by the social practices that underpin them (and this is Bernsteinian insight as well as a critical realist insight). Developing knowledge within a discipline is always a relational process (socially and epistemically) with other disciplines. Our study *of* disciplines consequently needs to include a study of their relations with each other to establish the way in which these relations partially constitute the field of knowledge *within* disciplines, and the way in which the disciplines specify their objects of knowledge and establish their methodological procedures (López 2003: 83). This emphasizes Bernstein's (2000) insight about the way in which the relations of insulation between disciplines is an important structuring feature of the disciplines.

Rather than negating disciplinary boundaries, the explicit negotiation of these boundaries helps us to understand when we are drawing on one discipline to develop another and to develop a better understanding of the complexity of these concepts and their contribution. This cannot occur in an atomistic way. While Cruickshank (2003: 6) refers below to the role of metaphor in theory development within the disciplines, his point also applies to the social practices and methods underpinning the disciplines in saying that:

> we need to recognise that in drawing upon metaphors we are drawing upon the world-view – and its associated practices – of a different discipline, which will in turn carry its assumptions over into the new discipline.

Failure to negotiate disciplinary boundaries will result in these assumptions remaining implicit and invisible to analysis. For example, the disciplinary imperialism of economics has resulted in the unproblematic importation of the rational, self-interested and self-maximizing actor of rational choice theory into many domains and disciplines, and this is problematic because these assumptions are taken out of their disciplinary context (and they are dubious even there) and transplanted in new contexts without the accompanying theorization and justification. It renders concepts such as the rational, self-maximizing actor opaque to analysis *unless* it is situated within the system of meaning that gives the concept its meaning, and doing so will render the concept more open to critique.

Proponents of the negation of the disciplines have a model of the disciplines that is rigid and positivist, and reducible to power relations (in the case of relativists) or to a world long past (as in the Gibbons *et al.* mode 1 and mode 2 thesis).[10] The disciplines are not closed conceptual networks; they must draw on society's available conceptual and linguistic repertoire, and so will be drawing on overlapping concepts particularly by the use of metaphor and analogy (López 2003). Consequently, their boundaries change and they are in continual processes of development, concept borrowing, renegotiation and transformation.

This point is not always appreciated by critical realists who emphasize the importance of interdisciplinary work in understanding complex realities. Their argument is premised on the need to focus on the object of study, its relationships to other objects and the various disciplines that are necessary to explore these, all of which is justified as far as it goes. In many cases, the argument is an ontological one against proponents within particular disciplines who draw on Humean notions of causation and methodological individualism. However, this sometimes leads to unhelpful language such as calls for transdisciplinarity which suggests the negation of disciplinary boundaries (see, for example Dickens 2003). This is so even while the analysis is predicated on the stratified nature of the real which requires different disciplinary insights. It is evident that critical realism has some way to go in debating and exploring these issues, and one issue that needs further exploration is the way in which disciplinary boundaries can be negotiated, rather than just asserting that it is necessary to do so.

The analysis presented in this and the previous chapter may seem to limit the importance of disciplinary knowledge to the natural and social sciences and leave less scope for the humanities and creative arts because the emphasis is on the way in which the disciplines relate to the natural and social worlds. However, the humanities and creative arts are also important parts of the social world, and in some cases draw on materials provided by the natural world as in many creative arts. The humanities are in part a sustained exploration of humanity's relationship to the natural world as well as of human nature and the complexities of our social and inner lives. Each is shaped by its relationship to its object, to the methods it uses to explore its objects and to the social relations that underpin it. For example, Carter and Sealey (2004: 118) explain that language is a 'cultural emergent property', and although language is the emergent outcome arising from the interplay of human practice in a material world, it cannot be reduced to an epiphenomenonal consequence of human practice. Its construction and emergent properties are complex and it must be understood in its own right and on its own terms. We can extend their example: while a study of the nature, structure and properties of language provides important insights for poetry, it does not explain poetry. Students need to be inducted into systems of meaning within the humanities and creative arts as with any other discipline if they are to become 'suitably knowing subjects' who are able to extend knowledge and engage in debates and controversies within their discipline.

Conclusion: implications for curriculum

This chapter analyses the relationship between disciplinary knowledge and the objects such knowledge is about, and the way in which disciplinary knowledge is developed and changed. It does so by distinguishing between the transitive and intransitive dimensions and in so doing, demonstrates that knowledge and the objects of knowledge have different conditions for their realization and different properties. It also distinguishes between disciplinary and everyday knowledge, because while both are theory laden and concept dependent, the former is distinguished from the latter because it represents the systematization of knowledge that 'extends and supersedes our ordinary understanding of things' and the relations between them (Taylor 1982: 101). The disciplines provide students with access to the *relational* connections within a field of study and between fields, and students need access to the disciplinary 'style of reasoning' (Muller 2000: 88) to move beyond a focus on isolated examples of content. Specific content is the *product* of disciplinary knowledge, and not the relational connections that allow students to produce that content. Unless students have access to these relational systems of meaning they will not be able to drive the production of knowledge, or determine the criteria they need to evaluate knowledge.

Disciplinary knowledge also needs to be distinguished from everyday knowledge and considered as an ontological object in its own right. This is part of considering the different properties of knowledge and the objects of knowledge and the conditions required for the realization of each. The structures of disciplinary knowledge have their own causal properties as do the social practices that mediate the production of knowledge. Such an analysis allows for a comparison of the different social practices used by disciplines to produce knowledge, but also to compare everyday and disciplinary knowledge. Disciplinary knowledge is the emergent outcome of the interplay between agency, social context, social resources, social relations between knowledge producers, the aspect of the world which the discipline focuses upon, and the objective structure of knowledge within the field. Both the epistemic and social relations of knowledge have causal properties that shape the way knowledge is produced.

This analysis provides grounds for both defending the objectivity of knowledge and for critiquing social practices used to create further knowledge because the source of objectivity is not located exclusively in these social practices (although these are important); it is also located in the objects of knowledge.

Because disciplines are (in part) humankind's way of dealing with the stratification of the world, the boundaries between the disciplines are perhaps more permeable in this analysis than in Bernstein's analysis. Changes in disciplinary knowledge and in the boundaries between them must occur as we develop greater insights into the objects of study, and not just as a consequence of shifting relations of insulation between boundaries. However, these boundaries are important precisely *because* they reflect the stratified world (even if they do so imperfectly) and so this analysis *complements* Bernstein's analysis.

Drawing Bernstein and critical realism together is an argument for social and epistemic access to the disciplines. Bernstein demonstrates that access to disciplinary knowledge is access to socially powerful knowledge; critical realism demonstrates that social access to disciplinary knowledge can only be mediated by epistemic access. Moreover, Bernsteinian insights into the structures of knowledge and the social relations that underpin its production complement critical realist insights about the nature of knowledge and the relationship it has to its intransitive object. Both see the production of disciplinary knowledge as consisting of specific social practices that are distinguished from social practices used to produce everyday knowledge by their purpose and by the nature of those practices. While some critical realists may argue for greater emphasis on interdisciplinarity, this is not at the expense of disciplinary boundaries or recognition of their importance. It is an argument about where the boundaries should lie and the nature of their permeability. The critical realist arguments cited in this chapter, particularly those by Collier, emphasize the relationship between stratification in the natural and social worlds and disciplinary boundaries as the basis for negotiating the relationship between them.

Together, this establishes the centrality of disciplinary knowledge for curriculum and it has implications for the way curriculum should be structured. The first implication is that the pursuit of truth should be a normative goal of curriculum, but tempered by an awareness of the fallibility of knowledge and the need to revise it in the light of new evidence. However, fallibility here is not relativism which permits no judgement to be made between competing theories; knowledge is fallible precisely because it is more or less associated with truth, and the aim of knowledge creation (and curriculum) is to try to get closer to the truth. Bhaskar (1998d: 63) explains 'that truth *is* a good (*ceteris paribus*) is not only a condition of moral discourse, it is a condition of any discourse at all.' Fallibility must be associated with judgemental rationality.

The second implication is that the fallibility of our knowledge means that curriculum cannot be presented as 'the truth', but as our best approximation to the truth in light of the available evidence (Norris 2008). That is, curriculum cannot and should not present theoretical knowledge as timeless truths that cannot be questioned. This distinguishes the approach outlined here from traditional, conservative models of curriculum that take the current disciplinary configuration and state of knowledge as a given. Traditional conservative approaches to curriculum also proclaim the importance of truth, but they do so in the absence of judgemental rationality because truth is a given. Consequently, the basis of truth claims in traditional conservative approaches is *authority* and not the relationship between knowledge and its intransitive object.

The third implication is that curriculum must provide students with the means to *test* disciplinary (and other kinds of) knowledge and make judgements about it, while being open to alternative ways of thinking. This requires grounding in disciplinary knowledge and attention to the contexts of learning because it is by practice and application that such knowledge can be tested (Clarke and Winch 2004). The methods of the disciplines provide frameworks for testing knowledge because they provide access to ordered explanatory systems (Muller 2000: 51). This also exposes the methods of the disciplines to critical evaluation and provides a framework for evaluating cross-disciplinary knowledge, because the standards and rules of evidence are made explicit rather than rendered opaque.

The following chapters now move to an exploration of the reasons why knowledge has been displaced from the centre curriculum and the resulting crisis of curriculum. They also critique instrumentalist and constructivist approaches that emphasize the contextual as the principle of curricular construction and illustrate the way they deny students the access to the knowledge they need to participate in debates and controversies in their intended or existing field of practice, and in society's debates and controversies more broadly.

6 How knowledge was dethroned in society and displaced in curriculum

Introduction

The paradox of knowledge is that even though it is more important in late modernity and in the 'knowledge society', social trust in its truthfulness and objectivity has been severely undermined. The consequence is that while students' need for access to knowledge has never been greater, it has been displaced from the centre of curriculum. How are we to account for this? Bhaskar (1998d: 121) argues that it is not enough to demonstrate that something is problematic, we have to explain why problematic approaches persist and are valorized and the deleterious social consequences that occur as a result. The chapter is thus a sociological analysis of the social conditions for, and the consequences arising from, the relativizing of knowledge in society as the basis for its displacement in curriculum.

The chapter argues that the 'dethroning' of knowledge in society and in curriculum is the result of complex and iterative social changes over the last half century in the way knowledge is produced and used. This includes changes associated with globalization, the nature of work and weakened insulation between knowledge production and society. These processes were reflected in the academy in new conceptions of the human actor and in the rise of post-modernism. The result was that the focus of the academic disciplines that underpin the construction of curriculum moved from knowledge to knowers. The consequence was a crisis in curriculum theory which laid the basis for the triumph of the 'new vocationalism' thus further contributing to the relativizing of knowledge because of its emphasis on relevance to the workplace, which values knowledge only for its instrumental purposes.

While this compressed explanation of the arguments in this chapter seems almost deterministic and teleological, this is a problem that is common to any retrospective sociological analysis. However, it will become apparent that things could have been otherwise and indeed can be otherwise. Many of the changes discussed in this chapter were not the consequence of the unfurling of inexorable and impersonal social forces; rather, they were (and are) the result of deliberate neo-liberal government policies. While broad social, cultural and economic structures provide the parameters within which governments can act, they do not determine the course of action governments are required to take. The 'space' for the political remains important. This is why we need to understand why problematic approaches are valorized and persist despite their deleterious social consequences.

This chapter is in two sections: the first considers the relationship between knowledge and society. It has three parts that include a discussion of: globalization and reflexive modernization; changes to the nature of work; and the weakened insulation between the field of knowledge production and society more broadly. The second considers the consequences of the changed relationship between knowledge and society for the field of knowledge recontextualization. It has two parts: the first discusses changes in the field of knowledge production and the field of knowledge recontextualization, while the second discusses the triumph of vocationalism in curriculum.

The changed relationship between knowledge and society

Changes in the way knowledge is produced and used in society and in work have contributed to, and are the result of, changed social relations *between* knowledge and society. The status of knowledge is more important in the 'knowledge society' and 'knowledge economy', yet its nature, status and validity are under threat. This is reflected in the increased importance of knowledge and the way it is implicated in the social, cultural and economic wellbeing of societies on the one hand, and doubts about its objectivity and truthfulness on the other. The changes described in this section are complex and interrelated, and it is structured in three parts only to facilitate analysis even though they can only be understood in the way they relate to each other. Globalization and reflexive modernization have contributed to new relations between labour and capital at work, and to the new relationship between knowledge and society. Some are the consequence of broad social, economic and cultural processes of change, while others are the result of government policies and the way governments have mediated these social changes.

Globalization, the risk society and reflexive modernization

Even though there is debate over the nature and scope of globalization, profound changes have occurred in society and the economy so that each is characterized by perpetual change which is mediated through interconnected global networks. Castells (2000: 77), a leading globalization theorist, says that the result is a globalized economy that has three distinctive, but mutually reinforcing features: first, the globalized economy is informational, because the creation of knowledge is now a crucial factor of production; second, the production, consumption and circulation of goods are organized on a global scale; and third, production and competition are realized through global business networks that interact with, and are enmeshed within, each other. The interconnectedness of the international economy has been dramatically demonstrated by the 2008 crisis of the world financial system, which has ushered in the worst economic recession since the Great Depression of the 1930s.

This economic crisis demonstrates the way in which lives on one side of the globe are affected by decisions taken on the other, but the effects go beyond the economic. While globalization was initially driven by powerful Western nations to expand markets based on neo-liberal policies (Olssen and Peters 2005), it has since developed its own dynamic. Marginson (2000: 1) argues that globalization has social and cultural roots as well as economic roots, and these social and cultural changes have most affected the way we live and work. Globalization is, he argues, associated with world systems that bring people into more intensive and extensive relations with each other within nations and across national borders.

The interconnectedness of all our lives amidst perpetual change has led theorists such as Ulrich Beck (1994) to argue that we live in a society characterized by risk and permanent reflexivity. This is why processes characteristic of late capitalism or late modernity are referred to as reflexive modernization. The risks we face have been produced by our scientific–technical society and are of our own making; they are *manufactured* risks rather than risks from *natural* phenomena so that our concerns now centre around 'food scares and radioactive contamination, say, rather than plague and famine' (Field 2006: 70). However, even if one accepts this argument, it is, perhaps, important to emphasize the restriction of this analysis to the comfortable West; natural disasters (such as famine, drought, flood and tsunamis) combine with manufactured disasters in ways that compound the former and continue to wreak havoc on poor countries, while wealthier nations remain relatively more insulated from their effects. Global warming is, arguably, the best example of a manufactured risk that transcends borders. Manufactured risks such as global warming have contributed to less trust in scientific knowledge because it has, in part, contributed to its creation.

Beck argues that the institutions of the modern nation state – government, the army, science and commerce – cannot insulate citizens against these risks because they transcend borders. More than that, he says that these institutions: 'are no longer seen only as instruments of risk management, but also as a source of risk' (Beck 2006b: 336). This is because the rationalism and technicism of modernity have produced the risk society and traditional solutions within the nation state cannot resolve society's problems. This affects both institutions and individuals. Institutions must perpetually revise their strategies based on new and often uncertain information, whereas the individual 'must cope with the uncertainty of the global world by him- or herself. Here individualization is a default outcome of a failure of expert systems to manage risks' (Beck 2006b: 336). Uncertainty, risk and perpetual change have, he argues, weakened traditional social institutions such as the nuclear family, social class and the nation state and the social forms of solidarity they engender. He argues that individualization breaks the nexus between class culture and social class and unequal exposure to risk has replaced social class as the principal source of inequality (Beck 2007). Anthony Giddens (1994: 57), another leading theorist of the risk society, argues that on the one hand, we have had the globalizing and universalizing of modern institutions, but on the other, 'the disinterring and problematizing of tradition'. Individuals are compelled to be authors of their own biographies amidst conditions of uncertainty and are *forced* to engage in 'every-day experiments'. The problematizing of tradition gives rise to individualization because, according to Giddens (1999: 4):

> In a world where one can no longer simply rely on tradition to establish what to do in a given range of contexts, people have to take a more active and risk-infused orientation to their relationships and involvements.

How are we to assess these arguments? There is merit in arguments about reflexive modernization to the extent that they point to the impact perpetual change has on our identities and the nature of our institutions, and, as we will see in a later section, to changes in the social relations of knowledge production. This does not mean, however, that social class and the nation state have been transcended. It is important to distinguish between globalizing tendencies and neo-liberal government policies rather than conflating the two, as do Beck and Giddens, so that neo-liberalism comes to be seen as an intrinsic part of globalization (Jarvis 2007). Nation states continue to play a central role in world politics and the world economy, and while capital is mobile it is not global – capital has become more concentrated in wealthy countries, not less. Rather, nation states have used globalization as a mechanism to drive internal change and to implement neo-liberal reforms (Jarvis 2007).

Using globalization and reflexive modernization to explain all features of life that have changed over-simplifies the nature of these changes. Reflexivity becomes tied to, and reducible to individualization in the case of agents and positioning strategies in the case of institutions. It leads to teleological (and normative) arguments about the nature of globalization and concomitant changes to social structures and agency. This is because analyses of reflexive modernization often emphasize the individual and active agency (as emphasized by Giddens' quote above) while delocating agents from social and class structures that mediate their access to society's resources and power. There are particular consequences for education. Analysis of structural relations recedes, while those associated with agency and individualization are emphasized with individual decisions about participation in education and training redefined as purposeful and 'agential' (Avis 2006: 345), thus investing arguments of individualization with normative content. The agential is defined as good and non-agential as not good. The potential for learning to act as a process of individual transformation is emphasized, rather than the way in which education can (and often does) act as a mechanism for class reproduction. This is quite an effective way of blaming the victim and naturalizing inequality.

Moreover, the 'individualization thesis' can result in tying reflexivity to the instrumental self-maximizing rational economic actor in the case of individuals, market reflexivities in the case of enterprises, or customer satisfaction reflexivity in the case of government agencies and statutory bodies (such as tertiary education institutions) situated within quasi-markets. This is because each must develop self-interested 'positioning' strategies as other forms of social solidarity and the social institutions that underpin them have been eroded where neo-liberalism is naturalized as an inescapable and intrinsic feature of globalization.

Reflexivity of knowledge is thus tied to these strategies and in the process is reduced to the instrumental, whereas there are many different types of reflexivity because the production of knowledge and the way it is used is not reducible to the economic. The 'way things are' becomes reducible to the TINA argument – 'there is no alternative'. Such analyses fail to distinguish between the *discourse* of individualization intrinsic to models of citizenship that reassert consumer sovereignty, particularly in Anglophone nations, and the way in which social relations of power continue to structure patterns of opportunity in society. While globalization and market reforms are often regarded as synonymous, they are not the same, because many phenomena associated with globalization are 'in fact the result of deliberate policies aimed at deregulating markets' (Field 2006: 27). This means that the 'evolution of government, education and economic organisation ... *might have been different*' (Marginson 1997a: xii-xiii, emphasis in original).

Work and the new relations of subordination

That things may have been different is helpful in understanding debates about changes to the nature of work and the role of knowledge in work, and the extent to which both have been fundamentally transformed as a consequence of globalization and neo-liberal government policies. There is debate over the extent to which globalization has transformed work and the industrial division of labour from Fordist to post-Fordist principles of production, and the extent to which the current structure of work is a product of deregulatory market reforms, particularly in Anglophone nations (Moore 2004: 63). Proponents of the globalization and post-Fordism thesis argue that 'knowledge work' is now the crucial factor driving the world economy and innovation (and hence of globalization), and that firms that can produce and use knowledge most effectively will maintain the competitive edge (The World Bank 2002: 1).

Proponents of this thesis argue that the advent of knowledge-work has changed the nature of work and the nature of the industrial division of labour. Under Fordism production is geared to manufactured goods and mass markets. Management is responsible for the conceptualization and execution of tasks and the outcomes that are achieved, while workers on the floor are responsible for a small component of the productive process with no responsibility for outcomes (Braverman 1974). In contrast, post-Fordist workplaces (putatively) produce for niche markets, and have flatter organizational structures and devolved responsibilities for planning, implementing quality assurance and continuous improvement processes and for achieving work outcomes in line with enterprise or institutional strategic priorities.

Robert Reich (1992), a leading economist in the United States and advisor to United States' President Bill Clinton, explains in his famous analysis of the nature of work, that work can be divided into three broad categories: symbolic analytical services (high-skilled 'knowledge work'); in-person services (which involve direct contact with customers); and routine production services (which are in decline). In discussing Reich's work, Robinson (2003: 21) explains that we need to view each category 'according to their exposure to globalisation if we are to truly understand how the labour market is changing'. The first group is 'positively' exposed to globalization, and involves high skill levels that are globally traded and in high demand with the consequence that this group of workers benefits from globalization; the second contains jobs that are high, medium and low skilled but, as they are based on service occupations they are largely insulated from the effects of globalization (we will always need doctors, chefs and waiters locally, for example); and, the third is the most vulnerable to globalization, with both high- and low-skilled jobs in areas that are being overtaken by technology and easily transferable to lower cost economies.

On the other side are those theorists who accept that fundamental changes have occurred to societies, economies, culture and politics as a consequence of globalizing tendencies, but that the changes to the nature of work have been exaggerated.[1] Even theorists who think that globalization is a qualitatively new phenomenon that is reshaping our world argue that routine work is still the norm for many workers, characterized by little or no discretion by workers over the content, pace, or method of their work (Marginson 2000). The transformation of work has not been even, with many still employed in low-skilled jobs in organizational hierarchies and Fordist forms of work organization (Avis 2006). Moreover, Cully (2003: 5) explains that the relationship between a 'knowledge economy' and an increase in overall levels of skill cannot be assumed because knowledge can be codified into machinery, technology, or work-processes, while the execution of work may require little cognitive skill.

Work *has* changed in important ways for people engaged in work at all skill levels because the structure of occupations has changed, along with the nature of the employment contract. Cully (2008: 5–6), in an explanation which seems to lend some support to Reich's thesis, says that there has been a shift in Australia towards more highly skilled jobs at the expense of middle-ranking skilled jobs such as in the trades and advanced clerical and service jobs, while the share of less-skilled jobs has fallen only slightly. Where there has been growth in low-skilled occupations, it has been in service work and support tasks which have been 'created by knowledge workers' demand for services which previously would have been provided within the household' (Cully 2008: 6). In Australia, as in other Anglophone countries, participation rates by women have increased; union membership and award protection have declined as a result of deregulated markets; the labour market has become increasingly casualized (Wanrooy *et al.* 2007), and there is more heterogeneity in work arrangements with those working the 'standard' full-time week now in the minority (Cully 2008: 4).

The work relationship has also changed. Mounier (2001) describes this as the changed 'psychological contract' between labour and management. Under traditional Fordist relations, workers were responsible for undertaking work under supervision but without responsibility for the outcomes that were produced. Under post-Fordism,[2] workers are now required to take responsibility for outcomes, and to 'accept a part of the risk of the profit-making operations' (Mounier 2001: 18). Chappell *et al.* (2003: 3) argue that the overall level of skill required of lower and medium skilled workers has increased because the *work process* has changed as a consequence of flatter management structures, fewer core staff and increased levels of responsibility at lower levels of the enterprise.

This means that in addition to technical skills, workers need 'person-oriented' skills to take responsibility for quality assurance, collaboration with suppliers and customers, and all aspects of production and the provision of services (Chappell *et al.* 2003: 3). Moreover, in flatter, leaner enterprises, workers need to be 'multiskilled' because the knowledge and processes needed by the enterprise change with every innovation in technology or every innovation implemented by a competitor. Both reasons mean that there is less emphasis on the *specific* knowledge and skills of workers and the nature of knowledge and skill has consequently been redefined from technical knowledge and skills to include 'an array of general and person capacities and attitudes' (Chappell *et al.* 2003: 5). Increasing emphasis is placed on workers' personal attributes such as team-work, communication and problem-solving skills, but this also extends to attributes such as commitment and personal loyalty. In other words, workers' identities are now seen as central elements of the employment contract.

The focus on personal attributes is part of the new relations of subordination in the labour force. Mounier (2001: 18) argues that coercion in Fordist forms of work organization was achieved with economic devices (such as financial incentives) and forms of military organization (such as process lines in factories), however, this is now achieved with 'democratic forms and psychological attachment to the enterprise objectives in the post-Fordist era'. Part of workers' commitment is evidenced in their preparedness to 'invest' in themselves by developing their workplace competence and skills by undertaking education and training; however, they bear the risk and it is their fault if they do not invest wisely. The responsibility for ensuring individuals have the skills needed in the workplace has moved from the employer to the individual. This is particularly the case for those who are in part-time, casual and contingent employment even though these are the individuals with the greatest need and the least resources.

An even more compelling reason why individuals must invest in education and training is because it has replaced welfare as the 'social safety net' that protects against the risk of unemployment. Successive waves of neo-liberal reforms since the 1970s and 1980s have resulted in the winding back of the welfare state and its replacement by education and training as insurance against social risk (Mounier 2001). Indeed, access to welfare in Australia is contingent on welfare recipients' willingness to undertake formal education and training to acquire the skills needed for work. However, different levels of access to education and training are available to welfare recipients because the emphasis is on short-term training for entry-level jobs regardless of its quality, and this limits the range of educational and occupational pathways that are subsequently available to them.[3] Gamble (2004a: 187), in discussing South Africa, refers to this as a shift from employment to employability: the focus of governments is to make people *employable* through education and training rather than ensuring sufficient jobs exist.

The investment in the self is not in high-level, industry-specific skills because volatile labour mobility in (particularly Anglo) liberal market economies makes such an investment risky (Hall and Soskice 2001).[4] The emphasis moves from knowledge to knowers and to their attributes and identities, particularly as expressed through 'employability skills'. Consequently, even though globalization, technological change and perpetual change all require the production and use of more knowledge, the changed nature of the work relationship, particularly within Anglo liberal market economies, means that there is less emphasis on *specific* knowledge, and this has contributed to the displacement of knowledge from the centre of curriculum so that the focus is on generic attributes and skills.

Knowledge and the fall from grace

The insulation between society and the field of knowledge production have changed, as has the way society uses knowledge, thus contributing to its importance on the one hand, and on the other, to doubts about its objectivity. The elevated status of knowledge is in part due to the exponential growth of the scientific community which, in turn, was produced by a major expansion of higher education over the last 40 years. Trow (1974, 2005) describes a higher education system in which up to 15 per cent of the relevant age group participate as elite, one with 16–50 per cent participation as mass, and one in which half the population or more of the relevant age group participates as a universal system. Most industrialized countries have been progressively moving from elite to universal systems over the last 30–40 years in response to changes in society, the economy and technology (Trow 2005). The growth of higher education led to the production of more knowledge within a much bigger system, but also in the proliferation of new sites beyond the academy where knowledge was created and applied by a greatly expanded pool of knowledge workers (Bernstein 2000). Knowledge and knowledge production were no longer the exclusive preserve of tiny and closed elites.

All of this occurred in response to increasing social demand for knowledge-mediated products, but with profound social effects. The more society has recourse to knowledge, the more uncertainties proliferate, thereby increasing demand for further knowledge. Moreover, while increased knowledge production may make greater self-determination possible, it also leads to heightened social indeterminacy, greater social complexity and loss of trust in expert knowledge (Muller 2000: 147).[5] Global and spectacular failures of science (such as global warming) have contributed to this loss of trust. We now have, in part as a consequence of these failures, the 'tragedy of the commons' which has arisen from the exploitation of the world's resources by a few, even though this harms the long-term interests of all (including those few) (Collier 1999: 87).

Part of the loss of trust in expert knowledge arises because there are now many more scientists and debates between them are now conducted in public rather than behind the closed doors of academe. Muller (2000: 147) argues that this led to suspicions within the public sphere that scientists were acting on their particular interests and ideologies rather than a disinterested pursuit of truth, and that their different positions could be explained as, and reduced to, self-interest. He argues that the fact that scientists do not agree is not new, for they have never agreed. What is different is that the insulation between science and the public domain has been eroded.

The nexus between politics and science has also changed (Muller 2000). Before this change, the high status and unquestioned validity of knowledge was predicated on the distinction between values, which were the domain of politics and value-neutral science, which solved problems put to it by politics (through the state) and society more broadly. Researchers undertook value-neutral research and produced knowledge that could be counted on to be 'true', and politicians decided how it would be used. Muller (2000: 146) explains that 'This tradition has come to an end.' It led to doubt about the epistemic relation between science and objects studied by science and the collapse of the epistemic relation into the social relation.

Muller (2000: 145) explains that the changes in the social relations of knowledge production have led to curriculum debates about knowledge that are cast in apocalyptic polarities. On the one hand, there are those who argue for a return to the basics and for the reassertion of (an unquestioned) truth. This is to be achieved by the state playing a leading role in 'a quick but devastating attack on post-modern cynicism and irony and a clear rededication of faith and resources to the enterprise of research of useful knowledge for politics' (Muller 2000: 145). In this account, knowledge is disinterested and objective and deployed for different purposes following rational processes of decision-making. On the other hand, he says there are those who argue that the institution of science has been transformed because it now exists in different relationships to the (also transformed) worlds of politics, culture and the economy. Proponents of this thesis argue these new relations of knowledge production have replaced beliefs about the objectivity and neutrality of knowledge with views premised on the relativity of knowledge, and that this has changed the way knowledge is understood, the way it is produced and the way it is used (Muller 2000: 145).

A particularly influential example of the latter is Gibbons (2004, 2005) and his colleagues (Nowotny *et al.* 2001, 2003) who argue that society has been transformed from an industrial economy based on Fordist principles of production to a society in which the boundaries between different, and hitherto distinguishable and insulated domains, now transgress on each other. This analysis has led Gibbons and his colleagues to distinguish between mode 1 and mode 2 societies, and mode 1 and mode 2 knowledge. They argue that mode 1 society is characterized by distinct domains between politics, culture, the market, science, and civil society, with each having its own internal developmental logic and strongly insulated boundaries between it and the others. In contrast, they say that mode 2 society has transcended the distinct categories and domains of modernity, and is characterized by blurred boundaries where each domain transgresses upon and co-mingles with the other as a consequence of co-evolutionary trends (Nowotny *et al.* 2001: 4). They argue that mode 2 knowledge developed because society changed and became a mode 2 society.

Mode 1 knowledge is disciplinary based, often 'pure' research, conducted in universities by disciplinary specialists within a hierarchical framework that specifies the rules for knowledge creation, what counts as knowledge and who can contribute to it. The boundaries between different disciplines are strongly insulated, as are the boundaries between the academy as the principal site of knowledge production and society. Conversely, mode 2 knowledge is categorized by 'a distinct set of cognitive and social practices' suitable for cross-disciplinary, problem-oriented, applied and less hierarchical research that occurs at the site of application and which is, as a consequence, more socially accountable and reflexive than is mode 1 knowledge (Gibbons 1997: 3). Knowledge production now occurs in many sites and not just universities.

The mode 1/mode 2 thesis is problematic for many reasons, but the most important problem is that it is based on a faulty theory of ontology because it focusses on the contextual as constituting the limits of the real. As explained in the previous two chapters, critical realists argue that the natural and social worlds are characterized by ontological depth, stratification and emergence. The disciplines seek to understand this complexity by abstracting particular features from the contextual. This is necessary to understand causal mechanisms and the way they have interacted to produce the events that take place and our experiences of them. It means that, as Bhaskar (1998d: 146) explains, no moment ever contains its own 'truth', as the moment has always been multiply determined. However, to understand any particular moment requires multidisciplinary research precisely because it is multiply determined, but this occurs by navigating disciplinary boundaries rather than negating them. Consequently, the Gibbons thesis underestimates the extent to which mode 2 knowledge relies on mode 1 knowledge.

Muller (2000: 48) convincingly argues that the Gibbons thesis provides useful insights if it is used to argue that mode 2 approaches need to *supplement* and not *replace* mode 1 knowledge production. This is because access to mode 2 knowledge requires a good grounding in mode 1 knowledge to understand the structures of knowledge, its boundaries, evaluative criteria and how to work across the boundaries. He explains that the mode 1 and 2 thesis is an over-dichotomization of the different kinds of knowledge and the relationship between them. This is because disciplinary knowledge has always engaged with the applied and contextual (Muller 2000: 47), and indeed, this helps us to make sense of the development of *applied* disciplinary knowledge and the way in which the applied disciplines contribute to change in the 'pure' disciplines (Young 2006c). However, Muller (2000: 48) says that while mode 2 knowledge has existed for some time, it has become much more visible in late modernity for the reasons discussed above.

The collapse of the tradition of value-neutral research and the conflation of the epistemic and social relations of knowledge provided fertile ground for the growth of post-modernist arguments in disciplines such as sociology and other social sciences and humanities. The broader social consequences arising from the dominance of post-modernism in these disciplines was a belief (or at least suspicion) that scientists could not separate their interests from their research, and that the outcomes of research have no special authority because they are reducible to self-interest (Muller 2000: 148). This means that the advent of post-modernism was not just an internal phenomenon *within* the academy and in the fields of knowledge production; it had broader social origins in society and broader social consequences that contributed to the collapse of trust in knowledge more broadly.

The displacement of knowledge in curriculum

This section draws on the discussion in Chapter 2 of Bernstein's distinction between the field of knowledge production (such as the academic disciplines and other sites where knowledge is produced), the recontextualizing field (where knowledge is 'translated' into pedagogic knowledge) and the field of reproduction (where teaching takes place). The first is associated with knowledge production, the second with its transmission and the third with its acquisition (Bernstein 2000: 37). The recontextualizing field is further divided into the pedagogic recontextualizing field (PRF) and the official recontextualizing field (ORF). The PRF consists of teacher education departments and others implicated in the construction of pedagogic discourses. The ORF consists of government departments and associated bodies established by the state to oversee the construction of state pedagogic discourse (Bernstein 2000: 115). The PRF and ORF are, to a greater or lesser extent, in conflict over the principle of recontextualization because this determines 'what matters' in curriculum. The focus in the first component of this section is on the field of knowledge production and the recontextualizing field and the relationship between them to understand the social processes that led to the displacement of knowledge in curriculum. The focus in the second is on the triumph of vocationalism and the inability of the PRF to resist its imposition by the ORF, in part because there was no shared theory of knowledge within the PRF.

Changes in the fields of knowledge production and recontextualization

The changed social relations of knowledge production were reflected in disciplines that contributed to shaping curriculum in two ways: the first was through changed conceptions of the nature of the human actor and the second, somewhat later, was through the dominance of relativism in the social sciences and humanities.

Bernstein says that a remarkable convergence occurred around the principle of competence in the 1960s in the social and psychological sciences, which are the disciplines that inform curriculum and learning theory. He says this convergence involved 'disciplines with radically opposed epistemologies, methods of inquiry and principles of description', and he includes disciplines such as linguistics, psychology, social anthropology, sociology and sociolinguistics (Bernstein 2000: 41). While the focus and approach of these disciplines varied, their convergence around the principle of competence arose because they shared a humanist understanding of the intrinsic creativity and potential of human beings. The notion of competences was seemingly underpinned by emancipatory values and agendas and resonated with the rise of liberal, progressive and radical ideologies in the 1960s and 1970s.

Competence here is not to be confused with competency-based training (and associated behaviourism). Rather, it refers to those capacities that are developed creatively and tacitly by engaging in informal interactions which provide the basis for constructing meaning and the world. Competences are 'practical accomplishments' (Bernstein 2000: 42). Subjects actively and creatively construct their world of meanings and practices so that there are no deficits, only differences. It results in a sceptical view of hierarchical relations and emphasizes democratic practices because all possess the same inherent capacity for self-realization, even if they are realized differently (again there are no deficits). The goal is to help individuals become self-regulating, a process which is 'not advanced by formal instruction' (Bernstein 2000: 42). These humanist principles were drawing on much older traditions of humanism that emphasized the capacities intrinsic to all human beings rather than the formation of individuals from without (Bates *et al.* 1998: 110). The problem is, as Bernstein (2000: 43) argues, that this idealized notion of competence was bought at the price of abstracting individuals from their social relations and from an analysis of the way in which power differentially mediates access to the development of competences and their realization. It makes invisible the way in which the broader 'macro' social relations of power are implicated in structuring the 'micro'.

These changes in the field of knowledge production resulted in changes in the field of recontextualization so that competence replaced 'performance' as the principle of curricular recontextualization. Competence pedagogic modes are contrasted to performance pedagogic modes because the former seeks to develop the realization of capacities individuals already possess, whereas the latter is focused on the acquisition of that which students do not yet possess. In other words, the focus on performance modes is on an *absence* (and hence deficit), 'and as a consequence ... the emphasis [is placed] upon the text to be acquired and so upon the transmitter' (Bernstein 2000: 57). In performance modes, knowledge is strongly classified with sharply defined boundaries between the disciplines. Knowledge is strongly framed, and the pace and sequence of knowledge are external to the student. The rules for its realization are explicit. Performances of acquirers 'are graded, and stratification displaces differences between acquirers' (Bernstein 2000: 45). In contrast, competence modes tend to be weakly classified and framed, with implicit realization rules and invisible modes of pedagogy. The locus of control (apparently) lies with the student, and the emphasis is on differences between acquirers and not on stratification based on external measurements.

The replacement of performance pedagogic modes by competence pedagogic modes was the result of the convergence of a number of different factors. It was in part a consequence of moves in countries such as England and Australia away from education systems designed to serve elites towards comprehensive primary and secondary education where the aim was, among other things, to remove the bases for arbitrary privilege (even if this was not the outcome) (Bernstein 2000: 57; Connell *et al.* 1982; Marginson 1997a). This opened 'an autonomous local space for the construction of curriculum and the manner of its acquisition' (Bernstein 2000: 57). The creation of this space led to the strengthening of the PRF relative to the ORF and in both primary and secondary education 'there was a strong move to a competence modality and its modes, powerfully legitimised by the convergence in the field of production of discourse' (Bernstein 2000: 57). However, these changes in the disciplines which produce discourse about human beings facilitated the rise of competence modes in *both* the official and pedagogic recontextualizing fields, so that there was convergence between them and these notions of the human actor were reflected in teacher training programs (Bernstein 2000: 57–58). Under such conditions, the relative autonomy of the PRF is less of a problem for the ORF.

The relative autonomy of the PRF from the ORF was also strengthened by changes in the PRF. Teacher education programs in universities underwent dramatic expansion as a necessary condition for comprehensive primary and secondary education, and they became sites for contests about knowledge. Moreover, weakened boundaries between disciplines and their discourses were also reflected in that which could be constructed as legitimate concerns of the recontextualizing field. Bernstein explains that full employment and the massive expansion of higher education meant that the recontextualizing field began to focus on broader social relations such as youth cultures, multiculturalism and leisure: 'Not only were there new spaces at all levels of education from higher education to the infant school, but *new agendas* were filling these spaces' (Bernstein 2000: 58). The oppositions within the pedagogic recontextualizing field were now cast *within* the competence mode rather than between competence and performance modes, so that the contests were now between 'liberal-progressive, populist and radical modes' (Bernstein 2000: 57). This was until, as we will see, the reassertion by the state of control over the recontextualizing field based on a new principle of recontextualization, which was vocationalism.

The dominance of competence modes as the principle of recontextualization from the field of knowledge production to the field of its reproduction in education contributed to challenging the importance of disciplinary knowledge as a core component of the curriculum. The competence mode helped to reshape both the instructional and regulative discourses underpinning pedagogic practice. This is because the emphasis was on providing the conditions for self-actualization, and not on acquiring a body of knowledge that is (initially) external to the student. Knowers rather than knowledge became important, and questions about the different conditions of access to knowledge by knowers receded in importance. This helps to account for the continuing socially unequal outcomes of education despite developmental discourses that seek to valorize the voices of the hitherto excluded.

The emphasis on knowers intrinsic to competence pedagogic modes was consistent with the development and eventual dominance of relativist discourses of knowledge in academic disciplines that inform curriculum. Young identifies three factors that contributed to the rise of relativism in disciplines such as the sociology of education. The first was the unintended consequences of work in the 1970s (which included his own work as well as that of others), where, ironically 'the intention ... was to give centrality to the role of knowledge in education' (Young 2008a: 81). He says that this conceptualized curriculum as the expression of powerful interests and the problem with this is that while social interests and privilege are implicated in knowledge they can only be part of the explanation. The curriculum cannot be limited to such explanations as 'It leaves us with no independent criteria for curriculum decisions, only competing interests' (Young 2008a: 82). There are no grounds for assessing knowledge beyond the social conditions in which it is produced. Young (2008a: 82) says that the second trend emphasized on privileged curriculum as a social practice and this is characteristic of many socio-cultural theories of learning. The problem is, however, that such approaches are not able to distinguish between the knowledge we acquire in our daily lives from the knowledge we acquire from education, because both are embedded in social practices which are ultimately commensurable (this is discussed in more depth in the next chapter). This could not, consequently, address the issue of knowledge in the curriculum or provide guidance for debates about it. The third trend was the influence of post-modernism in the social sciences in general and on curriculum studies in particular. While post-modernism challenged existing concepts of knowledge, it was not able to offer a theory of knowledge that could inform curriculum, because not only was knowledge itself relativized, the very conditions for the possibility of knowledge were relativized.

The result is, Young argues, that we have a crisis in curriculum theory and many different curricula – a school, post-compulsory, vocational and higher education curriculum – 'all of which take for granted the assumptions upon which they are based. On the other hand we have a marginalized curriculum theory which offers critiques of the interests involved in existing curricula, but no alternatives' (Young 2008a: 82).

The new vocationalism – the reassertion of dominance by the ORF

The crisis of curriculum theory within the PRF meant that it could not mount an effective response to the increasing vocationalization of curriculum that began to occur in earnest in the 1980s in all sectors of education. If knowledge is reducible to social interests, then the argument becomes centred on those social interests rather than the intrinsic features of knowledge. Knowledge thus is an issue of power and debates over curriculum are reduced to debates about whose voices should be heard. This was answered resoundingly in government policy and enforced by the reassertion of dominance of the ORF over the PRF with the development of the 'new vocationalism'. Education needed to be taken out of the hands of 'producers' (that is, the PRF and teachers) and subordinated to the national economic interest (Marginson 1997a).

The social and economic basis of the new vocationalism lay in the long post-War economic boom and in the massive growth of education after the Second World War. Marginson (1997a) explains that this expansion was explicitly associated with and designed to facilitate vocational aspirations as governments sought to develop the human capital needed to support economic growth. Systems of education were expanded to fill the need for more highly skilled workers in many areas of the economy as a consequence of the technological, economic and social transformations of the 1960s, 1970s and 1980s, and to ensure students learnt the knowledge and skills needed for the changing workplace. However, the 'new vocationalism' as it became known, was a specific response to the economic crisis of the 1970s and the collapse of the youth employment markets which created the need to ensure that young people were gainfully occupied in the absence of suitable employment (Marginson 1997a). It encompassed education more broadly over the following decades, and was explicitly 'designed to bridge perceived gaps between educational provision and social and economic needs' (Skilbeck *et al.* 1994: 7). Skilbeck *et al.* (1994: 7) explain that the vocationalization of curriculum in compulsory and post-compulsory schooling occurred in most if not all OECD countries as well as in many less industrialized countries.[6]

While the economic and social conditions for vocationalism were laid earlier by post-War Keynesian economic policies, the *form* of the *new* vocationalism was a product of neo-liberal human capital discourses and the associated 'new public management' theories, which became the hegemonic policy drivers within western nation states in the 1970s and 1980s (Olssen and Peters 2005). Neo-liberalism views society as fundamentally a *market society* rather than simply a society that is supported by a market economy (Emy and Hughes 1988: 117). Pusey (1991: 10) explains that this has important consequences for the development of social policy: primacy is given to the economy, 'second place to the political order, and third place to the social order'. The pursuit of the market society has led to the reconstitution of domestic and global economic relations, in which the Keynesian welfare state was replaced by the neo-liberal state, with its emphasis on the marketization and privatization of public services and social infrastructure (Olssen and Peters 2005: 315). Marginson (1997a: 151) argues that education and training became subordinated to national economic policy by the reforms of the late 1980s and early 1990s, and that:

> Everywhere, education was seen as crucial to economic competitiveness, mobilised for economic reconstruction, and embedded in micro-economic reform, corporatisation and marketisation. The formation of citizens in

education was subordinated to its new economic mission. ... this time the objective was not so much the broad development of the skills and talents of the nation, as in the late Keynesian period, but the development of those specific aspects of education and research that assisted national economic competitiveness.

He explains that the consequences of this went beyond *how* education was delivered, to *what* education was designed to do:

the way of thinking about education, and the new systems and behaviours emerging from reform, were neoclassical and market liberal. More so than in the 1960s, the education citizen imagined in government was an *economic* citizen.

(Marginson 1997a: 152)

Economic citizens are those who participate in the market instead of depending on the state. Decision-making is exercised in the market through consumer sovereign models of citizenship rather than in social and political fora. The purpose of education shifted from preparing a citizenry capable of participating in the social, political and judicial debates and fora in society, to a purpose which is mainly vocational, and the systems of education, including curriculum, were reshaped to meet this goal. The new vocationalism was associated with valorizing education, but this was because of the contribution it could make to economic performance. Grubb (2005) refers to this as the 'education gospel', while Beck (1999: 223–34) refers to it as 'a thoroughly secular vision of national economic salvation achieved through raising educational standards by following government prescriptions'.

The focus in the new vocationalism is on preparing students for work in general, rather than specific occupations (Young 2006c; Bates *et al.* 1998). It emphasizes 'generic skills' or 'employability skills', because the skills and knowledge to which they refer are the skills and knowledge sought by the market. Skills and knowledge are thus decontextualized from the vocations in which they were originally embedded. It is not the occupation or vocation that defines what is necessary, it is the market, and it is assumed that because the market transcends most occupations these marketable skills also can be unproblematically translated from one context to another. As a consequence, knowledge (including vocational knowledge) recedes and is downplayed and regarded as transient and ephemeral. The principle for selecting knowledge is primarily instrumental and knowledge is valued in so far as it serves instrumental ends.

Marginson (1997a: 172) explains that the discourse of generic skills means that 'it became possible to govern *all* educational programs in terms of vocational objectives'. General and vocational education became conflated by the notion of generic skills, and the vocational became 'the prototype of all post-compulsory education and training' (Marginson 1997a: 172). Generic skills were universalized to apply to *all* social situations. For example, the Mayer Committee (1992: 5), which produced Australia's first generation 'generic skills' in its seven 'key competencies' in the early 1990s, argued that 'the key competencies are not only essential for effective participation in work but are also essential for effective participation in further education and adult life more generally'.

However, the discourse of generic skills was (and is) only part of the policy process whereby the vocationalization of curriculum was achieved. Equally important was (and is) the insistence that qualifications, particularly in vocational education and training (VET) and higher education, be 'relevant' to work. The emphasis on generic skills is thus a component of the process of vocationalization, but it is vocationalization more broadly which allows the discourse of relevance to be continually reasserted and used as the basis for policy intervention. Vocationalism is the means by which the different parts of curriculum are organized in relation to each other; generic skills on the one hand, and 'relevant' knowledge needed for work on the other.

All sectors of post-compulsory education and training in Australia, as in similar Anglophone countries, were reshaped through the prism of the new vocationalism, though in different ways. The 'generic' key competencies gradually entered the broad school curriculum (Smith and Keating 2003: 219), and 'VET in schools' is a key part of the senior school certificates in all states (National Centre for Vocational Education Research 2008). The economic modernizers in government have not had untrammelled power to change senior school curriculum because of the power of the elite universities, and elite private and selective public schools over university entrance requirements (Keating 2003: 3), but nonetheless the restructuring of senior school certificates in Australian states has emphasized the vocational purposes of education.

Compared to the higher education sector, government in Australia could exercise greater explicit control over VET and this occurred by mandating that VET qualifications be based on competency-based training (CBT) (Wheelahan and Carter 2001). There is much education policy borrowing between the United Kingdom and Australia, and Australia drew on the UK's CBT qualifications as the model for its qualifications in VET (Guthrie 2009). Australia's competency-based qualifications are called training packages, and they are similar to National Vocational Qualifications in England. The imposition of CBT was and is supported by both the labour and conservative parties at all levels of government in Australia. Qualifications are made up of 'industry-derived' units of competency that describe workplace performances, tasks or roles (Smith and Keating 2003). Vocationalism is thus expressed through the model of curriculum and qualifications, and this is unambiguous.

Such overt control has not been exercised over higher education, but higher education has still been subject to policy pressures to consult industry 'stakeholders', design 'relevant' programs and ensure that programs 'meet the needs of industry'. The Australian Department of Education Science and Training (2002: 14)[7] explains that 'The need for effective processes for industry and business engagement permeates the entire higher education enterprise, including institutional planning'. Such 'engagement' has occurred in two ways: first, through the discourse of generic attributes or graduate attributes,[8] and second, through the discourse of outcomes-based education which, even though it does not enjoy total dominance in higher education, valorizes the specification of learning outcomes as performances by defining what students will be able to do rather than what they know. However, the vocationalizing of higher education curriculum goes beyond the content of curriculum and is also expressed in processes of learning, particularly in the enthusiasm for problem-based learning in professional programs, and the enthusiasm for work-integrated learning more broadly.

The new vocationalism contributes to displacing knowledge from the centre of curriculum because knowledge has no intrinsic value beyond its instrumental purposes. The principle of workplace relevance means that the emphasis is on the contextual and situational, and in this approach, vocational knowledge is interpreted as contextually specific applications of theoretical knowledge. However, a richer notion of vocational knowledge is that it comprises complex and difficult bodies of knowledge that individuals acquire in the process of becoming a member of a community of practice, which they then use as a tool to transform practice and create new knowledge.

Conclusion

The main focus of this chapter has been to demonstrate the social basis for the displacement of theoretical, disciplinary knowledge from the centre of curriculum. This lays the basis for discussing the resulting crisis in curriculum theory in the next chapter. A sociological explanation for downplaying the importance of knowledge in the curriculum must be found in the transformed role of knowledge in society and work as a consequence of the economic, social, cultural and technological changes associated with globalization, and in the changing relationship between labour and capital at work. The pace of change means that individuals and institutions must continually access knowledge and revise existing knowledge in situating themselves in relation to these changes, while the changed relations between labour and capital in the workplace mean that a greater focus is placed on the attributes of knowers rather than the knowledge they use. Workers' identities and personal attributes are now part of the new relations of subordination between capital and labour. The relativizing of knowledge also occurred as a consequence of the weakened insulation between science and society with increased access to knowledge production by larger proportions of the population, and the changed social relation between knowledge production and society more generally with calls for greater accountability of knowledge producers to society (Muller 2000).

These changed social relations of knowledge production iteratively supported the rise of constructivist (particularly relativist) theories of the person and knowledge in academic disciplines that traditionally underpinned curriculum. Lacking a theory of knowledge, the PRF was not able effectively to resist the reassertion of dominance by the ORF and the imposition of vocationalism. Knowledge is further removed from the curriculum because the principle for curricular recontextualization is instrumentalism and relevance, not systematic access to structures of knowledge. The emphasis in both constructivist and instrumentalist approaches is thus on knowers, but knowers who live and work in a society in which knowledge has been relativized, regarded as ephemeral, transient and ultimately unreliable, even though its role has never been more important.

In an argument that is equally relevant to other countries, Grubb (2005) argues that vocationalism is now so deeply embedded in higher education in the United States that it cannot be wished away. He argues that the only possible strategy that can be used to overcome the narrow instrumentalism of the new vocationalism is to seek to 'integrate vocational purposes with broader civic, intellectual and moral goals' (Grubb 2005: 2). He argues that the notion of professionalism provides a bridge back to liberal education because each profession has an ethical dimension, is situated within a broader social, civic and political context, has a history and a relationship to knowledge, theories and concepts (Grubb 2005: 16). This provides a useful framework for thinking about different ways of responding to vocationalism, and for structuring the relationship between vocationally specific programs and the disciplines that underpin their field of practice.

A vocational education *can* provide students with access to 'society's conversation' if it provides them with explicit and systematic access to the relevant disciplines that underpins their field of practice, which includes the capacity to recognize different forms of knowledge and to traverse the boundaries between them. However, the crisis of curriculum theory means that traditional-conservative, instrumentalist and constructivist theories of curriculum are unable to respond to this challenge, because each focuses on the social relations of knowledge and not its epistemic relations. The discussion in the next chapter demonstrates that each, in different ways, is concerned with knowers rather than knowledge.

7   The crisis of curriculum

Introduction

The crisis of curriculum arises as a consequence of the displacement of knowledge from the centre of curriculum by the dominant models of curriculum. Conservative, technical-instrumentalist and constructivist models of curriculum regard knowledge instrumentally and not as a causally important objective in its own right because of the access it provides to the nature of the world and to society's conversation. Knowledge is subordinated to other curricular goals as each is primarily concerned about the social relations of knowledge rather than the epistemic relations. The conflict between these different approaches is, as Moore (2000: 27) explains, 'about how different *organisations* of knowledge can be held to represent conflicting models of society'.

The chapter uses a Bernsteinian analysis to explore these three approaches. It argues that they exist in relationships of affinity and opposition, and that the outcome of these relationships results in a 'pedagogic pallet' so that no model is implemented in its pure form. However, these relationships are shaped by the dominance of the official recontextualizing field (ORF) over the pedagogic recontextualizing field (PRF) and the imposition of an instrumentalism that selectively appropriates from conservatism and constructivism. In addressing each of these approaches on their own terms, the chapter demonstrates the theoretical problems intrinsic to each, the inconsistencies that result and the deleterious social outcomes that arise from their implementation (Bhaskar 1998d: 120). Each approach is outlined and this is followed by a discussion of the relationships of affinity and opposition between them.

Conservatism

Conservatism precludes a debate about knowledge in its own right because it is primarily concerned with a return to basics, traditional disciplines and the selection of social elites by processes of ranking. Its concerns are with social order and appropriate relations of deference rather than inducting students into the controversies and debates within the academic disciplines and in society more broadly. There are different conservative approaches and Bernstein distinguishes between 'old' and 'neo'-conservative pedagogic modes. He says that the purpose of old conservative pedagogic modes is to produce retrospective identities which are 'shaped by national religious, cultural, grand narratives of the past' (Bernstein 2000: 66). The past is used as the model for the future, and the purpose of education is to accommodate the future to the past (see also Dewey 1997 [1916]: 79). Bernstein (2000: 67, emphasis in original) contrasts this with neo-conservatism which draws selectively from the past '*to deal with cultural, economic and technological change*'. Neo-conservatism selectively appropriates discourses from the past that can be used to aid future economic performance in a market culture and reduced welfare state (Bernstein 2000: 67–68). He identifies Thatcher and Blair as heads of states who promote this position. The past is re-imagined and undergoes a process of recontextualization to project into the future (see also Beck 2006a). The retrospective conservative pedagogic mode is not dominant in most countries and has ceded to the prospective conservative pedagogic mode (Bernstein 2000). Consequently, rather than continually distinguish between old conservatism and neo-conservatism, conservatism as used in this chapter refers to neo-conservatism.

Conservatism endows the traditional division of the disciplines and disciplinary knowledge with timeless and universal features. The main role of curriculum in conservative approaches is to transmit timeless truths through contemplative processes that have their roots in the monastic tradition (Dewey 1997 [1916]: 280; Moore and Young 2001: 447). The central purpose is to inculcate appropriate deference to traditional bodies of knowledge in students, and to instil respect for authority and traditional values. Dewey (1997 [1916]: 280) explains that traditional approaches emphasize 'defining, expounding and interpreting the received material, rather than to inquiry'. It is not just *what* is taught, but *how* it is taught that matters. Donnelly (2004: 22) illustrates this when he proclaims the importance of 'memorisation, rote learning and mastering essential content' in subjects such as mathematics and English, implemented through 'whole class teaching' with the teacher out in front of the class.[1]

Real knowledge is that which is fixed, stands outside learners, and is not related to the socially mediated processes by which it was created. Knowledge is not created, it just is. Knowledge is transmitted, not socially produced. Young (1998: 23) describes this as the 'curriculum as fact' approach, in which curriculum is presented as unchangeable and as having a life of its own, thus obscuring the social contexts in which it is embedded. Bernstein (2000: 48) explains that pedagogic practice and the evaluation of students in 'performance' modes of pedagogy characteristic of conservatism:

> positions the acquirer, *invisibly*, in the past and its rituals which have produced the instructional discourse. Thus in the case of performance models, the future is made visible, but that which has constructed this future is a past invisible to the acquirer.[2]

The previous conservative Australian Minister for Education, Science and Training, Julie Bishop (2006b), provided a good illustration of the 'curriculum as fact' approach and the way conservatism positions students in the past when she insisted that Australian history be reinstated as a distinct subject taught in schools, but that it must be taught as a narrative. This is because 'students should be given a good grounding in key dates, facts and events of Australian history'. Bishop (2006b) said that 'History is not peace studies. History is not social justice awareness week. Or conscious-raising about ecological sustainability. History is history, and shouldn't be a political science course by another name.' Bishop (2006a) also wanted to introduce a values education programme to overcome the 'decline of civility' in Australia. There is, in her view, abundant evidence for this, including road rage, the ugly parent syndrome, the use of offensive language in public, young people who do not give up their seats to their elders on buses, and so forth. This decline was caused by an excessive emphasis during the last generation on teaching young people their rights and not enough emphasis on their responsibilities. She says that a 'rights-centric understanding of citizenship does not build good citizens of the future' (Bishop 2006a). Bishop (2006a) defines civility as comprising three core elements: 'respect, relations with strangers and self-regulation'. She explains that our notion of what constitutes civil behaviour is drawn from Australia's Judeo-Christian heritage and the English and Scottish Enlightenments. Students should respect themselves and others, schools, the national anthem,[3] and society's institutions. She argues that schools have an important role in instilling respect in students.

The purpose of performance modes of pedagogy is, as Bernstein (2003: 208) explains, to bring about 'specialized differences between individuals'. Intrinsic to the conservative approach is the insistence on external 'high stakes' examinations against externally derived and universally imposed standards. Like many other countries, Australia now conducts national literacy and numeracy tests commencing in the early years of school. Students' achievements are measured and ranked, and information is now published about individual school results and how the school compared to 'similar' schools, as well as information about the student population (Gillard 2008b). The process of stratification and ranking culminates in the senior school certificates which mediate access to post-school outcomes. In a pattern that is typical of most countries (Santiago *et al.* 2008a), those least likely to finish school and undertake the senior school certificate in Australia are students from low socio-economic backgrounds. If they do finish school, they are more likely to go to lower-status vocational education and training (VET) than are students from more privileged backgrounds who are far more likely to go to university (and to high status universities) (Teese *et al.* 2006b; Foley 2007; Wheelahan 2009).

Bernstein (2000: 57) argues that performance pedagogic modes draw from behaviourist theories 'which are atomistic in their emphasis'. 'Traditional' approaches to the structures of knowledge take these structures as self-evident givens and they exhibit features similar to empiricism, which is based on a denial 'that introversion could possibly be a source of knowledge' (Benton and Craib 2001: 82). In these approaches, the whole is to be constructed by building up the parts rather than by providing access to the system of meaning as the basis for understanding the parts. The locus of control, selection, sequencing, pacing and evaluation of knowledge are all external to the student. Contexts, discourses, knowledge, spaces and practices are separated, distinguished and marked by discontinuity (Bernstein 2000). Knowledge is acquired and evaluated atomistically and outcomes are evaluated, measured and ranked. Conservative approaches emphasize the external control and regulation of behaviour as the basis for developing internal beliefs and orientations. Induction into knowledge is initially premised on unquestioned authority, while those who survive these processes of screening and ranking are inducted into the 'mystery' of knowledge and its fallibility, openness and incoherence, but only once access to such knowledge has been mediated through the distributive rules of the pedagogic device (Bernstein 2000).

Instrumentalism

The technical–instrumental paradigm precludes a discussion about knowledge in its own right because it is primarily concerned with the needs of the economy. Its focus is on the way in which education contributes to the formation of human capital and it is premised on notions of the economic citizen, the commodification of knowledge and the marketization of social relations. Curriculum and knowledge are designed to create a 'form of society' peopled by those who have the attributes of trainability and flexibility as these are the fundamental attributes needed in the knowledge society (Moore and Young 2001: 447–48).

The civic, political, social and cultural purposes of education are subordinated to the goal of producing the knowledge and skills needed in the economy. Investment in education is investment in human capital. This is illustrated by the Australian Labor Party (2007a: 5), which was elected to government in 2007 with a commitment to implement an 'education revolution' so that Australia would 'become the most educated country, the most skilled economy and the best trained workforce in the world'. The 'education revolution' encompasses pre-school education to higher education. Its policy on early childhood education (that is, for children aged five years and under) begins with this statement 'Investing in human capital formation delivers significant benefits to individuals, society and the economy. International research demonstrates that earlier investment yields a higher rate of return' (Australian Labor Party 2007b: 2). The current Australian Labor Education Minister, Julia Gillard (2008a), argues that the 'progressive centre' of politics is concerned with two key questions, which are:

- How do we ensure that all of our citizens are able to take part in the dynamic, wealth-creating opportunity that the market and society combined represent?
- And how does this happen in a way that contributes to the battle against climate change?

The need to utilise the talents of every citizen in production and the long-term challenges to growth posed by climate change, mean that social equity, environmental sustainability and prosperity are part of the same overall process.

Building human capital is the way these concerns will be addressed because it is this that gives individuals the capacity to participate in the market. This is a key objective of government because markets have been naturalized as the best and most efficient way of organizing all aspects of social life. As an illustration, the Australian Prime Minister, Kevin Rudd (2008), argues it is important to recognize that markets fail, but nonetheless, 'As a matter of general principle we believe in using market mechanisms and incentives to design innovative approaches to these long-term challenges.'[4] The Australian Labor Government is in favour of 'market design' rather than laissez-faire markets, but markets remain the principal mechanism of social reform and for the allocation of public resources. Gillard (2008a), who is Australia's Deputy Prime Minister as well as Education Minister, says in explaining the policy of her government that:

> The next generation of reform challenges are all about how the power of the market interacts with the surrounding framework of institutions and the actions of individuals themselves.
>
> This means we are focussing on the fundamentals of *market design*.
>
> Whether it is an Emissions Trading Scheme – a market in carbon – or a national water market capable of incentivising water savings – or the growth of renewable energy sources – or the role of the labour market in lifting social mobility and workforce participation – or the adaptation of our tertiary education sector to a new global landscape – the same issues emerge. How can we develop markets which interact productively with strong public institutions and empower users to participate successfully in them?

In a market society the social benefits of education are defined instrumentally and reduced to the economic. Gilbert Jessup (1991: 6), one of the key figures associated with the implementation of competency-based National Vocational Qualifications (NVQs) in Britain, provides an example of this in his book which seeks to extend outcomes-based education to all sectors of education (and not just to NVQs) when he says:

> Happily, the needs of individuals to realise their potential, to develop their skills and knowledge, to take on more responsible and fulfilling work and to earn more money, seem to be largely compatible with the current needs of the country and the economy, for a workforce of more competent, responsible, flexible and autonomous employees.

The concern is to produce a particular kind of identity, but it is a market identity. The outcomes of learning need to be specified in advance so 'purchasers' can 'choose' what they will buy based on the criteria of relevance and utility. Knowledge becomes commodified and divorced from the disciplinary frameworks that give it meaning. Knowledge is selectively disaggregated from disciplinary frameworks and preferably tied to performance. Coherence is not derived from the hierarchically organized, systemized bodies of knowledge, because 'coherence is ultimately a matter for the individual learner' (Jessup 1991: 4). Bernstein (2000: 86) argues that this posits a fundamental split between knowers and knowledge:

> This new concept is a truly secular concept. Knowledge should flow like money to wherever it can create advantage and profit. Indeed knowledge is not like money, it *is* money. Knowledge is divorced from persons, their commitments, their personal dedications.

Instrumentalism evades the question of the nature of knowledge by focussing instead on developing the disposition of 'trainability', a disposition which is necessarily empty, because as Beck (2002: 624) explains 'its whole point is the fostering of receptiveness to whatever set of objectives and contents comes along next (or is next imposed)'. It is the *receptiveness* that must be developed by education and this turns the focus to generic skills and attributes (a generic receptiveness), rather than specific knowledge.

The specification of outcomes in a marketized system where outcomes are exchanged through buying and selling gives purchasers greater control over the development of outcomes, because producers aim to please the customer. This shifts the locus for determining educational outcomes to 'stakeholders' outside education, and these outcomes are in turn used to derive learning programmes (known in Australian VET as 'delivery strategies'), rather than structured systems of principled knowledge as in the academic disciplines or the applied academic disciplines. The specification of outcomes gives employers greater control, provides governments with mechanisms for evaluating the extent to which these outcomes have been met (defined as compliance with government objectives), results in a more 'efficient and effective system', and reduces the problem of 'producer capture'. Students also putatively have greater control through the 'choices' they exercise, thus ensuring they achieve their vocational objectives. However, their perceptions are often based on vague notions of the relationship between particular programmes of study and specific occupations at the end (James *et al.* 1999). Students' pursuit of instrumental returns from education is the inevitable consequence when social participation is defined by consumer choice in markets, and education the instrumental means to achieve these ends (Wheelahan 2002).[5] Performance indicators and league tables can be developed to provide more information for the 'market', and can be used as mechanisms to discipline educational providers and elicit particular behaviours. This is why 'it is a mis-recognition to see these reform processes as simply a strategy of de-regulation, they are processes of re-regulation' (Ball 2003: 217).

Instrumentalism is based on generic knowledge because it seeks generic performances defined by work outcomes. As explained in Chapter 2, 'generic' knowledge structures characteristic of instrumentalism originated independently of education and the recontextualizing field (Beck and Young 2005: 190; Bernstein 2000: 53). This occurred by reconstituting the relations within the recontextualizing field and asserting the dominance of the ORF over the PRF. Goozee (2001: 62) explains that in Australia the years 1987–90 were characterized by strong interventionist government policy designed to respond to national economic needs and this resulted in dislocation and constant restructuring for all sectors of education. Similar processes occurred in other countries, particularly in Anglophone nations which engaged in much policy borrowing, each from the others (Marginson 1993, 1997b). The role of the ORF in Anglophone countries was reconstituted as the conduit for translating externally derived requirements of employers based on idealized notions of ideal workers defined by the attributes of flexibility and trainability.

Bernstein argues that the 'generic mode' gives rise to a performance pedagogic mode rather than a competence pedagogic mode despite the superficial resemblance of the generic mode to the competence mode. Competence modes are characterized by 'similar to' relations that seek to develop attributes that are *shared* intrinsic propensities of the individual, community or group, whereas performance modes are characterized by 'different from' relations, in which the purpose is to differentiate, stratify and rank (Bernstein 2000, 2003). The superficial resemblance between generic pedagogic modes and competence pedagogic modes arise for two reasons. First (as discussed in the next chapter) generic pedagogic modes such as competency-based training have appropriated the language of empowerment from competence modes. Second, generic pedagogic modes do not seek to stratify and differentiate between students as do performance modes of pedagogy. Rather, the aim is to produce common outcomes by defining the generic skills or attributes all graduates need for work in the new 'globalized' economy (Bernstein 2000: 55). Generic modes develop suitable subjects for markets, and these attributes are shared. However, unlike competence modes, the learner identities intrinsic to generic modes do not turn inwards to facilitate the development of already existing (if latent) attributes. Instead, generic modes project outwards towards externally imposed outcomes that are derived from the functional requirements of the workplace, rather than 'personal, cultural or political ends' (Muller 2000: 107).

Both conservative and generic (instrumentalist) performance modes seek to develop an autonomous identity, but the nature of this autonomy differs in each case. The autonomous learner of conservative performance modes is one who has internalized appropriate values and orientations arising from deference to traditional bodies of knowledge, steeped in a discourse that is derived from the past (Bernstein 2000: 48). Bernstein (2000: 48–49) refers to this as an *introverted* modality in which the future consists of 'exploration of a specialised discourse ... as an autonomous activity'. However, the pedagogic practices and performances constructed by this process are 'subordinate to external curriculum regulation of the selection, sequence, pacing and criteria of that transmission' (Bernstein 2000: 49). Market or generic identities are in contrast *extroverted* modalities, in which 'the future is likely to be dependent upon some external regulation, for example, the economy or local markets' (Bernstein 2000: 49). These are market-projected identities and the demands of the market are the 'pull' of extroversion. Identity is constructed by outward market orientations and not inner dedication, in which 'Contract replaces covenant' (Bernstein 2000: 69). However, like traditional performance modes, the outcomes, evaluative criteria and standards are all externally imposed. The autonomous identity constructed by this process monitors 'the skill requirements of changing skill niches and "skill up" accordingly' (Muller 2000: 108).

Instrumentalism, as with conservatism, draws from behaviourist theories of learning and is also atomistic in its approach. The emphasis is on externally derived, precisely specified standards and assessment is based on performance against these standards. While instrumentalism is less concerned with ranking outcomes than is conservatism, it is concerned with quantifiable measurement of outcomes to facilitate quality assurance, efficiency, effectiveness, audit and monitoring. If outcomes are to be measured in this way, they must be in a form which permits measuring to take place. It is equally concerned with the external control and regulation of behaviour, though these are generally defined as generic skills or generic attributes, and now employability skills. In defining generic outcomes as unproblematic descriptions of skills, instrumentalism silences 'the cultural basis of skills, tasks, practices and areas of work and give[s] rise to a jejune concept of trainability' (Bernstein 2000: 53).

Constructivism

In contrast, constructivism emphasizes the cultural basis of skills, tasks and practices, but to the exclusion of the knowledge that is used to inform these practices and the knowledge that is produced as a consequence of these practices. Knowledge is either an epiphenomenal outcome of practices that is ephemeral and context bound and/or the reflection of differently positioned actors or voices. Constructivist theories vary in the extent to which they are based on post-modernism, and, as will become apparent, not all constructivist approaches share post-modernism's concern with unequal power relations to the same degree and they vary in the extent to which they are 'strongly' relativist (Muller 2000: 59). Generally speaking however, 'stronger' and 'weaker' forms of constructivism share a commitment to the social construction of meaning, and this means that they emphasize processes of meaning-making that focus on the tacit, contextual and applied at the expense of disciplinary knowledge.

While there are differences between strands of constructivism, they share three basic premises, each of which builds on the other (Young 2008a). The first is that knowledge is a product of social practices. The second is that different kinds of knowledge can be reduced to different social practices. The third is that the social practices of knowledge producers, and other kinds of social actors are commensurable so that the knowledge produced by the former has no special 'authority' compared to that produced by the latter. There is no fundamental distinction between theoretical and everyday knowledge because both are the product of social practices. The boundary between vertical and horizontal discourses is collapsed. The consequence is that knowledge does not have transcendent features beyond the social context in which it was produced and the social practices used to produce it.

Young (2006a: 114–15) distinguishes between two main strands of constructivism. He locates the intellectual roots of the first in Marxism, and the second in Dewey's pragmatism and Mead's symbolic interactionism. The first focuses on knowledge as the product of socially situated actors so that 'The ideas of the ruling class are in every epoch the ruling ideas, i.e. the class which is the ruling material force of society, is at the same time its ruling intellectual force' (Marx 1932). The second emphasizes processes of knowledge creation and meaning-making in which education is a 'continuous reconstruction of experience' (Dewey 1997 [1916]: 80). The emphasis is experiential, which means that the contextual and situated takes priority. For example, Dewey (1938: 83) argues that: 'When education is based in theory and practice upon experience, it goes without saying that the organized subject-matter of the adult and the specialist cannot provide the starting point.'

However, in both strands, the relativity of knowledge has been taken beyond the starting point of its intellectual origins. Marx and Engels distinguished between ideology and scientific knowledge, with the former reflecting the naturalized and hegemonic interests of the ruling class and the latter reflecting objective knowledge (or at least the *possibility* of objective knowledge) (Benton and Craib 2001: 52). Dewey (1997 [1916]: 326) says that 'Knowledge, grounded knowledge, is science; it represents objects which have been settled, ordered, disposed of rationally.' Moreover, Dewey's (1997 [1910]: 27) insistence on the scientific method of inquiry demonstrates his belief that the external world is not purely a social construction brought about by acts of signification. However, Dewey (1997 [1916]: 339) collapses the distinction between *knowledge* and *knowing* by focussing on the contextual in arguing that: 'knowledge is a perception of those connections of an object which determine its applicability in a given situation.'

Knowledge as power and standpoints

The first approach, which emphasizes knowledge as the expression of relations of power, gave rise to various 'standpoint' approaches culminating in post-modern theories in which knowledge is reduced to the situated perspective of differently positioned social actors marked by different access to power, and different relations of domination and subordination. Post-modern framings, according to Edwards and Usher (2001: 282), 'enable a critique of those overarching or totalizing schemes' of modernity and 'problematize the exclusions and oppressions that these inscribe'. Michelson (2006: 145) argues that the rationality of the Enlightenment purged knowledge and knowers of their 'origins in particularised experience' so that knowledge was 'abstracted from the place of its making, and dehistoricised.'

She argues that all experience is socially mediated and socially situated, and this means 'that experience and knowledge are neither chronologically nor logically distinct' (Michelson 2006: 150). Her conclusion is that the notion of objective and transcendental knowledge cannot be sustained. This is because experience is not transparent, and reason does not exist independently of knowers. Knowers are not universal and interchangeable, because they are socially situated and enmeshed in meaningful social practices, social practices which are 'sometimes shared and sometimes contested among people and social groups' (Michelson 2006: 154). Knowers are socially particularized by their gender, race, class and other attributes, histories and experiences (Michelson 2006: 145–46). The consequence is that:

> We thus arrive at an epistemology that holds knowledge to be at once a social product and invariably partial; different knowledge is available from different 'standpoints', that is, from social and historical locations.
>
> (Michelson 2006: 154)

Michelson (2006: 147) takes Kolb to task for accepting the Enlightenment distinction between experience and knowledge (it is a false body–mind distinction to say that we reflect on the former to arrive at the latter), and Knowles to task for 'epistemological individualism' that results in the self-actualizing autonomous individual learner. She also takes Habermas, Mezirow and Freire to task for 're-presentation' of the situated perspectives of the disenfranchised to arrive at objective truths (Michelson 2006: 148). However, arguably, if we were to consider this 're-presentation' from a Marxist perspective, it means that the disenfranchised would be free of the hegemonic ideology of the ruling class. Knowledge in this strand of constructivism consequently becomes a question of power and reducible to power. The academic disciplines are a reflection of these power relations in which particular situated perspectives are naturalized and universalized as objective knowledge (Edwards and Usher 1994: 93–94). Relations of power are problematized particularly in debates in adult education about the distinction between formal and informal learning and the extent to which informal learning should be recognized in formal education programmes (Colley *et al.* 2006). For example, according to Fenwick (2006: 45), it is problematic to argue that the excluded lack social capital, something which can be remedied by their inclusion in the academy, because this:

> colonizes their own knowledge, reifies the normalizing categories of the middle class whose values control the dominant cultural meanings and perpetuates an acquisitive conception of experience as *capital* to be obtained and parlayed into credit, income or profit.

Standpoint theories can be used on the one hand to support the incommensurability of situated perspectives, or on the other, to 'support claims that some standpoints give better views than others' (Benton and Craib 2001: 143).

Young (2006a: 115) argues that the problem with standpoint or interest-based approaches is that they 'lead to a reductionist view of all knowledge as power relations, hence the only question this leads to is who has the power.' The result is that post-modernism denies that knowledge has any transcendent features and displaces the knowledge/object relation of knowledge by 'dropping the idea that language has a referent' (Benton and Craib 2001: 171). This means not a great deal can be said about the relationship between knowledge and its object other than as the expression (or construction) of power or of particular situated standpoints. Benton and Craib (2001: 171) explain that the 'problem with trying to abandon vast and complex bodies of thought is that it cannot be done. One cannot think new thoughts out of nowhere.' They explain that critiques of the Enlightenment can only come from *within* the Enlightenment, based on Enlightenment principles as their reference point. Critics of the Enlightenment must *reason* and *argue* in attacking the Enlightenment, but reason and argument are Enlightenment principles. They argue that this places critics within the tradition they are critiquing, while refusing to recognize that the concepts they seek to advance, such as 'democracy, tolerance, multiculturalism, the equality of the sexes' were in many cases generated within traditions descended from the Enlightenment, and can be supported by principles from within these traditions (Benton and Craib 2001: 171).

By reducing knowledge to power or situated perspectives, standpoint theories (ironically) make it impossible to discern, as Marx and Engels did, between ideology and objective knowledge. This means that they are unable to identify the way in which power is or can be implicated in knowledge. Benton and Craib (2001: 74) argue that constructivists have a point when they emphasize that the questioning and revision of our beliefs and concepts must of necessity take place *within* discourses and social practices of human communication, but they are mistaken because they reduce the world *to* communication and discourse. Our practical engagement in living takes place in a world which is 'only partly made up of communication and discourse', which means that while 'we may lack unmediated access to external reality, we *do* have mediated access to it' (Benton and Craib 2001: 74). Understanding the socially mediated basis of our access to knowledge and its relationship to its referent (its aboutness) makes it possible to critique knowledge producing social practices that contribute to privilege and power while at the same time valuing the epistemic insights such knowledge provides.

Moreover, debunking academic knowledge is not necessarily in the interests of those who have been excluded, because the important insight that standpoint theories provide is that academic knowledge is powerful knowledge (Young 2006b: 322). 'Wishing away' the distinction between academic knowledge and knowledge of the excluded leaves them exactly where they started, as excluded. Strategies to 'transform the academy' implicitly recognizes that 'new knowledge' becomes powerful when it is admitted to the academy, yet this does not transform the academy as a site of power or remove the difference between knowledge that is included and knowledge that is not. In fact, asserting the commensurability of different kinds of knowledge runs the risk of diminishing the importance of access to the academy and in the process becoming 'an alibi for a lack of access to formal education' (Muller 2000: 86). Insisting on access to powerful knowledge becomes less important. For example, Muller explains that if print literacy has no cultural advantages over other literacies, then insisting on access to print literacy diminishes in importance. He quotes Latour to this effect: 'Is there a better way to finish off those one wants to save from condemnation?' (Muller 2000: 86).

Learning as a process

The second tradition of constructivism that draws from pragmatism and interactionism emphasizes learning as a process that arises from individuals' engagement in conscious goal-directed activities (Billett 2004: 192). While there are shared approaches, overlaps and commonalities with the first tradition discussed above, socio-cultural or situated learning theories in the second tradition are pervasive in adult and vocational education and training (and increasingly in higher education), particularly in the literature on workplace learning.

Theorists in this tradition start from a number of assumptions. First, we are active, social beings and it is our *nature* to learn from experience (Dewey 1938). Second, we construct knowledge through, as we learn from, our active and purposeful engagement in the world. Knowledge is understood as knowledge in action and knowledge in use. The distinction between knowledge and knowing is collapsed. Third, in creating knowledge, we create meaning, but this is always a negotiated process as we engage with others, so knowledge is socially constructed. Fourth, learning is a process of participation (Sfard 1998).[6] Among the most well known is Lave and Wenger's (1991) community of practice theory. Identities are constructed from learning to belong, and this occurs through a process of 'legitimate peripheral participation' in which novices learn to become experts by starting on the periphery and moving closer to the centre as their expertise develops (Lave and Wenger 1991: 29).

Billett provides one of the clearest examples of the way in which knowledge is equated with social practices, and his work establishes a continuity and commensurability of social practices between learning in the workplace and learning in the institution.[7] He says that:

> It is proposed that workplaces and educational institutions merely represent different instances of social practices in which learning occurs through participation. Learning in both kinds of social practice can be understood through a consideration of their respective participatory practices. Therefore, to distinguish between the two in terms of formalisms of social practice (ie, that one is formalised and the other informal) and propose some general consequences for learning arising from these bases is not helpful. Both these kinds of social practices are constituted historically, culturally

and situationally ... and share a common concern with continuity of practice.

(Billett 2002: 56–57)

Arguing that it is false to classify learning in educational institutions as formal and learning in workplaces as informal, with the latter valorized over the former as in some socio-cultural approaches, or the former over the latter as in traditional accounts (Billett 2002), allows Billett to focus on the *quality* of the social practices in each case, and the extent to which they facilitate learning.[8] This is helpful, because it provides a basis for critiquing many practices that pass as workplace learning and to argue that not all workplaces are good locations for learning, a problem which is rarely considered in many other situated learning accounts.

Situated learning theories in the workplace learning literature are problematic on two counts. First, in collapsing the distinction between vertical and horizontal discourses, situated learning theories privilege contextual and situated knowledge over decontextualized theoretical knowledge because of the closer relationship between horizontal discourse and workplace practices. The second problem, discussed below, is that these accounts lead to an impoverished notion of workplace learning – they cannot work on their own terms.

Socio-cultural learning theories critique traditional 'front-end' models of education because they are putatively based on the Cartesian mind–body distinction, and this is problematic because it results in education for the mind separate from the body (see Hager 2004). For example, Beckett and Hager (2002: 127) say that 'If humans are essentially minds that incidentally inhabit bodies, then development of mind remains the focus of education.' The way this Cartesian mind–body dualism is overcome is by equating knowledge with knowing, and knowing with holistic knowing that incorporates bodily (and thus tacit) knowing. Gonczi (2004: 29) in drawing on Hager's work, says that:

> knowledge as integrated in judgements is the capacity to act in and on the world, and that the acquisition of knowledge (and this includes know how of various kinds as well as propositional knowledge) alters both the world and the learner who is part of the world.

Consequently, it makes sense that holistic learning should be 'authentic', and take place where knowing that and knowing how are integrated in practice, which is primarily the workplace. This goes beyond arguing that the workplace could (or should) be the site in which propositional knowledge is acquired; the nature of the relationship between education and work changes and the nature of knowledge changes. Changes in society and the economy in late modernity mean that the boundaries between educational institutions and the workplace are breaking down. Curriculum is negotiated and designed to meet the needs of the employer and enterprise, in which 'The enduring disciplinary knowledge of the academy is replaced by a transdisciplinary understanding of knowledge in use' (Boud 2006: 85–86).

However, arguments about situated learning go beyond the workplace. Gonczi (2004: 21, emphasis added) argues that the best preparation 'for occupations and professional life, *and more generally for successful life*, is through some form of apprenticeship'. The 'remainder' left in formal institutions will need to engage in 'cross-disciplinary teaching, problem-based approaches, project work, use of portfolios to gather evidence of competence and so on' (Gonczi 2004: 21). This is an example of the way in which apparently 'progressive' socio-cultural approaches to learning can borrow from largely instrumentalist discourses about the changing nature of the world and work *and relevance* to justify their own approach and reduce learning to that which is needed for work.

Situated learning theories cannot work on their own terms because they fail to distinguish between the need to learn the context-specific knowledge required in the workplace, and access to theoretical knowledge codified in the disciplines or applied disciplines. Access to disciplinary knowledge is necessary because it is a condition for its contextually specific application in the workplace. Consequently, these accounts are not able to consider the conditions that are necessary for students to access and acquire decontextualized theoretical knowledge systematically and how they can draw on these bodies of knowledge in selecting and applying contextually specific applications in the workplace. Fuller *et al.* (2004: 3) explain, that 'stressing the situated character of knowledge fails to recognize that there are types of knowledge, such as theoretical ideas not connected to specific contexts, which are not always accessible on-the-job'. A focus on 'knowledge in use' may result in students being given access to contextually specific applications of disciplinary knowledge but not the system of meaning in which it is embedded and made meaningful. Students are not provided with the means to *select* appropriate contextual applications of knowledge in new situations. Barnett (2006: 150) explains the reason why people need access to the *structures* of knowledge and not just the 'information' that disciplines produce in the following way:

> Why not list a large number of topics and take them in alphabetical order in the manner of a modern encyclopaedia? This comes down to the difference between a textbook and a dictionary: broadly speaking, a dictionary of subject knowledge would not be learner friendly because alphabetical lists are a means of ordering information which suppresses any knowledge structure that the subject may possess. In knowledge terms, it is an arbitrary form of sequencing which arbitrarily separates things that belong together and conceals, rather than reveals, significant patterns.

Power is also a problem for that strand of constructivism that draws on pragmatism and interactionism, but it is the *absence* of power that is problematic. Curiously, in contrast to Dewey (1997 [1916]) who was concerned with power and democracy, many modern situated learning theorists do not focus on relations of power and social inequality, and relations of power do not figure sufficiently in accounts of the workplace. In approaches such as Wenger's communities of practice, the workplace is defined unproblematically as being an undifferentiated collective entity and contrasted to individuals for determining the presence or absence of conflict. Wenger (1998: 147) says that whether there is or is not conflict between the two needs to be decided individually, and not derived from a fundamental dichotomy.

Boud (2006: 79) identifies a number of tensions that arise from work-based learning partnerships between organizations, employees and universities. He says that tensions arise from: being both a worker and a learner; the difficulties for the academy 'in judging knowledge as legitimate when they are not involved in its codification'; the different time-scales between short-term work pressures and longer term learning expectations of the university; and, the need to rework relationships 'between adviser and learner when the "teacher" is necessarily not a subject-matter expert'. Missing from this is any analysis of power arising from conflicts between labour and capital, and from power relations arising from social class, ethnicity and the gendered nature of the workplace.[9] Later Boud (2006: 84) refers to the 'vexed' problem that arises when supervisors act as 'learning facilitators' because workers don't want to portray themselves as incompetent in front of their boss. That's it. In later work, Boud *et al.* (2009) argue that one of the problems with trying to formalize informal workplace learning practices is that it distorts them and workers feel that they are subject to surveillance, and they don't like it. But this does not lead them to problematize the nature of power in the workplace.

Even socio-cultural theories that *do* place conflict at the centre of analysis, such as in Engeström's (2004) 'third generation' of activity theory, can result in a slide towards a conservative pedagogy by their emphasis on the contextual. While power, contradiction and conflict are to the fore in activity theory,[10] the emphasis is on the 'expansive transformations' that result from conflict and the resolution of that conflict. This results in unitary conceptions of workplaces that are focussed on unproblematic concepts of development (Avis 2007). The consequence is, Avis (2007: 169) argues, that often there is little to distinguish approaches such as Engeström's from systems theory, and from 'developmental work research, which is no more than a form of consultancy aiming to improve work practices'.

The emphasis on collective competence, an approach Engeström shares with many other socio-cultural learning theorists, marginalizes the Marxist notion of the fundamental antagonism in the *relations* of production in favour of secondary contradictions in the *process* of production itself, thus downplaying antagonistic relations between labour and capital (Avis 2007: 169). Conflicts are resolved and new conflicts ensue because of contradictions intrinsic to the activity system, but these conflicts are underpinned by an underlying consensus and identity of interest between labour and management. Power relations in the workplace are trivialized in such analyses because 'antagonistic relations at the site of waged labour are bracketed in as much as the collective worker is deemed not to embody class antagonism' (Avis 2007: 172). An example of this is provided by Hager and Smith (2004: 39), who say of the 'new workplace' that 'Here the focus shifts from the competencies of individuals to an organisational capacity to function in ways that effectively employ the combined assets of the organisation's staff and resources.'

The end result is a description of workplace learning that is premised on social partnerships in which the employer, employee (aka student) and educational institution are *partners* in shaping the programme of learning. For example, Gonczi (2004: 33) says that 'these learning arrangements are a three-way partnership between the work organisation, the learner and the university. The learning program is linked to the strategic goals of the organisation, while assessment and accreditation are the responsibility of the university.' No power differences here!

If learning is viewed solely as a participative activity it risks trivializing power relations in the workplace and the way opportunities for workplace learning are shaped by work organization, the employment relationship and organizational structures (Fuller *et al.* 2004: 6). 'Failure' to learn appropriately can be attributed to individuals rather than the way in which the nature of, access to and outcomes from, workplace learning are shaped by broader relations of power. Preparedness to engage in both informal and formal workplace learning can be construed as a commitment to the organization's strategic goals no matter how problematic these goals or processes of learning, and in this way they may be another mechanism for control in the workplace. An example that comes to mind is staff development processes designed to 'teach' teachers in VET institutions about entrepreneurship, team-working and customer service. The notion that there should be a 'conversation' in the workplace about the nature of knowledge is evaded, and with it, the possibility of a discussion about what counts as knowledge and how it should be structured and accessed. Teachers in VET are rarely asked if they think programmes to teach them entrepreneurship and customer service provide them with access to the knowledge they need to become better teachers.

Moreover, insufficient attention to power relations means that much of the literature on workplace learning tends to present an idealized account of the *possibilities* rather than the *realities*. For example, the Victorian Workcover Authority (2006: 3), which is a statutory body of the Victorian State Government in Australia, reports that 49 per cent of respondents to a 2006 survey on the incidence of workplace bullying reported that bullying took place in their workplace, and 33 per cent said they had taken time off due to workplace bullying. Apprentices and casual and temporary staff were more likely to have experienced bullying, but less likely to report it and less likely to have it resolved. In a majority of cases, the bullies were the targets' supervisors but this did not exclude bullying by co-workers (The Victorian Workcover Authority 2006: 2–3). Kelly (2005: 5) argues that the careers of the bullies are rarely disrupted in contrast to those who have been bullied, in part because 'tough management can become a euphemism for bullying'.

Unwin *et al.* (2007) explain that the contextual relationships shaping work-place learning are not just internal to the enterprise or organization, but also include the wider economic, social, regulatory and political environment. This is because the 'primary function of any workplace is not learning but the production of goods and services and the achievement of organisational goals' (Unwin *et al.* 2007: 334). The broader environment helps shape workplace learning but it does not fully determine it and it is possible to distinguish between workplaces' learning environments. Fuller and Unwin (2004) do so in distinguishing between workplaces that offer expansive learning environments and those that offer restrictive environments. Whether it is one or the other is often related to the way work is designed, which includes the level of discretion workers have in performing their roles, the strength of the boundaries between roles and the extent of the knowledge that workers need to perform their jobs. Expansive learning is more likely to take place:

> when knowledge was seen to be a central component of all jobs and that employees needed to cross workplace boundaries in order to both demonstrate their existing knowledge and acquire new knowledge.
>
> (Fuller and Unwin 2004: 137)

They argue that off-the-job learning can support expansive learning by providing opportunities for workers to expand their networks, to reflect on workplace practice and to 'pursue knowledge-based courses and qualifications' (Fuller and Unwin 2004: 139). The latter is helpful because it gives participants access to knowledge they are unlikely to acquire from workplace experience, and provides the basis for career progression.

Furthermore, the interests of employers and employees are not always the same. Power relations shape the purpose and definition of learning *outcomes* as well as access to learning and the type of learning that takes place. Even assuming that workers want to invest in learning that is useful to their current workplace, it is not always in workers' interests to have learning so closely identified with the workplace or with the organization's 'strategic goals' when these goals are themselves contested. And nor is it in workers' interests when training results in more limited or impoverished access to learning than would be where students have *relative* independence from the workplace. Too close an identification between the workplace and educational institution can lead to social reproduction rather than social change (Granville 2004). This is because, arguably, students who do not have access to off-site learning where they are not under surveillance have less opportunity to develop a critical perspective on workplace practices. Learning that occurs over two sites – the workplace and the educational institution – potentially provides students with access to empowering learning, because it can provide access to society's conversation expressed in systematized theoretical knowledge, relative independence from the workplace as a basis for developing a critical practice and access to the workplace as the site where different kinds of knowledge must be integrated through practice.

Both strands of constructivism give rise to competence modes of pedagogy. Constructivism gives rise to weak classification because knowledge is reducible to commensurable social practices and weak framing in which the student has apparent control over the selection, sequencing, pacing and evaluation of knowledge because knowledge is constructed through processes of participation. The focus is not on external knowledge, but rather on developing the individual, group, or collective (depending on the type of constructivism and whether it has an individualist or holist premise). The purpose is not to differentiate and rank, but to develop shared capacities and understandings.

While some workplace training may in fact look like this, the *practice* of workplace training may be altogether different. It may consist of weak external classification of knowledge so that the boundaries between theoretical, abstract knowledge and everyday knowledge are weakly defined, but strong *internal* classification with strongly defined relations between people, objects and spaces. Thus speaks the voice of power, because it is, in many cases, up to the employer or management to decide on the nature and type of workplace training. Framing may be weak so that the student controls the sequencing, pacing and evaluation of the outcome, or it may be strong with little student control and strong evaluation at the end, particularly if participation is required for job permanence or promotion. The problem arises when workplace learning theory is used to justify a practice to which it is diametrically opposed. This is one example of the complex relationship between constructivism and instrumentalism and the reason why it can be difficult in practice to distinguish between the two.

Relations of affinity and opposition

Conservative, instrumentalist and constructivist theories of curriculum are enmeshed in complex relations of affinity and opposition. Bernstein (2000: 56) explains that different pedagogic modes and associated pedagogic identities may give rise to a 'mixed pedagogic pallet'. This is because curriculum is always the outcome of struggles about what matters and this is never settled. Contests occur *within* the ORF and PRF as well as between them, reflecting broader social and class investments and interests in these debates (Bernstein 2000: 115). An example of a 'mixed pedagogic pallet' is the way that developmental discourses of competence modes can 'be inserted in an economic mode, retaining its original name and resonances, whilst giving rise to an opposing practice' (Bernstein 2000: 56). As will be discussed in the next chapter, this is exemplified when apparently 'student-centred' socio-cultural learning theories and discourses are used to implement competency-based training.

Bernstein (2000: 61) says that all sectors of education are subjected to managerialist discourses with the result that educational institutions have been required to create management structures to enable them to compete in the educational 'market' and to create internal entrepreneurial cultures. This has been the means by which the ORF exerts dominance over the PRF. The mediating discourse is instrumentalism because of its hegemonic dominance within the ORF, and this brings instrumentalism into different relationships with conservatism and constructivism. The current relative dominance of instrumentalism has restructured the relationship between different pedagogic modes and identities so that each can be mobilized in the employ of instrumentalism.

Arguably, conservative curricular discourses are influential in schools because concerns about the nature of the *person* are more strongly emphasized in school discourses as a consequence of the role of schools in shaping identities. In contrast, constructivist discourses and concerns about *contexts* are particularly influential in tertiary education (vocational education and training and higher education) because of the emphasis on relevance for the economy. However, while tertiary education focusses on contexts, it is also concerned with the person as evidenced by the policy preoccupation with generic skills and attributes. While the relationships between conservatism and instrumentalism, and between instrumentalism and constructivism, may be emphasized more strongly in one sector or the other, these relationships are present in all sectors and contribute to shaping curriculum, although in ways that are contradictory and incomplete.

Instrumentalism must draw on conservatism's concerns about the person and on constructivism's concerns about contexts otherwise it cannot be realized as a mode of pedagogic practice. It can only effectively operate through the constitution of market identities, but such an identity cannot be constituted in isolation even if the market identity is 'socially empty' through its emphasis on perpetual trainability. The market citizen requires a particular habitus to engage in market behaviours, invest in the self and project the self appropriately into these relations (Bourdieu and Wacquant 1992). The successful operation of markets requires intrinsic respect for the rules and institutions that establish the rules (Hobbes 1985 [1651]). Consequently, instrumentalism draws from conservatism through the *bourgeois liberal individual*. The bourgeois liberal individual stands in a relationship of ownership of the self as proprietor of the self as the basis for engaging in relations of exchange between proprietors, with society the sum total of these exchange relations (Macpherson 1962: 3). The values of entrepreneurship and commitments to individualism and self-reliance (rather than reliance on the welfare state) are the principles upon which the market identity can develop. The person constructed by the school system is the proprietor of the self who is able to position themselves in the market, acquire knowledge and skill in response to external signals and invest in themselves appropriately. Thus conservatism blends unproblematically with the instrumentalism of the neo-liberal market identity.

Constructivist discourses are selectively appropriated by instrumentalism through affinities they share around the nature of the individual and the nature of knowledge through their shared focus on the contextual. This is the focus of the next chapter. It explains the affinities that arise between the two through the discourse of reflexive modernization, the fluid nature of individual identities and the self as a project and the consequence is that the voluntarism of much constructivism accords with the voluntarism of instrumentalism in which the self is a continuing project. Each draws on the language of empowerment and student-centredness, even though instrumentalists privilege the empowered *consumer*, whereas constructivists privilege developmental discourses of the self, group, or workplace. Both view academic knowledge as elitist and ideological, but they differ over who should control knowledge (Moore and Young 2001: 446).

The dominance of instrumentalism is reinforced in countries such as Britain and Australia by the increasing intervention by the state in the preparation of teachers by insisting on instrumentally relevant forms of educational theory, at the expense of the philosophy, history and sociology of education, all of which are intrinsic to theorizing the role of knowledge in curriculum and qualifications.[11] This is a 'silencing' of the theoretical basis of teaching practice and the possibility of criticism, and lays the basis for the dominance of instrumentalism in constructing qualifications in all sectors of education (Beck and Young 2005: 193).

Conclusion

The consequence of the crisis in curriculum theory is that the dominant approaches – conservatism, instrumentalism and constructivism – are not able to address knowledge as a causal and emergent property at the core of the curriculum because each collapses the epistemic relation of knowledge into the social relation. However, the state of the curriculum at any time is the outcome of power struggles for control of the pedagogic device, because the curriculum defines that which is important. This means that these theories of curriculum do not exist in pure form, even though they have different philosophical premises and social bases. The ORF is itself ideologically divided between those who support the 'traditional' curriculum and 'educational modernizers' who support instrumentalism and seek the development of generic skills and capacities (Hickox and Moore 1995; Marginson 1997a: 172). The PRF on the other hand, is dominated by varieties of constructivism and this is problematic because it means there is no real basis for developing a theory of knowledge to underpin curriculum or for constructivism to serve as an opposition to either the conservatives or instrumentalist–modernizers in the ORF. However, instrumentalists can also be found within the PRF, particularly in vocational education and training, as can constructivists who have unproblematically built a bridge between constructivism and instrumentalism.

The consequence is that a 'pedagogic pallet' emerges in different forms in each of the sectors. This arises from relations of power and control between the dominant approaches and their supporters. This chapter has argued that instrumentalism is the dominant theory of curriculum that selectively appropriates elements from conservatism and constructivism, but in ways that do not challenge the fundamental premises of instrumentalism, which is that education is mainly an economic tool. The next chapter theorizes the relations of affinity and opposition between instrumentalism and constructivism in more detail by analysing the way in which these relations facilitated the introduction of competency-based training in VET.

8 The appropriation of constructivism by instrumentalism

The case of competency-based training

Competency-based training models of curriculum are now the basis of vocational education and training (VET) qualifications in many countries because governments believe that they meet the needs of industry and ensure industry 'control' over VET. Many countries have, or are in the process of introducing, competency-based training (CBT) qualifications in their VET systems as part of constructing national qualifications frameworks (Tuck 2007). National Vocational Qualifications (NVQs) in England, Wales and Northern Ireland are based on CBT models of curriculum, as are Scottish Vocational Qualifications (Misko 2006). CBT is also a feature of many vocational qualifications in South Africa (Allais 2007b) and New Zealand (Melles 2008). Australia is of particular interest because it has gone further than most other countries in insisting that all and not just some of its publicly funded qualifications in VET be based on CBT. Australian VET qualifications are derived from 'training packages', which are the equivalents of British NVQs. Guthrie (2009: 6) explains that the Australian model of CBT in VET was strongly based on the UK NVQ model and drew heavily on the UK experience and literature so there are many parallels between the two countries.

Yet the introduction of CBT has been controversial wherever it has been implemented and it has evoked strong opposition because of concerns that it downplays the importance of underpinning knowledge.[1] Guthrie (2009: 6) illustrates this controversy in Australia by quoting Collins who, in 1993, said that the introduction of CBT evoked responses which included:

> the enthusiastic commitment of the campaigner; the 'no choice' acceptance of the bureaucrat; the 'we can subvert this and get it to work educationally' argument of the educational policy advisor; the cries of pain from those seeing good education being replaced by jargonistic ritual; the exploration of research work that suggests that at least part of the competencies agenda cannot work; and the arguments that the whole current discourse is dangerous because it shifts the balance of power in the wrong direction and threatens crucial educational purposes in a democratic society.

CBT still provokes similar controversies today. However, as we will see, one thing that has allowed CBT proselytizers to carry the day is that CBT is tied to a putatively progressive policy which promises to empower the most disempowered. This occurs in part because instrumentalism is able to appropriate progressive discourses of student-centred learning from constructivism, and also to appropriate from constructivism a focus on situated learning and the contextualized nature of knowledge. This appropriation contributes to the legitimation of CBT and to its continuing theorization and development. As a consequence, knowledge is displaced from the centre of curriculum in competency-based qualifications thereby denying students access to the theoretical knowledge that they need in the workplace, even though the purpose of competency-based qualifications is to prepare students for the workplace.

This is not just an esoteric argument; there are real practical consequences for students and society. Competency-based qualifications in most countries are usually located in institutions in lower-status, vocationally oriented 'second' tiers of tertiary education rather than in universities, or as an alternative stream to 'academic' pathways in senior secondary school. Working-class students are more likely to go to lower status institutions and undertake competency-based qualifications while more privileged students are more likely to go to higher education (Santiago *et al.* 2008a). Consequently, the structuring of knowledge in competency-based qualifications is a matter of distributional justice.

The definition of competency and units of competency in VET in Australia is typical of CBT in other countries. Competency is defined as the application of specified knowledge, skill and attitudes needed to undertake a work role or task to the required standard in the workplace (Department of Education Science and Training [DEST] 2006: 69) and units of competency (which make up qualifications) 'define the various competencies required for effective workplace performance' (DEST 2006: 109). Learning outcomes are described as a demonstration of workplace tasks or roles and knowledge and skill is inferred from this performance. Knowledge is included in units of competency, but only if it is 'actually applied at work' (DEST 2006: 114). Knowledge is integrated into the performance specification in the performance criteria, range statements or evidence guides thus tying it tightly to the contextual. This demonstrates that knowledge is included, but it is only contextually specific knowledge which has been delocated from the system of meaning in which it is embedded.

The first section of the chapter explains that the new vocationalism in general, and CBT in particular, was in part made possible by the instrumentalist appropriation of progressivism at the broad policy level, and by the continuing appropriation of concepts and language drawn from constructivism in developing a conceptual basis for CBT. The section that follows discusses the way in which the atomistic ontology of CBT facilitates its capacity to appropriate concepts selectively from opposing theoretical premises, while the final section discusses the commonalities between instrumentalism and constructivism around knowledge and the implications for curriculum. The chapter uses the Bernsteinian concepts of regulative and instructional discourses to illustrate the process used by instrumentalism to appropriate constructivism in justifying and legitimating CBT, while both Bernsteinian and critical realist concepts of the structure and nature of knowledge and processes of acquiring knowledge are used to critique constructivist and instrumentalist approaches to knowledge.

The introduction of CBT and the language of progressivism

In a pattern typical of similar Anglophone countries, the introduction of CBT in VET in the 1980s and 1990s in Australia was a key component of neo-liberal reforms to education that sought to create a 'training market' and an 'industry-led' training system as part of broader industry restructuring and micro-economic reform (Goozee 2001: 62). However, its introduction was mediated through the emancipatory language associated with the developmental discourse of the 'new vocationalism' which was tied to new conceptions about work and society. The new vocationalism sought to foster the knowledge and skills necessary for a changing world and to prepare people for changes to work and the way knowledge was used at work. This meant, as Bates *et al.* (1998: 113) explain in discussing the introduction of the new vocationalism in England, that it aimed to prepare people for work in general rather than for specific jobs. They argue that the new vocationalism of the 1980s was infused with the language of progressivism despite the historical antipathy between vocationalism and progressivism.

The language of progressivism was also strongly associated with the introduction of CBT in Australia. Indeed, the Australian Council of Trade Unions was among the most enthusiastic supporters of the introduction of CBT and helped to develop and implement the new VET system and new VET qualifications by their participation in corporatist mechanisms established by the then Labor government (Goozee 2001). It was argued that the introduction of CBT would: increase participation in education and training; provide unparalleled access to education and training for people from disadvantaged backgrounds; recognize and certify the skills of existing workers; create access to on and off the job training for workers; help to overcome occupational segregation based on gender divisions or outdated craft divisions; increase private and public investment in training; and, improve the quality and flexibility of the training system (Goozee 2001: 63–64). It was also to be used to develop formal training for occupational areas where there were no existing qualifications (Guthrie 2009: 5). Moira Scollay (2000), who was the chief executive officer of the Australian statutory body responsible for VET at the time, described the introduction of CBT and training packages in these terms:

> A revolutionary tide has swept through Australia's vocational education and training system over the past decade, bringing with it new and better ways of linking the world of work and the world of learning.

However, in Australia as in England, the 'new vocationalism' of the 1970s and early 1980s was transformed into 'controlled vocationalism' that granted increased control to the state and to employers in specifying the outcomes of VET (Bates *et al.* 1998: 114). VET policy was restructured so that it was aligned with the world of work imagined in policy (at least in Anglophone, liberal market economies), and this world of work consisted of the 'natural' free market populated by entrepreneurial, *flexible* workers who took responsibility for their firm's outcomes, but without the hierarchical (and expensive) management structures characteristic of Fordism (Bates *et al.* 1998: 116). The model of work and workers envisaged was (and remains) a unitary one where the interests of management and workers are the same, untroubled by relations of power or the possibility of conflicting interests. The outcomes of work are not problematized and policy takes for granted that the purpose of education is to 'revolve around the cultivation of appropriate skills and attitudes for employment' (Bates *et al.* 1998: 115). The outcomes of education were similarly redefined as unproblematic 'descriptions' of the skills needed by employers.

Empowerment as a deficit discourse

The move from the new vocationalism to controlled vocationalism occurred despite the language of empowerment that described the way students and teachers would be empowered, language that was used at the beginning of the introduction of CBT and in its subsequent implementation as NVQs in England and as training packages in Australia. Indeed, a stronger argument is possible: the language of empowerment *facilitated* the move from the new vocationalism to controlled vocationalism. This language is *still* being used in Australia. Students are putatively empowered not just because they can 'choose' what, when and how they will study, but also because learning is now a negotiated activity in which 'learners have a part to play in developing their own learning processes, contexts and outcomes' (Smith and Blake 2005: 6).

However, in practice, students' freedom is limited to the way in which 'the tightly prescribed learning objectives are to be achieved', so that students have responsibility for learning, but not control over learning (Bates 1998: 188). This is because all the key elements are specified in the competency-outcomes, performance criteria and assessment guidelines. The autonomy students have is as consumers; they can choose to buy this and not that commodified, pre-packaged product. However, choices are not made by abstract market individuals who have the necessary knowledge and capacity to choose programmes that meet their well understood and transparent instrumental (and commensurable) purposes. Rather, choices are exercised by socially specific individuals with differing life histories within a field in which 'players have differing resources, but where the rules are determined by their unequal interactions' (Hodkinson 1998: 160). Knowledge of the 'game' and its rules and capacity to play are differentially distributed through social hierarchies that are produced by underlying social inequalities (Bourdieu 1984 [1979]). This is a consequence of the instantiation of the distributive rules of the pedagogic device and the way these rules work to, as Bernstein (2003: 182–83) explains, distribute access to forms of consciousness, identity and desire.

The language of empowerment is not limited to students. Teachers are putatively empowered because training packages allow 'trainers' creatively to develop and apply their pedagogic skills and knowledge and 'to develop and promote their expertise as flexible learning managers' (Scollay 2000). In fact, according to Scollay (2000), training packages give teachers a *more* active role than they had hitherto, because teachers no longer function as the 'mere deliverer of courses'.

It is clear, however, that teachers do not feel empowered. In their high-level review of training packages in Australia in 2004, Schofield and McDonald (2004: 27) found that there was an 'unacceptably high level of confusion amongst educators in particular about the relationship between Training Packages and teaching, learning and assessment.' They continue:

> Many do not seem to understand how Training Packages work, or how to work with them, and blame them for what may well be their own planning and practice or inadequate management support. After seven years, we would have expected a more widespread understanding.
>
> (Schofield and McDonald 2004: 27)

They argued that teachers do not understand CBT. A similar observation was made by a visiting Organisation for Economic Cooperation and Development (OECD) team to Australia that reviewed Australia's VET system which found that training packages are 'frequently too complex to follow for teachers and trainers, who are not involved in their development' (Hoeckel *et al.* 2008: 36). Schofield and McDonald (2004: 27) argued that teachers confuse and conflate training packages with curriculum (which they define as learning design), methods of teaching (pedagogy) and resources to support teaching and learning. It appears from this analysis that all these dimensions are separate and distinguishable. As will be argued later in this chapter, it is these distinctions that in part allow instrumentalists to co-opt the language of constructivism.

Furthermore, it was not just that teachers do not understand training packages, they are also hostile to them, and Schofield and McDonald (2004: 33) argued that this legacy needed to be dealt with if training packages were to be based on a 'new settlement'. 'All parties' needed to acknowledge that the introduction of training packages could have been better handled as a first step in engaging 'clients' (that is, teachers in this instance). Poor planning and management are cited as contributing factors to the apparently widespread misunderstanding of the purpose and nature of training packages, as are teachers' lack of skills in constructing appropriate curriculum and learning materials (Down 2003a, 2003b; Harris *et al.* 2005; Guthrie 2009).

Consequently, the 'problem' is one of implementation, and while some responsibility is directed towards broad policy and the way that it is implemented, most is steeped in a deficit discourse around teachers' skills.[2] This is not limited to Australia. Wolf (2002: 76–77) explains that failures of NVQs in England are not attributed to the model itself, but to problems of implementation. In Australia the problem was how to unlock the 'revolutionary' potential of training packages (ANTA 2003: 22), and while teachers were (and are) regarded the key, they are also the problem. The language of empowerment is thus used to construct a deficit discourse about teachers. In their research, Clayton and Blom (2004: 5) cite experts they interviewed about the capacities of VET teachers who thought that:

> many teachers and trainers had difficulty in interpreting training packages and translating them into teaching and learning strategies, while some also had difficulty in structuring, focusing and systematically addressing underpinning knowledge and higher order cognitive skills.

They argue that while many teachers have adapted to training packages, many have not, and teachers need support in 'translating competency standards into learning experiences' and to develop skills in working with industry and with diverse groups of learners (Clayton and Blom 2004: 5). Mitchell *et al.* (2006a: 6) argue that teachers need to be reskilled because the demands upon them have changed; the contexts in which learning takes place are more diverse and now include workplace learning as well as flexible modes of delivery. Teachers have to adapt to new assessment practices and to a more diverse range of clients that includes industry, employers and individual students, and they have to be able to 'customize' learning appropriately. The language of progressivism is used to describe the kinds of changes teachers need to make, and simultaneously to construct the discourse around their deficits. They need to be innovative, flexible and creative, be able to understand and apply adult learning theory and principles and empower learners through this process (Mitchell *et al.* 2006a; Harris *et al.* 2005). Guthrie (2009: 25) argues that there is now a large measure of support for CBT despite lingering disquiet among providers (that is, educational institutions) using CBT and some academics, and that moreover, 'On the whole, a strong case has not been made for an alternative approach.' This does not prevent him from later arguing that better change management strategies are still needed, and that 'The secret will be to focus attention on those who are sceptical about training products and processes to convince them of the change required' (Guthrie 2009: 27). One wonders why this would be necessary if there is a large measure of support for CBT.

The incorporation of progressivism into instrumentalism

How are we to understand this? Jones and Moore (1995: 81) explain that educational policy must be located within the political context in which it arises, and this helps us to understand the way in which the progressivism of the new vocationalism was transformed into controlled vocationalism. They explain that educational policy development is characterized by two processes: the first is the process of recontextualization and the second is the process of incorporation (Jones and Moore 1995: 83–84). In the first, ideas and concepts are selectively appropriated into an instructional discourse and embedded within a regulative discourse. The principle of recontextualization points backwards; it tells us where the discourse has come from. They use a Bernsteinian framework to explain that the broader policy context is the dominant regulative discourse which is used to construct the explicit, instructional discourse. Jones and Moore (1995: 81–82) explain that the:

> political and policy context act selectively upon the realisation of the various *possibilities* suggested by different approaches to competence ... Whether it is the controlling or emancipatory possibilities that come to be realised will be settled not by theoretical or definitional debates but within real world, institutional contexts.

The regulative discourse provides the principle of recontextualization which is used to selectively appropriate concepts and then reassemble them as the instructional discourse so that the appropriated discourse is ideologically congruent with the regulative discourse (Bernstein 2000: 32–33). The parameters of the regulative discourse are shaped by the particular model of social order, which in this case is neo-liberalism. The instructional discourse is consequently embedded within the dominant regulative discourse.

In the case of CBT, the (regulative) policy discourse of competence borrowed concepts and language from theories that were originally developed within academic disciplines, and then reassembled within the framework of 'an approach appropriate to the particular objectives of the agency assembling it' (Jones and Moore 1995: 83). This occurred by the process of incorporation, which refers to the way 'in which the discourse incorporates those aspects of social life that are the primary concern of the agency' (Jones and Moore 1995: 83–84). This tells us the direction in which the discourse is going. The introduction of CBT in England (and in Australia) incorporated ' "the world of work" according to its own particular principles and rules' (Jones and Moore 1995: 84).

Elements of progressivism were selectively drawn from humanism and reassembled within instrumentalism at the broad policy level, while elements of constructivism that emphasized situated learning and a focus on the student were selectively used in the implementation of CBT with its focus on workplace learning. Vocationalism drew from progressivism a rejection of 'the centrality of disciplinary knowledge and school subjects in definitions of the curriculum' (Bates *et al.* 1998: 111). Progressivism was concerned primarily with the development of the intrinsic capacities of the student, and so the task of the teacher was not to instil disciplinary knowledge, but to provide students with opportunities to construct their knowledge of the world (Bates *et al.* 1998: 111).

Bloomer (1998: 168) explains that the reworked progressivism drew the language of 'consumer rights, freedom and individuality' from the liberal market ideologies that were driving the new vocationalism, because these were seen as 'inherently and morally good'. It was, however, the instrumentalist policy objectives that dominated and shaped borrowed concepts. The developmental language of empowerment is tied to the 'project of the self', but it is a self that is constructed as a market identity using 'the products and services which the market provides' (Hartley 2007: 2). Progressive concepts consequently are not used to broaden the scope of education and resist the subordination of education to economic ends, but to better serve these economic ends (Bates 1998: 189).

The processes of recontextualization and incorporation make it possible, for example, for Smith and Blake (2005: 1) to say on the one hand, that teaching in VET is moving away from 'a teacher-centred and supplier-driven approach towards an approach where learners are viewed as clients and individuals', and on the other, to argue that teaching in VET is now underpinned by constructivism, instead of instructivism (Smith and Blake 2005: 2). VET staff development programmes champion approaches such as communities of practice, action learning and professional conversations for staff development in VET in Australia and as a model of work-based learning more broadly,[3] while at the same time, arguing that these models enable VET to build human capital in the workforce, and thus meet the Australian government's aims for skill development (Mitchell *et al.* 2007).

CBT policy as pastiche – the mechanism of appropriation

The theoretical premise within instrumentalism that allows CBT to appropriate from constructivism is the way in which CBT divorces learning outcomes from processes of learning. Such appropriation is also possible because of theoretical commonalities between instrumentalism and constructivism, and this is addressed in the next section. CBT is a form of empirical realism based on atomism in ontology and epistemology, in which the 'real' consists of discrete, atomistic events that can be translated into unproblematic (empirical) descriptions of those events. This is expressed in units of competency which are unproblematic descriptions of workplace roles or tasks. The ontology of CBT means that each of the components of the model can be considered independently of the other and adjusted as appropriate to 'fix' deficiencies. The model is then reassembled through an aggregative process rather than a relational one in which the components are changed by their relationship to the whole and to each other.

For example, the design of units of competency has been augmented to accommodate concerns about, among other things, the inclusion of underpinning knowledge and to ensure that a broad range of contexts was specified in units of competency as protection against overly narrow training (Rumsey 2003: 13–15). However, the underlying definition of competency has not changed fundamentally in Australia since the early 1990s, although the words may have changed slightly (Guthrie 2009: 17). The notion of competency was then and is now based on four components: task skills task management skills, contingency management skills and job/environment skills (DEST 2006: 110). The 'solution' to every perceived deficiency was to add required and optional components to the model and tight specifications for their inclusion.[4]

This process of augmentation and aggregation makes it possible to distinguish between competency outcomes (learning outcomes), curriculum, pedagogy and the resources used to support teaching and learning. If each is considered independently rather than relationally, then it is possible to invest each with differing content. In the case of CBT proselytizers, the outcomes of learning are held constant while other aspects are changed as needed. This is necessary because the underlying premise of CBT is that *employers* (or more charitably and inclusively, sometimes 'industry') should determine what is needed in the workplace.[5] This is what an industry-led VET system is supposed to mean, with the result that *this* component of the model – industry specification of outcomes – is not negotiable.

The result is policy that uses as its justification and source of legitimation a pastiche of theories and approaches that draw from sometimes opposing theoretical premises, which are then blended by processes of recontextualization. Constructivist theories of learning are mobilized to support human capital objectives, even though human capital theory is based on the self-maximizing rational economic individual. Individualistic theories of learning styles (that ascribe learning styles as relatively fixed attributes of individuals) are unproblematically blended with theories that emphasize learning as a participative process (in which the construction of meaning is a shared process).[6] This process of selection, augmentation, blending and incorporation is achieved with the principle of recontextualization which is derived from the broader human capital policy. As argued in previous chapters, the principle of recontextualization in all sectors of education is increasingly dominated by the principle of market relevance and genericism and, in VET, this is expressed in the notion of an industry-led system in which 'industry' determines the outcomes it wants and VET delivers those outcomes.

The recontextualizing field and the production of knowledge

This analysis explains *how* the process of recontextualization and incorporation takes place, but it doesn't explain *who* is driving it. Bernstein (2000: 42) argues that the recontextualizing field as a whole largely recontextualizes from the field of knowledge production in other disciplines such as (but not limited to) psychology and sociology. He implies that university teacher education departments are primarily knowledge recontextualizers rather than knowledge producers, because their purpose is to select, translate and relocate knowledge from the field in which it was produced to reproduce it (in transformed form) in curriculum and to teach teachers. The main concern of the field as a whole, and the official recontextualizing field (ORF) and pedagogic recontextualizing field (PRF), is the structure of, and struggle for control over, the pedagogic device.

While agreeing with Bernstein's argument about the primary focus of the recontextualizing field, part of the work in constructing (contested) models of the pedagogic device *itself* may include the *production* of knowledge and not merely its recontextualization. Theorization about the nature of the pedagogic device draws from other disciplines, particularly those that conceptualize the nature of the actor and society, but theorization *about* the pedagogic device takes place within the field of recontextualization by building on these other disciplines. The lines between the production and recontextualization of knowledge are perhaps more permeable, with teacher education departments contributing to knowledge production even if this is often within the context of other disciplines. For example, the sociology of education is embedded within the discipline of sociology, but often conducted in university teacher education departments. Such knowledge production may draw on its foundational disciplines, but its development and application in the field of education invests it with relative autonomy, which may in turn act back on the foundational discipline. It is this knowledge that is 'recruitable' because it is already developed within the field of education and selectively reappropriated by the ORF.

Just as the lines between knowledge recontextualization and knowledge production are permeable within the recontextualizing field, so too are the lines between recontextualizers located primarily in the ORF and those located primarily within the PRF. Both are drawn upon to develop policy and staff development programmes and to undertake evaluative studies to advise government on how existing policy can be implemented better. The PRF is particularly drawn on to undertake evaluative studies of existing policy and many in the PRF rely on funds provided by the ORF to conduct research, but these studies mostly take the existing policy parameters as a given. This makes it very difficult for such work to say, 'The emperor has no clothes' (Wheelahan 2003, 2006).

There are those within the PRF who have maintained more independence from the ORF. Their relative independence gives them more autonomy and enables them to develop a more critical stance towards the policies and approaches of the ORF. Indeed, much of this work has been important in developing a critical understanding of VET policy in Australia, the UK and similar Anglophone countries. It also means that this work is theoretically consistent and generally not mashed together as a pastiche of inconsistent ontological premises. Arguably, however, the relative independence of these knowledge producers has not protected them from having their work plundered by the recontextualizers in the ORF, and this is particularly so for those who are (different varieties of) constructivists. This is not just because CBT can unproblematically 'add' whatever seems like a good idea at the time as a consequence of its atomistic and aggregative ontology. This bridge is made because there are important similarities between instrumentalism and constructivism, which also facilitate the incorporation of the latter by the former.

The problem of knowledge

The relationship between instrumentalism and constructivism makes CBT possible not just at the level of its legitimation and justification, but also in its theorization and development. Even though constructivists differ among themselves about the nature of contexts (Edwards and Miller 2007), they share a common concern about context with instrumentalists and with the contextual, situated and problem-oriented nature of knowledge creation and learning. Both could agree with the statement that: 'Current thinking emphasises knowledge constructed as practical, interdisciplinary, informal, applied and contextual over knowledge constructed as theoretical, disciplinary, formal, foundational and generalisable' (Chappell *et al.* 2003: 7). Both privilege the workplace as the site of learning and knowledge production at the expense of disciplinary knowledge based on the assumption that the process of *creating, acquiring* and *applying* knowledge are the same. Both emphasize the context specific features of knowledge rather than its decontextualized features.

As a consequence of their emphasis on the contextual, both posit a 'flattened' ontology in which 'the real' exists at the level of events and experiences and in so doing reduce knowledge to experience, although they do so in different ways. Absent from both is an analysis of emergent outcomes arising from the interaction of generative mechanisms in a stratified, complex reality (Bhaskar 1998d). Consequently, neither has the capacity to distinguish *between* contexts by identifying commonalities and differences, or to identify features of the context that are necessary and those that are contingent because all aspects of the context are rendered equal. The structuring mechanisms of events and experiences are thus rendered invisible, so any analysis of context is necessarily always partial and incomplete.

Because experience is the basis of knowledge, both minimize the differences between knowledge acquired at work and that acquired in education. This enables both to emphasize the commensurability of vertical and horizontal discourses rather than their differences because each consists of experiences that form the basis of knowledge. Indeed, a stronger argument can be made; both privilege horizontal discourses over vertical discourses because of their emphasis on 'authentic' learning in the workplace and in sites other than the academy, because it is in the former that knowledge can be contextualized and applied. Knowledge is not valued *unless* it has application in the workplace or can be used to solve a problem, as in problem-based learning approaches to curriculum. The privileging of horizontal discourses is also demonstrated by the way both valorize informal learning even if they do so for different reasons. Instrumentalism valorizes informal learning to support efficiency and effectiveness, whereas constructivism does so as part of the process of (individual or shared) knowledge construction and developmental discourses, or as a way of challenging the power relations of the academy (Harris 1999, 2000).

Where the existence and necessity of codified knowledge is admitted, both see it in instrumental terms and subordinate to 'authentic learning' rather than as systemized, structured bodies of knowledge; structures that have pedagogic implications for the selection and sequencing of this knowledge and for the way students engage with it. Consequently, both are unable to theorize the relationship between theoretical abstract knowledge and knowledge acquired in the workplace. This is a problem because, as Young (2006a: 113) explains: 'It is the connections between the codified knowledge of the college-based curriculum and the tacit and often uncodifiable knowledge that is acquired in workplaces that is the basis for what is distinctive about vocational knowledge.' The boundaries between the two sites and the kinds of knowledge in each are the basis for navigating between the two, yet neither instrumentalism nor constructivism can adequately theorize this relationship because they collapse the distinction between the kinds of knowledge available in each.

Instrumentalism

Bernstein's insights allow us to see that in tying knowledge to workplace tasks and roles within units of competency, CBT fundamentally transforms the nature of knowledge by delocating it from the vertical discourse in which it is classified and relocating it into a horizontal and segmented knowledge structure (if not necessarily a horizontal *discourse*). The process of recontextualization that occurs is quite different from the recontextualization of academic disciplines into curriculum, which maintains the disciplinary boundaries and their visibility in the process of translation. In contrast, CBT severs the relationship between the field of knowledge production and its associated field of reproduction in curriculum by divorcing knowledge from the system of meaning in which it is embedded and the way this is distinguished from other areas of knowledge, and by tying it to the specific.

This changes the nature of knowledge and the processes by which it is acquired. Rather than integration of meanings characteristic of vertical discourses, we have integration within a context characteristic of horizontal discourses. It results in a segmental pedagogy in which, as Maton (2007: 6) explains, 'meaning is more strongly tied to its social context of acquisition or use'. Consequently, students are provided with access to contextually specific applications of disciplinary knowledge rather than the disciplinary system of meaning. However, contextually specific applications of knowledge are the products of the discipline (and each has lots of 'products'); they are not the principles used within the discipline to create relationships between components or to evaluate and critique knowledge. A focus on the specific does not provide students with access to debates and controversies within disciplines. Nor does a focus on the specific provide the criteria needed to *select* the knowledge needed in new contexts. This is because content is disaggregated so that it consists of isolated 'bits' of knowledge. A focus on specific content for a specific context means that the meaning of that content is, as Bernstein (2000) would say, 'exhausted' or 'consumed' by the context. For example, apprentice motor mechanics will have difficulty understanding when and if they should use particular mathematical formulas in other contexts if they have been taught that this *particular* formula is used in a *particular* context. They will be able to relate the specific context and the specific formula, but will not have been provided with the tools to choose, select and apply other formulas within that context or a range of other contexts. Knowledge is not under their control.

Critical realism extends these Bernsteinian insights, because a focus on the specific content of disciplines denies students access to the 'collective representations' that provide access to the stratified and emergent nature of the real. This 'absence' arises from the atomistic, empirical ontology and epistemology of CBT. CBT collapses the domain of the real (of generative mechanisms) and the domain of the actual (where events take place) into the domain of the empirical (that which is observable). It does this by focussing on the knowledge and skills that people need to 'do' their job and by insisting that assessment be aligned directly with these outcomes (in the workplace or in a simulated workplace), rather than the generative mechanisms (and their interplay) that produce those outcomes. One of these generative mechanisms is knowledge, in which the general is recruited to understand the specific.

Because CBT is based on descriptions of discrete, atomistic events, it considers tasks and roles independently of their broader relationship to each other, the workplace or society more broadly, and this means that the same task or role can be identified in many workplaces. The task or role takes on universal properties because it is considered independently and non-relationally. It is the task or role that is unique even if it is applied over many contexts, and it is this that is translated into an unproblematic description within units of competency. There is a presumed 'correspondence' between the task or role that the unit of competency describes, so that the description results in objective statements that incorporate all aspects of the relevant task and role and associated skill. Assessment then becomes a straightforward matter of providing 'evidence' that the specified performance criteria have been met. That which can be specified and measured is measured, that which cannot be specified is not measured. The limits of the real thus become defined by the limits of language.[7] Units of competency are then added up, moved about and reconfigured to make different qualifications with common core competencies (and employability skills). That is, the total equals the sum of the parts, and different sums (comprising many of the same elements) make different totals. This is the method that *aggregates*, and is less concerned with understanding the relationship between elements and how these elements are transformed in the context of such a relationship.

Consequently, despite claims that CBT is premised on contextualized learning, the only real contextualization is in the way in which competency is demonstrated, not in defining the task or role itself. This is a positivist, atomistic understanding of skill and the elements that contribute to it. Constructivists also critique CBT because it is premised on a limited, positivist notion of contextualized learning (see Hager and Smith 2004: 39), however, as we will see, their 'solution' is to tie learning and knowledge even more tightly to contexts rather than emphasizing the transcendental features of knowledge.

In collapsing the domains of the real and actual into the empirical, CBT assumes that outcomes can be achieved by teaching to the outcomes directly, and in doing so ignores the complexity that is needed to create *capacity* which goes beyond the level of experience in the contextual and situated, while not ignoring the importance of such experience. Capacity implies the possibility of responding appropriately to that which has not yet happened, as well as to that which has. Absences can be conceptualized and alternative realizations envisaged. However, envisaging alternative futures requires access to knowledge. In focussing on aggregations of specific skills, CBT limits the focus to what people have demonstrated they can do in one context, not what they know or could potentially do by creatively and innovatively considering how they can use what they know (Wheelahan 2005). In contrast, CBT downplays the importance of knowledge as a causal mechanism by emphasizing skill as demonstrated in observable outcomes. It also (ironically) downplays the importance of embodied and tacit knowledge because such knowledge does not easily translate to demonstrable and observable outcomes that can be measured and specified. The consequence is, as Butler (2000: 334) explains, that 'Knowledge has largely been redefined in VET as "industry relevant", "just-in-time", ephemeral and disposable skills, with short use-by dates.'

CBT's simplistic and atomistic notion of skill is what allows current Australian state and Commonwealth government policy to insist that apprenticeships can be shortened (see Callan 2008). However, learning how to become a member of a trade, occupation, or profession is not simply a matter of meeting all the specified learning outcomes, particularly when these are tied to specific tasks or roles. The holistic development of the person in the context of their profession or occupation is excluded, and this involves forming an identity as part of that profession or occupation. This cannot be easily codified as observable outcomes tied to specific skills. Bernstein (2000: 59) explains that 'This identity arises out of a particular social order, through relations which the identity enters into with other identities of reciprocal recognition, support, mutual legitimisation and finally through a negotiated collective purpose.' CBT denies the importance of knowledge in orienting to work, but also in forming working identities.

Teaching and learning must engage the real and the actual and not just the empirical, because this is the only way to generate a varying and contextually sensitive performance in a variety of contexts, and to build capacity for dealing with the future. By focussing on workplace roles and tasks rather than holistically preparing students for an occupation, CBT abstracts knowledge and skill from the bodies of those who must apply that knowledge and skill. *People* apply knowledge and skill, and education and training needs to address the enabling conditions that allow them to engage in knowledgeable and skilful work. One of the structuring mechanisms that shape particular workplace contexts is the broader knowledge and skills that workers bring with them as well as the way that they apply that knowledge and skill. This is why the aims of education and training should be to develop the knowledge, skills and capacities of workers and citizens in broad terms.

Constructivism

Constructivism is related to instrumentalism in two ways. The first is because each is committed to a foundationalist notion of justified true belief in which there is a correspondence between objects and our knowledge of those objects with the possibility of law-like statements about their operation. The difference is that, whereas positivism thinks that access to such knowledge is possible,[8] constructivism denies that it is so.[9] Moore (2007a: 35) explains that for positivism ' "things" give order to words' whereas for constructivism 'words give order to "things".' For constructivism, different words (and different meanings) consequently invest different kinds of order in things, none of which is more true than others because 'the ordering' of social reality is constructed through discourse and the meaning that actors invest in these creative acts.

The second way in which instrumentalism and constructivism are related is by their commitment to *experience* as the basis of knowledge. Unlike the empiricism (and positivism) of CBT, constructivists do not restrict themselves to the empirical *world*, while still privileging experience as the basis of knowledge. They are also generally not guilty of atomism in the same way as is empiricism, with the exception of some versions when considering the natural world (Bhaskar 2008). The focus in constructivism on contextualized social practices and processes of meaning-making means that the empirical world recedes in importance (where the existence of the empirical is admitted at all). Bhaskar (2008: 28) critiques transcendental idealism because while it rejects 'the empiricist account of science, it tacitly takes over the empiricist account of being'. Idealism (and relativist accounts are idealist) shares with empiricism a commitment to 'the use of the category of experience to define the world. This involves giving what is in effect a particular epistemological concept a general ontological function' (Bhaskar 2008: 28). The limits of the world become identified with our knowledge of the world. The result is that both positivism and relativism are not able to distinguish between knowledge of objects and the objects of knowledge. Both conflate the transitive domain (the domain of knowledge) and the intransitive domain (the domain of the real which exists independently of our conceptions of it) (Bhaskar 1998d: 142). However, whereas positivism collapses the transitive into the intransitive domain, relativism collapses the intransitive into the transitive.

Bhaskar (1998d: 142) explains that knowledge of objects and the objects of knowledge are causally related, but they are not the same. As discussed in Chapter 5, the objects of our knowledge have properties that do not depend on what we think about them, while our access to such objects is through our socially mediated engagement with them, and we use socially produced knowledge as one mechanism of engagement. Knowledge and objects thus have different properties and each may require different forms of access, using different procedures. So while we may use knowledge about objects to understand those objects, a condition of using knowledge in that way may require access to previously existing knowledge. For example, the use and application of mathematical knowledge to understand an object requires some understanding of the nature of mathematical knowledge itself, how it is constructed and how it can be used. Knowledge differs from the object it is about because it is a 'social product much like any other ... which has its own craftsmen, technicians, publicists, standards and skills and which is no less subject to change than any other commodity' (Bhaskar 2008: 21). However, as Bhaskar (2008: 21) explains, the other side of knowledge is that it is *of* things that exist independently of our thoughts about them. Knowledge is therefore not arbitrary because it is causally related to its object, but it is also fallible, because it is a social product and as such it is dependent for its production on many factors, including the pre-existing state of knowledge.

The consequence is that gaining access to knowledge and using that knowledge to gain access to objects are two related but distinct processes. Since knowledge and objects have different properties, processes of gaining access to each may not take place at the same time, because knowledge must exist (have been socially produced) if we are to use it and change it. Bhaskar (2008: 60) explains that 'if all our knowledge is acquired in perception and perception constitutes the world, there can be no place for an antecedent cause of knowledge (or of perception)'. Knowledge consists of 'antecedently established facts and theories, paradigms and models, methods and techniques of inquiry available to a particular school or worker' (Bhaskar 2008: 21). The production of new knowledge depends in part on knowledge-like antecedents, because without it we could not use it to explore 'the unknown (but knowable) intransitive structure of the world' (Bhaskar 2008: 23). In insisting on the causal, but non-identical relation between the object of knowledge and knowledge of the object, Bhaskar (1998d: 146) explains that:

> this has the profoundly anti-Cartesian implication that no moment ever contains its own truth, or act its own criteria of intelligibility. In particular, society is not constituted by the way it makes itself intelligible to itself: it is not, as it were, an 'intelligible', but a possible object of *scientific* investigation – that is, of a non-identical but internal relation to itself.

In focussing on the contextual, constructivism seeks to find the criteria of intelligibility within that context – the conditions *for* intelligibility are identical *with* the context, and the possibilities of the real are identified with the limits of experience of the context. This leads to a stronger emphasis on context than is the case with CBT and instrumentalism. Learning outcomes are not (generally) divorced from processes of learning, because, according to Hager and Smith (2004: 35), 'both the nature of work processes, as well as the standards that are applicable to those processes, are significantly shaped by contextual influences'. They explain that socio-cultural approaches focus 'on processes rather than entities or structures, and [stress] the inseparability of the individual and the social' (Hager and Smith 2004: 35). They argue that a focus on context leads to an integrated notion of competence because knowledge, skills, abilities and attributes are not demonstrated atomistically, but through complex, intentional actions that simultaneously enact several competencies but which at the same time demonstrate situational understanding (Hager and Smith 2004: 37). However, arguably, Hager and Smith concede more to CBT than would many other constructivist theorists because they say that competency standards can only ever be a partial description of what is required because of its focus on discrete tasks and roles as they cannot 'contain all that is needed to represent and describe the work' (Hager and Smith 2004: 36). This means that the standards consequently 'need to be supplemented by details of the particular context in order to arrive at suitable descriptions' (Hager and Smith 2004: 36). In making this concession they are implicitly endorsing the notion that 'industry-endorsed' standards can provide at least a partial basis for education, and the workplace context the rest.[10]

Situational understanding is thus contextualized and intersubjective, and this reduces all that is important to the intersubjective in ways that exclude the importance of (and reality of) theoretical knowledge. To insist on the externality and reality of knowledge is to be guilty of reification (see, for example, Hager 2004: 5). The emphasis instead is placed on process and tacit knowledge and skill and the way in which the social construction of both authorizes a performance in one instance as skilled and in another as unskilled (and does not address the question of whether or not the performance really *is* skilled). The focus becomes the way in which meaning is constructed and in some versions of constructivism, truth defined intersubjectively in ways that exclude and include. The problem with this analysis is that it accounts for only part of the context it seeks to describe because it focuses on a discourse that is internal to itself and devoid of external referents. Moore (2006a: 123) explains, 'The fact that all human embeddedness, consciousness and action is, in the first instance, local does not mean that it is nothing *but* local'. In focussing on the contextual, constructivists must discount the way in which social and cultural structures provide the parameters for purposeful activity by setting the 'degrees of freedom' which facilitate or impede purposeful action. To admit that social and cultural structures exist independently of processes of instantiation by agents is to be once again guilty of the sin of reification. This is because constructivists insist 'that the elementary structures of society are nothing but (relatively enduring) sets of interpretations' which consequently do not have a material dimension or a relatively autonomous existence independent of individuals in society (Archer 1988: 198).

Consequences for curriculum

Both constructivists and instrumentalists emphasize 'authentic' practices in the workplace as the best way to access applied theoretical knowledge. In contrast, Clarke and Winch (2004: 515) argue that while applied theoretical knowledge is 'theoretical knowledge [that is] to some extent embedded in practical skills', this does not mean that the best way to access that knowledge is primarily by first practicing those skills. A practice-based model of curriculum (as arguably exists in constructivism and instrumentalism) provides access to theoretical knowledge only through processes of induction so that students learn individual propositions and then inductively form generalizations (Clarke and Winch 2004: 516). Students have access only to the specific elements of theory that are relevant to the particular context, so that the emphasis is on *elements* of content rather than the system of meaning.

Clarke and Winch (2004: 516) argue that there are significant problems if theory is learnt primarily by processes of induction. While they discuss these problems as ones that arise in learning applied disciplinary knowledge relevant to workplace learning, these problems arguably would also apply to learning 'pure' disciplinary knowledge, although the emphasis may differ. Problems arise because first, students require access to a *sufficient* and adequate empirical base upon which they can form generalizations. Their learning experiences must be sufficiently varied and complex to ensure that they have access to the range of individual propositions that they need to form appropriate generalizations. Second, the capacity to form generalizations presupposes a grasp of technical concepts and the capacity to recognize instances of those concepts as the basis for theory-building. Students must have concepts for recognizing and determining that an object, instance, or process is this and not that, but also that a particular object, instance or process could be this *and* that. Third, there is a danger that students will form fallacious inferences and generalizations by attributing observed states of affairs to a particular theoretical framework when it may belong to other theoretical frameworks. Critical realists would elaborate this proposition by explaining that a focus on the contextual results in a flat ontology that omits the domain of the real so students are not able to identify the structuring mechanisms of the object or phenomena they are exploring. This is another form of misattribution. Fourth, while generalizations may be accurate, they may not be complete and students' experiences may not give them access to these complete generalizations. Finally, 'the ability to reason inductively is not a context-independent ability, but depends crucially on a grasp of the context in which inductive reasoning is to be carried out' (Clarke and Winch 2004: 516). An understanding of the context is important in determining the scope of inductive generalizations and whether they can be applied in that particular context, the nature of the empirical base that is required to support these generalizations, and the risks associated from failures in the inductive reasoning.

Students must learn to distinguish theory and contexts if they are to recognize and determine contextually appropriate applications of that theory. Clarke and Winch (2004: 516) argue for an alternative model based on a deductive method in which students 'learn relevant theory and then learn to recognize instances of theoretical propositions in practical situations to which they can then apply appropriate means'. This provides students with access to the system of meaning and the way in which experts have dealt with problems in developing and applying theory and in determining its scope. However, the capacity to recognize contexts and to apply theories appropriately cannot be learnt solely in the classroom; students need to learn to relate the general to particular instances and different kinds of instances. They also need access to the workplace if they are to learn to integrate theory and practice skilfully, but also to integrate theory and practice with the tacit understandings of the workplace. This is because it is not possible to become proficient at anything or to develop 'embodied' knowledge without practising it. Consequently, learning for the workplace must include learning *in* the workplace, but learning cannot be limited *to* the workplace. The task of vocational pedagogy is to 'face both ways' to theory and the workplace as the basis for their integration in vocational practice (Barnett 2006).

Bhaskar's (1998d: 146) argument that 'no moment ever contains its own truth, or act its own criteria of intelligibility' has important implications for pedagogy. By seeking meaning within the contextual, constructivism and instrumentalism deny students access to the conditions of knowledge needed to understand the contextual. This is because the complexity contributing to the structuring of the contextual is denied, as is the means to access the contextual by using the general to understand the particular. Not all knowledge that we need to use emerges from practice, and we need the means to move beyond the contextual to access systems of knowledge and their generative principles. If the world is characterized by ontological depth, stratification, emergence and co-determination then students need to understand these processes, and not have their understanding restricted to the level of events or experiences.

Conclusion

Neither instrumentalism nor constructivism can theorize the relationship between theoretical knowledge and workplace practice, and consequently for the complementary roles of educational institutions and the workplace and the kind of knowledge that is available in each. Blurring the distinctions between each results in segmental pedagogies; knowledge is delocated from the system of meaning in which it is embedded and knowledge becomes tied to the contextual. Students do not have access to the criteria they need to select knowledge and use it in new and creative ways, and knowledge is not under their control.

While instrumentalism has appropriated the language of progressivism and student-centredness from constructivism in legitimating and justifying CBT, constructivism has aided and abetted in this process by the commitment it shares with instrumentalism to the contextual and the experiential. The key criticism constructivism makes of instrumentalism is the atomistic way in which the latter conceives of contexts and skills. However, the alternative offered by constructivism is to tie knowledge more tightly to the contextual and, as a consequence, constructivism is not able to mount a coherent critique of instrumentalism or CBT. This is because the most important feature of each approach is the privileging of horizontal discourse over vertical discourse. Consequently, both are complicit in locking VET students out of access to disciplinary knowledge.

Whilst higher education qualifications were not analysed in this chapter, the relations of affinity and opposition between instrumentalism and constructivism characterize much of this provision. The prioritizing of workplace relevance and contextualized learning also represent powerful discourses that have shaped higher education qualifications, particularly those that have emerged in 'new' fields and occupations over the last thirty years. This is expressed in approaches that privilege work-integrated learning, work-based learning and problem-based learning as dominant models for constructing curriculum. The difference is that the shape, structure and content of higher education qualifications are more contested than are vocational education qualifications based on CBT.

9 Conclusion: What type of curriculum do we need?

The social realist alternative

Introduction

The key argument in this book is that knowledge should be at the centre of curriculum in all sectors of education – schools, further education/vocational education and training (VET) and higher education. Access to theoretical knowledge is an issue of distributional justice because society uses it to conduct its conversation about what it should be like. Society uses theoretical knowledge to think the unthinkable and the not-yet-thought, and this makes such knowledge socially powerful and endows it with the capacity to disrupt existing power relations. It plays this role because it is society's collective representations about the social and natural worlds, and we use it to access these worlds to understand how they are constructed, their processes of development and how they can be changed. Knowledge is continually revised as we engage with the world using knowledge that others have created before us, and in that process we change it and often change the world, or some aspect of it.

Social access and epistemic access to knowledge are causally related, because the latter is a condition for the former. Unless we have epistemic access to knowledge we cannot be part of the conversation, and unless we understand how to access knowledge using the specialized social practices developed for this purpose by communities of knowledge producers, we are not able to create, change, or add to it in a systematic and enduring way. This is relevant not just for changing knowledge that is organized in the academic disciplines, but also for changing the relationship between occupational fields of practice and the knowledge base that underpins practice, so that each can be changed in the process. It is only when we understand the rules that we can meaningfully and purposefully change the rules. This is why theoretical knowledge must be at the centre of all educational qualifications, including vocational qualifications.

This concluding chapter defends this argument by bringing together the analysis in preceding chapters to develop a social realist argument about knowledge and the way it should be structured in curriculum. It does so by considering a number of different questions which are: 'What is the nature of theoretical knowledge and how is it accessed?' 'What role should theoretical knowledge play in curriculum and why should it play this role?' 'Why has knowledge been marginalized in curriculum and how have instrumentalism and constructivism contributed?' The next two questions apply this analysis to examine the structuring of knowledge in qualifications. These two questions are: 'What is the difference between academic and vocational qualifications?' and 'What kind of access do different types of vocational qualifications provide to theoretical knowledge?' The particular focus is on vocational qualifications for two reasons: first, while knowledge has been displaced in both academic and vocational qualifications, this displacement has been more extensive in vocational qualifications than in academic qualifications. Second, most education in all sectors of education is now vocational. The way in which vocational qualifications mediate access to knowledge consequently matters a great deal. Equitable access to knowledge will not be achieved unless and until vocational qualifications are structured so that they provide students with this access. As we will see, while some types of vocational qualifications provide students with this access, not all do. The distributive rules within education do not function just by streaming students into academic and vocational pathways, they also function by the way access is mediated to different types of vocational pathways. This last section also considers the way that vocational qualifications can be structured to provide students with access to knowledge.

What is the nature of theoretical knowledge and how is it accessed?

The arguments in this book about the nature of knowledge and the way it is accessed have been developed by using Bernstein's social theory and the philosophy of critical realism as complementary modes of analysis. Bernstein's ontological premises are largely Durkheimian and rationalist while critical realism's are materialist, but there are affinities between the two that make it possible to take this approach. While their analysis of society differs in important respects, they both regard society as consisting of objective, socially differentiated social structures and in this sense both are realist. Their analysis of knowledge also differs, but they agree on the *sui generis* reality of knowledge, and they also agree that it has properties that transcend the conditions under which it was produced. Both see knowledge as historically and socially constructed, and agree that the social mediates practice and the creation of knowledge. Both seek to go beyond 'the facts' to identify the 'invisibles', that is, the objects and their generative mechanisms that structure the world, and each emphasizes the role of theory in understanding and accessing the world and in building knowledge (Johnson *et al.* 1984: 24). Indeed, the purpose of systematized, theoretical knowledge is to identify these invisibles, even if this is, and only ever can be, imperfect. Both are committed to a 'depth' ontology in which generative mechanisms in the domain of 'the real' interact in necessary and contingent ways to produce events and experiences in the domains of 'the actual' and 'the empirical' respectively (Bhaskar 1998d, 2008). This means both are committed to a notion of *alternative possibilities* because their analysis identifies the ways in which generative mechanisms interact and the ways in which they *could* interact to give rise to different outcomes (Bhaskar 1998d; Moore 2006b). This is, as Bernstein emphasizes, one of the key roles of theory, which is to think the unthinkable and not-yet-thought and to imagine alternative futures.

However, because they have different ontological premises, each emphasizes different aspects of knowledge. Word comes before world for Bernstein (2000: 82), and world comes before word for critical realism (Collier 2003). The distinctions between esoteric and mundane knowledge structures social practices and social relations for Bernstein, whereas critical realists argue that social practices in the world are the basis of our knowledge about the world. They argue that even though society depends on these social practices for knowledge production, the structures of the natural and social worlds contribute to the structuring of knowledge because they exist independently of these practices (Bhaskar 1998d; Collier 1994). For example, while sociology provides insights into society and often results in social change as a consequence, society does not depend on sociology for its existence and did without it for a long time, although it used other means to theorize about itself. Our intervention in the natural world may be changing it through global warming, but our intervention does not alter the laws of physics, chemistry, or biology. This means that the structure and properties of knowledge and the objects of knowledge are different.

These differences remain important, but each nonetheless approaches the other in some way. Bernstein insists that the theoretical must be capable of an empirical language of description and he insists on the need to focus on the 'external ontological imperative' (Moore 2004: 142). Knowledge about objects cannot therefore be reduced to statements about knowers which change depending on the position of the knower, because the objects of knowledge are not arbitrary. The distinction between esoteric and mundane knowledge may be fundamental for the structure of social relations, but these social relations are situated within a society that must engage with the natural world and reproduce itself. Critical realism distinguishes between theory and the objects of theory with its distinction between the transitive and intransitive dimensions: the transitive refers to knowledge of the real, while the intransitive refers to the domain of the real (Collier 1994: 50). Knowledge depends on knowledge-like antecedents and the specialized social practices that agents use to construct it, and these social practices in turn depend on a social division of labour and the social relations that have structured this division of labour.

Bernstein and critical realism thus reveal the emergent properties of knowledge and identify 'invisibles' that are fundamental to knowledge from their respective ontological premises. Bernstein reveals the complexity of the social relations of knowledge and in doing so provides the basis for the argument that access to knowledge is a question of distributional justice, but his argument goes beyond this. Bernstein identifies the causal and emergent properties of the structures of knowledge *qua* knowledge through his distinction between theoretical knowledge as vertical discourse and everyday knowledge as horizontal discourse. He further differentiates within vertical discourses, between those with hierarchical knowledge structures (such as physics) and those with horizontal knowledge structures (such as sociology) and between horizontal knowledge structures with strong grammars (such as economics) and weak grammars (such as cultural studies). He thus provides the basis for connecting knowledge production with its reproduction in curriculum, and for theoretically grounding the latter in the former. His analysis of vertical and horizontal discourses provides the connection between these discourses and his analysis of the pedagogic device, pedagogic discourses and the way in which the classification and framing of knowledge mediate access to the esoteric. Bernstein's insights can enrich critical realism which does not, generally speaking, pay sufficient attention to the structures of knowledge as a generative mechanism.

Critical realism identifies the casual and emergent properties of knowledge that arise from the aboutness of knowledge and through its notions of ontological depth, emergence, stratification and co-determination. It also provides a way of theorizing the way knowledge changes through the relationship it posits between practice and knowledge, and through theorizing the nature of the fallibility of knowledge by distinguishing between the transitive and intransitive domains of knowledge. In doing so, it places knowledge on a firm realist foundation by demonstrating that the fallibility of knowledge arises *because* the world exists independently of our imaginations and therefore cannot be construed in any way we please (Sayer 1992: 67). It links the fallibility of knowledge to judgemental rationality in arguing that just because all knowledge is fallible does not mean it is equally fallible (Moore 2007a). The fallibility of knowledge and judgemental rationality are based on the need to choose between competing accounts of the same world, whereas relativism construes different and largely incommensurable worlds as the basis of knowledge claims (Bhaskar 1998d).

Critical realism also provides a useful way for considering the objectivity of knowledge and its relationship to theoretical and everyday knowledge. Theoretical knowledge cannot be distinguished from everyday knowledge because the former is objective and the latter is not, and many realists contrast the irrationalism of relativism with the objective knowledge required to navigate a real world filled with objects, other people and aeroplanes (Gellner 1982; Horton 1982; Sayer 2000). Collier (2003: 135) explains that knowledge (including everyday knowledge) is objective if: first, it is objectively true regardless of what anyone thinks about it; second, if knowledge about the object was caused by the person's or knowledge producers' orientation to the object; and third, if the person or knowledge producers actively seek objective knowledge as a human attitude. Consequently, knowledge can still be objective in the second and third sense because it is formed by an openness and orientation to and desire to understand the object, but it can still be fallible because there is not a perfect correspondence between our knowledge and the objects of our knowledge. This framework provides criteria for criticizing the ways in which disciplines produce knowledge, particularly those dominated by relativism or positivism, because both are based on normative epistemologies (Moore 2004), and for arguing for processes of change and, in so doing, enriches Bernstein's approach.

Critical realist insights are also helpful for distinguishing between theoretical and everyday knowledge by highlighting what is different about each. This strengthens Bernstein's argument about the importance of the structures of knowledge and the social practices used to produce knowledge. The theoretical is distinguished from the everyday because it represents the systematization of our knowledge about relations between things, and because, as Taylor (1982: 101) explains, it 'extends and supersedes our ordinary understanding of things'. The *raison d'être* of theoretical knowledge is to create knowledge of the objects it studies (Bhaskar 1998d: 11–12), whereas everyday knowledge is not gained for its own sake, but as part of our intentional, goal-oriented, purposeful activity. We think *with* concepts in the everyday, but we think *about* concepts in the theoretical (Sayer 1992: 25). To develop and extend objective knowledge, we need to think about our concepts as well as with them and explore the relationship between our concepts and the things to which they refer. The specialized social practices of the different disciplines have been developed for this purpose and they have (to a greater or lesser extent) demonstrated that they provide access to the objects they study (Collier 2003: 39). This helps us distinguish between the processes of producing and acquiring knowledge in the theoretical and the everyday. Because we need to think about our concepts in the theoretical we need to enter the system of meaning. In contrast, in the everyday, we mobilize and use concepts because of their utility in particular contexts so that their meaning is closely connected to the context. Theoretical knowledge is differentiated from everyday knowledge because it is *general, principled* knowledge, while everyday knowledge is *particularized* knowledge (Gamble 2006b). In this way, critical realism ends up at the same point as Bernstein, but the difference is that critical realism regards the extent to which theoretical or everyday knowledge is objective or not as an empirical question to be resolved using the criteria Collier provides.

Theoretical knowledge that is organized in disciplinary frameworks is society's collective representations about the causal mechanisms the disciplines study by exploring the relationship between the real, actual and empirical. This is why theoretical knowledge enables society to transcend the everyday and provide access to the structure of the social and natural worlds, worlds that are characterized by ontological depth, stratification, emergence and co-determination. Disciplinary knowledge is a social product and is as a consequence marked by the social conditions of its production which include power and privilege. However, its aboutness and the methods used to explore this aboutness endow it with transcendent features that provide epistemic insights into their objects of study. Theoretical knowledge is society's work in progress.

What role should theoretical knowledge play in curriculum and why should it play this role?

There are two, equally important, implications for the way in which knowledge is structured in curriculum that arise from the above analysis. The first is that access to theoretical knowledge equips students to be part of society's conversation, and to shape their field of practice by questioning and critiquing the knowledge base of practice and the relationship between knowledge and practice. Knowledge thus must be at the centre of curriculum. The second is that the pursuit of *truth* should be a normative goal of curriculum, but tempered by an awareness of the fallibility of our knowledge and the need to revise it in light of new evidence. Curriculum should not present knowledge as 'the truth' because this would be to misrepresent the nature of knowledge and the way it is produced and changed. This distinguishes social realism from conservatism in which tradition and authority are the basis of knowledge and truth, rather than the access such knowledge provides to the social and natural world. Consequently, the emphasis in curriculum needs to be on the way knowledge is produced and shaped rather than presenting knowledge as a finished product. The focus must be on how students can *test* disciplinary (and other kinds of) knowledge and make judgements about it, while being open to alternative ways of thinking. If students are to do this they must be able to access knowledge as general, principled knowledge and not just as particularized knowledge.

A focus on the system of meaning and its relational connections also equips students with the capacity to use the decontextualized features of knowledge in new and creative ways and in a variety of contexts. Students cannot mobilize theoretical knowledge to understand the contextual unless they can recognize particular applications as appropriate instances of the relevant theory (Clarke and Winch 2004: 516). They need to be able to do so if they are to have control over knowledge and how it can be used. Alternatively, if they have been provided only with access to contextually specific applications of theory, they have no criteria to differentiate between appropriate and inappropriate applications of that theory and why this may be so.

Ensuring that students develop the capacity to use knowledge in this way is thus a key purpose of education (Young 2003b: 560). Education must help students distinguish between theoretical and everyday knowledge by helping them to recognize the boundaries between different kinds of knowledge and to be able to work productively with knowledge. The way in which knowledge is classified and framed in curriculum consequently needs to be made explicit and visible so that students can develop the recognition and realization rules they need to enter knowledge as a system of meaning and demonstrate that they have effectively engaged with such knowledge (Bernstein 2000). This is particularly so for working-class students who, in contrast to middle-class students, do not have extensive family resources to draw on as a second site of pedagogic acquisition for theoretical, abstract knowledge (Arnot and Reay 2004: 149). Strong relations of classification and framing consequently provide the basis for equitable access to knowledge and the capacity to use it.

Bernstein (2000) demonstrates that the way in which vertical discourses are produced and structured has implications for the way in which they are classified and framed and recontextualized in curriculum. Students' induction into and progression through hierarchical knowledge structures depends on their capacity to integrate shared meanings within the discipline at higher levels of abstraction, and this means they have to understand basic propositions before they can understand complex ones. The structure of knowledge thus has implications for the way in which it is sequenced (Muller 2006a, 2006b). Students' induction into horizontal knowledge structures, particularly those with weak grammars, necessitates the capacity to identify different languages, authoritative speakers and the texts of different languages within the discipline and to keep these distinct, while being able to integrate meanings with the language adopted as one's own (Bernstein 2000: 164). This also has implications for the sequencing of knowledge because students have to be provided with a map of the different perspectives and the tools to recognize them.

The disciplines are differentiated by the cognitive demands made on students, the kinds of outcomes that are expected and associated teaching, learning and assessment practices (Neumann *et al.* 2002). Disciplinary configurations are not fixed and will change, but the boundaries between different kinds of knowledge will remain important. Ignoring disciplinary divisions risks undermining processes of teaching and learning in different areas and, as a consequence, the outcomes of learning (Neumann *et al.* 2002). Moreover, engaging with disciplinary boundaries provides students with the basis for navigating those boundaries in multidisciplinary and interdisciplinary work. This is because, in understanding disciplinary boundaries, students are provided with criteria for legitimate and illegitimate uses of theory, for determining commensurability and incommensurability and for judging the validity of knowledge claims (Freebody 2006). Disciplinarity can only become a 'pragmatic recruitable resource' (Freebody 2006) in the service of interdisciplinarity and 'real-world' applications by explicitly navigating disciplinary boundaries and engaging with criteria for judging knowledge claims, rather than negating these boundaries.

Why has knowledge been marginalized in curriculum and how have instrumentalism and constructivism contributed?

Knowledge has been marginalized in curriculum despite its importance to students and society. This is as a consequence of a crisis in curriculum theory which has led to the dominance of instrumentalism in all sectors of education, achieved in part by its selective appropriation of elements of constructivism and conservatism. It is necessary to understand the social processes that resulted in this outcome because it is insufficient to demonstrate why a theory or approach is wrong; we have to account for why it is valorized and persists despite the deleterious social outcomes that result from its application if we are to develop a credible and realistic alternative (Bhaskar 1998d).

The key argument developed in the book to account for the relativizing of knowledge in curriculum is that the social relations of knowledge production changed, and this provided the social basis for the rise of relativist and instrumental theories of knowledge characteristic of constructivism and instrumentalism respectively. Transformations in technology, work, culture and society associated with globalization resulted in the proliferation of sites of knowledge production beyond the academy, heightened uncertainty arising from rapid and perpetual change and weakened boundaries insulating the sphere of knowledge production from society more broadly. Individuals, enterprises and governments all must continually revise their 'strategies' as the flow of new knowledge augments or transforms the old. Moreover, the relationship between labour and capital was also transformed as a consequence of these processes, particularly in Anglophone countries, so that the emphasis is now on personal attributes and generic skills and less on technical knowledge and skill, thus moving the focus in curriculum to ensuring students are 'employable' and have these generic attributes.

The nature and scope of education and knowledge production also changed. The massive growth of education in wealthy nations following the Second World War resulted in similar growth in the number of knowledge workers. Consequently, the production of knowledge was no longer the preserve of a tiny elite and the 'mystery' of knowledge was now more public, as were debates between knowledge producers and their sometimes spectacular failures (as in global warming). These broad social, cultural, political and economic changes contributed to a collapse in trust in knowledge as objective truth. The social character of knowledge production was now highlighted and it came to be identified with, and reduced to, the social interests of cloistered communities of knowledge producers, rather than the epistemic insights it provided (Muller 2000).

These changed social relations of knowledge production iteratively supported the rise of relativist theories of the person and knowledge in disciplines that traditionally underpin curriculum, including (but not limited to) disciplines such as sociology and psychology. As a consequence, the theoretical basis was laid for the rise of constructivism in the pedagogic recontextualizing field (PRF) and later, for the rise of instrumentalism in the official recontextualizing field (ORF). Knowledge was reduced to an issue of power in both approaches, although each differed in their analysis of power and the voices that should be valorized. This was resolved by the dominance of instrumentalism through the imposition of 'generic' modes of curriculum in the new vocationalism, in which the principle of curricular coherence is market relevance based on the notion of 'trainability' (Bernstein 2000; Beck and Young 2005; Young 2006a).

The pedagogic pallet

The dominance of instrumentalism enables it selectively to appropriate and draw from constructivism and conservatism and, in this way, to contribute to its continuing legitimation and justification. This results in a 'pedagogic pallet' (Bernstein 2000) which takes different forms in the school and tertiary education sectors, although there are overlaps between the two. The emphasis in schools is on the appropriation from conservatism because of the role of schools in creating persons. Instrumentalism selectively borrows from conservatism by appropriating the bourgeois–liberal individual as the proprietor of the self (Macpherson 1962) who has the knowledge, skills, dispositions and attributes required to invest in the self as appropriate in response to external cues from the market (Bourdieu and

Wacquant 1992). The emphasis in tertiary education (further education/VET and higher education) is on the appropriation of constructivism by instrumentalism because the focus is on relevance and context as a consequence of the role of tertiary education in producing skilled labour. However, both these relationships exist in all sectors even if the emphasis is different. The generic skills and attributes in tertiary education are implicitly underpinned by the bourgeois-liberal individual, and this explains why the focus on the 'person' in school is not in conflict with ensuring that senior school certificates prepare students for work and endow them with the attributes or 'employability skills' needed for work.

The relationships of affinity and opposition between instrumentalism and constructivism have been fundamental in facilitating the imposition of the new vocationalism in all sectors of education and training, and in particular, to the imposition of competency-based training (CBT) in lower-status, vocationally oriented 'second' tiers of tertiary education such as further education in the UK and VET in Australia. This has contributed to the marginalization of knowledge in curriculum because knowledge is regarded instrumentally and included in curriculum through the criterion of relevance. Constructivist, developmental discourses of student-centred learning, situated learning and the contextualized nature of knowledge were appropriated and reworked through the prism of instrumentalism, thereby contributing to the justification and legitimation of CBT, but also to its continuing theorization and development. Consequently, the relationship between constructivism and instrumentalism has had most impact on CBT in VET, but this relationship increasingly characterizes learning for the workplace more broadly, including in higher education.

The shared commitment by instrumentalism and constructivism to the contextual

The synergies between constructivism and instrumentalism arise because both are committed to the experiential within the contextual as the source of knowledge and this provides the scope for instrumentalism to further plunder constructivism. Both emphasize the contextual, situated and problem-oriented nature of knowledge creation and learning and curriculum based on 'authentic' learning in the workplace. The complexity and depth of vocational knowledge is replaced by knowledge that is ephemeral and transient. The most important feature of each is their flat ontology which results in privileging horizontal discourse over vertical discourse and this occurs because both are tied to the notion of context, even though they theorize contexts differently. Instrumentalism privileges the empirical *world*, whereas constructivism privileges *experience* while denying (to varying degrees) the existence of an empirical world. Instrumentalism defines contexts atomistically by identifying contexts with work roles or tasks which lead to atomistic and aggregative notions of knowledge and skill. In contrast, constructivism defines contexts more relationally, but the result is to tie knowledge more tightly to the situational.

Their shared 'flat' ontology means that the complexity that contributes to the structuring of contexts is not visible. Each seeks the criteria of intelligibility or 'truth' of the context within the context itself, rather than understanding the way in which the context has been constructed by processes of emergence and co-determination (Bhaskar 1998d: 146). Any analysis which is limited to the contextual is necessarily always partial and incomplete because the structuring mechanisms of events and experiences are not made visible. The differences between contexts cannot be effectively distinguished by identifying commonalities and differences, or features that are necessary and those that are contingent. In particular, neither instrumentalism nor constructivism is able to theorize the way knowledge can be used contextually, because they collapse the distinction between producing, acquiring and applying knowledge.

Constructivism and instrumentalism have particular implications for vocationally oriented qualifications because their focus on context leads both to posit a unitary conception of the workplace that brackets out wider relations of power and conflict. This again places constructivism at the service of instrumentalism. Neither the collective and distributed competence of constructivism nor the individual competence of instrumentalism is able to problematize the way in which the specification of competence is shaped, and the relationship between competence and wider relations of power within the workplace and society more broadly. While some constructivist approaches identify conflict and power as an important part of workplaces, this mostly focuses on work *processes* and not on the fundamental antagonisms intrinsic to the *relations* of production which may find expression in conflicts over work processes (Avis 2007). Developmental discourses ensue that identify common interests between employers and employees, but because these are defined contextually the outcomes of learning become identified with the enterprise's business, rather than problematizing the nature of this business. It is identity of interest expressed through the 'workplace' that has allowed the recontextualizers within the ORF to develop such a pervasive deficit discourse around teachers' knowledge and skills in further education/VET and increasingly in higher education in discourses about workplace learning and work-integrated learning. The 'problem' of workplace learning is not defined as a fundamental disagreement about the nature of, processes of and outcomes from, learning but rather as teachers' lack of knowledge and skills to work in the new (unproblematic and unproblematized) world of work.[1] The focus on learning for work also means that the broader purposes of education recede in importance.

The different purposes of academic and vocational education

While education needs to prepare us for work, it also needs to prepare us to live in the world of which we are part. The vocational and educational purposes of education are not in conflict, even though they are often construed that way in policy and curriculum debates. Dewey explains the broad purposes that all education must serve, including vocational education, when he says:

> each individual has of necessity a variety of callings, in each of which he should be intelligently effective; and ... any one occupation loses its meaning

and becomes a routine keeping busy at something in the degree in which it is isolated from other interests ... No one is just an artist and nothing else ... He must, at some period of his life, be a member of a family; he must have friends and companions; he must either support himself or be supported by others, and thus he has a business career. He is a member of some organized political unit, and so on. We naturally *name* his vocation from that one of the callings which distinguishes him, rather than from those which he has in common with all others. But we should not allow ourselves to be so subject to words as to ignore and virtually deny his other callings when it comes to a consideration of the vocational phases of education.

(Dewey 1997 [1916]: 307)

Knowledge is central to curriculum regardless of whether the purpose is to prepare students for the academic disciplines or to prepare them for occupational fields of practice, even though the orientation and focus of knowledge in curriculum will differ in each case. Academic pathways are generally well understood – they focus on the academic disciplines in the senior school curriculum and provide access to the academic disciplines in universities, and also to the elite professions in universities. The purpose of academic pathways is to induct students into the academic disciplines and these pathways consequently face one way, to the knowledge and structures of knowledge within the disciplines (Barnett 2006). The focus of academic pathways will be on the 'pure' disciplines or the disciplinary structures of knowledge.

The notion of occupational or vocational pathways is more contested. This is so even though most education in universities, further education/VET or schools is now vocationally oriented. 'Professional' education in universities is often distinguished from 'vocational' education in VET, yet there is continuity between the two because the purpose of both is to prepare students for an occupational field of practice. Universities traditionally prepare students for the elite professions but their role has broadened with the massive growth of higher education systems over the last 30 years. They now also prepare students for a much wider range of new occupations as society's demands for a higher skilled workforce have increased in response to the technological, economic, social and cultural changes of late modernity (Trow 2005). Lower-status, vocationally oriented 'second' tiers of tertiary education such as further education in the UK and VET in Australia have similarly grown in response to the same pressures, and in Anglophone countries VET is explicitly (and narrowly) designed to prepare students for the labour market. Government policies on increasing school retention and completion rates are also tied to preparing students for work and/or post-school education and training pathways that will prepare them for work. Vocational pathways thus encompass all vocationally oriented education in senior secondary schools, further education/VET and higher education. In contrast to academic pathways, the focus in vocational pathways is on the *applied* disciplinary knowledge that underpins occupational practice.

However, regardless of the differences between them, knowledge needs to be structured in both academic and vocational pathways so that students are provided with access to it. The problem is that in both cases the place of knowledge in curriculum has been undermined by vocationalism and by curriculum theories that privilege the contextual, situated and transdisciplinary nature of knowledge. Academic education becomes conflated with general education, which in turn becomes conflated with generic skills and attributes which are expressed through the vocational (Marginson 1997a: 172). This is exemplified by the Australian Department of Education Science and Training (2002: 3) which explains that:

> A liberal, general education and a professionally focused education are not necessarily mutually exclusive. The broad conceptions of a liberal education as espoused by Cardinal Newman in 1852 may be unsustainable, but the development of generic skills and knowledge should remain an essential part of all undergraduate education.

Knowledge has also been displaced in academic curriculum by curricular approaches that emphasizes problem-based learning which is based on multi-disciplinary problem solving. The context is presumed to provide all the clues about the type of knowledge that is needed. Moreover, knowledge is marginalized by 'smorgasbord' approaches so that relatively unlimited student choice of subject selection replaces the need for students to choose major areas of study that comprise sequenced subjects of increasing depth and complexity thus providing them with access to the relational complexities within disciplinary systems of meaning. Student choice is not the problem; rather it is that their choice is not structured to induct them into coherent fields of knowledge. However, student choice can be further and helpfully enhanced by program 'rules' that require students to undertake studies outside their major areas of study. This may help them to develop a wider understanding of the world through the prism of different fields of knowledge, but also to gain a better appreciation of the structuring of knowledge and underpinning assumptions in their own field. Such an approach is based, however, on an understanding of the relations of classification between different fields of knowledge and an appreciation of the criteria used in different fields to judge knowledge claims – insights which are more difficult to access through problem-based learning.

What access do different types of vocational qualifications provide to theoretical knowledge and how should they be structured?

The displacement of knowledge has been driven further in vocationally oriented education by the emphasis on preparing students for occupational fields of practice. The classification of knowledge within vocational qualifications is weaker than in academic pathways because the principles used to select and translate knowledge are the requirements of the field of practice rather than the structures of disciplinary knowledge. However, vocational pathways can be structured so that they provide more or less access to knowledge and they must be evaluated by the extent to which they do provide students with this access.

Young (2006c) explains that vocational curriculum consists of *applied* disciplinary knowledge, which is occupationally recontextualized disciplinary knowledge. It is disciplinary knowledge that has first been recontextualized for application in the field of practice, and then again recontextualized for curriculum. This means that a 'double' process of recontextualization takes place compared to the 'single' process in academic curriculum which maintains disciplinary boundaries and their relations of insulation in the process. The process of occupational recontextualization of knowledge has implications for the process of pedagogic recontextualization (Barnett 2006: 147). Occupationally recontextualized knowledge must be translated for vocational curriculum so students can access this knowledge, but also so they can relate theory to practice. The contextualized and situated knowledge of the workplace must also be translated and pedagogically recontextualized for curriculum (Barnett 2006: 146). Such knowledge is context specific and not easily translatable outside those contexts. This knowledge is the focus of practical and work-based components of curriculum. Vocational pedagogy thus needs to face *both* ways to occupationally recontextualized disciplinary knowledge and to the field of practice itself. Barnett (2006: 156) points out that these multiple processes of recontextualization present far more demands on vocational teachers than those teaching single academic disciplines. It also means that the relationship between theory and practice cannot be specified too tightly because, as Gamble (2006b: 99) explains, 'each refers to a different kind of knowledge. If the relationship is too direct, there is a danger that one kind of knowledge becomes the other.'

Vocational qualifications based on strongly classified and framed applied disciplinary knowledge provide more access to knowledge than do those based on weak relations of classification and framing (Young 2006c). The unproblematized nature of knowledge means that the extent to which vocational qualifications are based on applied disciplinary knowledge that is strongly or weakly classified and framed depends on relations that are *external* to education. Rather than concerns about the way knowledge should be structured so that all students have access to it, its place and structure in curriculum instead depends on relations within occupational fields of practice. Young (2006c) explains that vocational qualifications are differentiated by the nature of the field of practice they are oriented to, by whether they are a traditional field of practice such as in the professions or trades, or in a newer field of practice such as business studies, hospitality and tourism, or community services.

Occupational fields of practice differ in the complexity of knowledge that underpins practice and qualifications designed to prepare students for knowledge-rich occupations provide more access to applied disciplinary knowledge than those where the knowledge base is less clearly developed. One reason for this is that 'traditional' qualifications mostly prepare students for specific occupations within industries, so medical degrees prepare students to become doctors, and electrical apprenticeships prepare apprentices to become electricians. In contrast, the 'newer' regions that have emerged over the last thirty years focus on preparing students for an industry or field of practice, as in the new 'business studies' in senior school curriculum, further education/VET and higher education (Bates *et al.* 1998; Young 2006c). The knowledge base of the traditional fields is more defined than that of the newer ones, and they are more likely to be underpinned by communities of interest in which 'there is a substantial and widely agreed body' of knowledge (Young 2006c: 56). In contrast, 'newer' fields of practice are more likely to have a variable relationship to disciplinary knowledge because the knowledge base is less developed and articulated. There is also less of a tradition of education and training within newer fields and there is less likely to be defined (and powerful) communities of practice that can shape and build occupational knowledge.

Furthermore, while 'genericism' as the principle of curricular recontextualization is pervasive in all sectors of education and training and all types of qualifications, it is strongest within the newer fields. This is because the selection and inclusion of knowledge in newer fields of practice tends to be more shaped by the demands of the market in the absence of strong communities of interest. Qualifications for traditional, elite professions place knowledge under the control of practitioners, whereas the newer professions and occupations are driven by the tyranny of relevance, defined by and through the market.

Vocational qualifications can be further differentiated by whether they are offered within further education/VET or within higher education. This difference is exacerbated where VET qualifications are based on CBT because CBT is a poor basis for providing students with access to disciplinary knowledge. The 'rules' of CBT mean that knowledge must be tied to the contextual in the workplace, and workplace tasks and roles are used to define, distinguish and insulate 'spaces' in curriculum so that theoretical knowledge is weakly classified and framed. This denies VET students access to theoretical knowledge underpinning practice because such knowledge is fragmented and disaggregated from the system of meaning in which it is embedded.

The access to knowledge provided by different types of occupational qualifications reflects the hierarchical structuring of vocational qualifications which is, in turn, the outcome of and condition for reproducing relations of social advantage and disadvantage. Vocational qualifications are hierarchically structured so that the elite 'traditional' professions are at the top. Next are the newer professions that have emerged over the last thirty years in new fields such as information technology, recreation, tourism and hospitality. At the bottom are the vocational qualifications in further education/VET which prepare students for lower-level positions within these newer fields. The traditional trades, particularly the highly skilled trades, occupy an intermediate position in the occupational hierarchy in VET, in part because of their traditional association with male, working-class 'outdoor' work.[2] They are, however, regarded much more highly than the newer 'traineeships' which, like apprenticeships, combine work with training and mostly prepare people for lower level occupations in newer fields and occupations (such as in hospitality and office administration). This professional/occupational hierarchy reflects the class structure in society more broadly. The professions are dominated by the social elites, while at the other end, lower level VET qualifications in new fields are dominated by students from low socio-economic backgrounds (James *et al.* 2004; Foley 2007). As the occupational hierarchy ascends, so does social class.

How should vocational qualifications be structured?

There are five implications arising from the above analysis for the way in which vocational qualifications should be structured. First, the disciplinary basis of vocational qualifications needs to be made explicit. Students need access to this knowledge if they are to participate in society's conversation and in shaping their field by participating in its debates and controversies. That education should provide students with this access is an intrinsic part of the role it plays in contributing to social justice and in supporting democracy and democratic institutions within society. Vocational qualifications *can* equip students in this way *only* by providing them with access to knowledge. Grubb (2005: 16) argues that the notion of professionalism is the bridge back to liberal education because each profession has an ethical dimension, is situated within a broader social, civic and political context, has a history and a relationship to knowledge, theories and concepts. This notion is not limited to the professions and can be applied to all occupations, as is demonstrated in VET in Germany (Winch 2002). Clarke and Winch (2006: 262) cite Streeck to explain that the German:

> concept of 'occupation', or *Beruf*, signifies 'a body of systematically related theoretical knowledge [*Wissen*] and a set of practical skills [*Können*], as well as the social identity of the person who has acquired these.

This is a much richer and broader notion of skill and occupation than current Anglophone concepts, where education is reduced to skills that are tied to the performance of specific tasks or roles (Winch and Hyland 2007). In Germany, the nature and content of knowledge that is taught and assessed is negotiated and agreed by the industrial social partners.[3] The curriculum incorporates a broad social understanding of the nature of the work, industry and occupation for which students are being prepared, as well as the theoretical knowledge and 'technical and practical knowledge needed to practise a particular *Beruf* in its current, likely future and even past state of development' (Clarke and Winch 2006: 264). Clarke and Winch (2006: 264) explain that 'Vocational education in Germany is, therefore, closely bound to preparation for citizenship, just as in other Continental countries.' Vocational education focuses on preparing students for particular occupations, but importantly contextualizes that occupation in its wider social relations.

Second, the distinction between education and the workplace as sites of learning is important. Vocational curriculum that 'faces both ways' to the knowledge base underpinning practice and to the field of practice is predicated on maintaining the distinction between knowledge that is available in educational institutions and that which is available in the workplace. Learning *for* work needs to go *beyond* work and include educational institutions as a site of learning as well as the workplace.[4] Learning that is restricted to the workplace does not provide students with access to disciplinary knowledge as a system of meaning, because it is tied to the contextual. Similarly, educational institutions cannot provide students with access to the situated knowledge of the workplace, or with realistic opportunities to select, apply and evaluate contextually specific applications of theoretical knowledge. *Both* are needed, and both need to be recontextualized in curriculum as the basis of effective pedagogic practice (Barnett 2006). Collapsing the distinction between the two impoverishes both because it traduces that which is distinctive about each. Moreover, identifying education too closely with the workplace, is also, as Granville (2004) points out, likely to result in reproduction rather than transformation and innovation. Students need some distance from the workplace to reflect critically on practice.

Third, we need new partnerships with qualifications based on communities of interest, and not the precise specification of (commodified) outcomes (Young 2001, 2008a). Processes of learning cannot be divorced from outcomes of learning, because the nature of the learning process shapes the outcomes. The precise specification of learning outcomes narrows learning by emphasizing the measurable, and results in atomistic outcomes that are fragmented and decontextualized. The same learning outcomes will mean different things regardless of how precisely different aspects are specified, because learning outcomes cannot be 'unpacked' without reference to curriculum. Young (2003a) explains that a qualification will be valued only if it is trusted by those who have a stake in the outcomes, regardless of what the learning outcomes specify. It is the content of curriculum, processes of learning and assessment that provide the basis of trust in qualifications and for pathways to qualifications at higher levels (Lolwana 2005). Grounding qualifications in communities of trust means that there must be debate about what matters, and this focusses attention on knowledge and its relationship to practice.

Fourth, building and sustaining relationships between education and communities of interest is essential as the basis for envisaging alternative vocational practices and ensuring that the relationship between theory and practice is dynamic and contributes to change and innovation. Such a relationship is essential for the continuing vitality of the regions as the site in which students are prepared for fields of practice. It brings the different reflexivities of workplace practice on the one hand, and the production and recontextualization of disciplinary knowledge on the other, into a relationship with each other and enables each to contribute to change in the other. The innovation literature argues that innovation is a much broader concept than research and development; innovation also requires transformations to workplace practices if it is to be effective (Moodie 2006). The relationship between education and communities of interest thus must be based on recognizing the distinctive contribution each makes, but also on the necessity of building relationships between them. The aim of policy should be to build those partnerships where they are weak, particularly in newer fields of practice. This is in contrast to policy in Anglophone countries which structure this relationship so that education is the supplicant of industry and its only role is to deliver what industry 'wants' in the form of predetermined learning outcomes (Wheelahan 2004).

Finally, *all* vocational qualifications should include two outcomes: the first is to prepare students for a field of practice and the second is to provide students with the basis for educational progression as the basis underpinning occupational progression (Young 2005, 2006c). The growing complexity of work requires use of increasingly abstract theoretical knowledge in a much wider range of occupations and at different levels within occupations. Occupational progression will be tied to the capacity to use knowledge in this way and the way most people access such knowledge is through education. Occupational progression and educational progression are thus linked, although this relationship is tighter in some occupations and professions than in others. The 'dual outcomes' also provide the basis of a 'climbing framework' (Lolwana 2005) and in so doing, provide a basis for equitable access to knowledge, particularly for those hitherto excluded. It demonstrates that social mobility and equity are related to access to knowledge, and that qualifications must be structured so that they provide this access. Ensuring that vocational qualifications contain these two outcomes is one way in which the weak knowledge base of newer fields of practice can be addressed, because students' access to knowledge will not depend entirely on the state of knowledge within those fields.

Students' participation within their occupational field of practice mediates their participation in society's broader conversation. Consequently, while vocational qualifications need to prepare students for a *particular* field of practice, this is for a field of practice that is shaped within, and part of, broader social relations. Winch (2006: 421) sums this up when he says that:

> Once one sees that a society is a plurality of internally related practices, among which educational ones occupy a central role, it is no complaint against a form of education that it is a preparation for another practice or that it straddles practices. The important point for the success of education is that it prepares for or straddles them *effectively*, thus enhancing those practices for which it is a preparation.

Conclusion

Access to theoretical knowledge is fundamentally a question of distributional justice, but this question is made invisible in education policy in Anglophone countries such as the UK and Australia. The emphasis in policy is on completing school leading to pathways in tertiary education without differentiating between the way these pathways mediate social patterns of inclusion and exclusion. The esoteric is the site for alternative possibilities, yet access to such knowledge is just as strongly governed by distributional rules within a universal tertiary education system as it was within an elite higher education system. The difference is that access is not solely determined by *absence* from higher education, it is also determined by the *type* of participation within tertiary education.

Social realism differs from the dominant approaches to curriculum because it treats knowledge as causally important in its own right. It does not just critique conservatism, instrumentalism and constructivism; it is also able to theorize the place of knowledge in curriculum. The two principles upon which curriculum must be based are: first, a commitment to objective knowledge; and second, to the pursuit of truth as a normative goal of curriculum. However, because knowledge is always revisable in light of new evidence gained from our social practices, social realism argues that students must have the tools to evaluate, critique and judge knowledge claims based on credible evidence. Our aim therefore is to provide the means for students to participate in debates and conversations, not to accept eternal truths dispensed by those in authority.

Theorizing the nature of knowledge is also itself a work in progress for social realists and this will continue as social realism develops further as an important perspective within the sociology of education and curriculum studies more broadly. We are at just the beginning and the conversation is still wide open. It is demonstrated by this book which draws on Bernsteinian social theory and the philosophy of critical realism as complementary modes of analysis. Not all social realists necessarily agree with critical realism, although all acknowledge their debt to Bernstein. There is much to do. One area that has not been addressed in any depth in this book is the range of specific pedagogic practices that are needed to ensure all students have access to knowledge. Many students, particularly working-class students, have become disengaged from education as a consequence of the way in which their access to knowledge has been mediated throughout their education. Insisting that they 'learn science' or 'learn English literature' may just lead to further humiliation and alienation. However, in placing knowledge at the centre of curriculum we have the opportunity to begin to consider the way in which these students may be provided with access. There is no such possibility when knowledge is displaced in and replaced by a 'practical' and 'relevant' curriculum that is usually offered as an alternative to working-class students. Bernsteinian theorists and social realists have engaged in theorizing an inclusive pedagogy elsewhere to develop the elements of a 'radical' visible pedagogy (Muller 2004),[5] but the pedagogic implications arising from a realist analysis of knowledge need further development.

Knowledge is a social product and marked by the conditions under which it is produced. This includes relations of power and privilege. However, to reduce knowledge to power and privilege is to take the easy way out because it continues to give those who are already powerful inequitable access to powerful knowledge while excluding the less powerful. This problem will not be addressed by insisting that other 'ways of knowing' are also valuable and need recognition. Arguing for equitable access to powerful knowledge is not an argument against insisting that other ways of knowledge are valuable or that students should be able to recognize themselves in curriculum. The academy has changed and education has changed and this will continue. Similarly, the nature of knowledge and disciplinary configurations will change and new areas of knowledge will emerge as our knowledge is enlarged and reshaped. Knowledge will *always* bear traces of the knowledge producers who produced it and the conditions under which it was produced. This is why equitable access to knowledge really matters. Unless curriculum is organized so that working-class students and others who are excluded have equitable access to knowledge they will always be on the outside looking in, largely excluded from society's conversation about what it should be like.

Notes

1 Introduction: what should we teach?

1 The work of Teese and Polesel in Australia on secondary school curriculum is an exception. See Teese (2000), Teese and Polesel (2003) and Polesel (2008).

2 A Bernsteinian analysis of knowledge and the implications for curriculum

1 Arguably, this account is too focussed on Britain. While Britain certainly played a key role in the development of the structures of the disciplines, other countries and cultures also contributed.

2 While Bernstein locates the origins 'inner/outer' distinction in Christianity, others do not even though they accept religion's role in constructing the inner/outer distinction. Wexler (1995: 114) argued that both Bernstein and Durkheim drew on traditional Judaism's principle 'of *havdalah* or differentiation' to explore the distinction between the sacred and profane, and that this was not a distinction that was unique to Christianity. Bernstein (1995: 397) rejects Wexler's interpretation of his work, arguing that his analysis explored 'a *particular* conception of the sacred; a Christian conception, and that other conceptions, for example Judaic or Islamic, would not signify such a dislocation'. Dumont (1985: 94) provides an alternative account for the development of early Christianity where he argues that the individual of early Christianity is not the same as the individual of modern individualism today, and that the process of transition from one to the other took seventeen centuries. He argues that the Christian distinction between an inner self and outer practice had its origins in a social division of labour within the holistic society of the time, which acknowledged the religious elect who renounced living *in* the world as their way to God. This resulted in relativizing life in the world because 'the real' was to be found in Christ, not in 'worldly' affairs. However, religious communities still required contact with the profane world to subsist, and the Church mediated this relationship. Throughout these centuries of transition the distinction between those in-the-world and those out-of-the-world became expressed within individuals as the 'Christian individual becomes here more intensely involved in this world' (Dumont 1985: 111). This process culminated in the Protestant Reformation and Calvinism in the 1500s which removed the Church as the intermediary between the individual and God, and located the individual in the world but one who communicates directly with God. Dumont says that the 'outworldly' beginning of Christianity was not unique, and he draws parallels with ancient Indian religions.

3 Teese cites Bernstein elsewhere in this book, and he uses a Bernsteinian framework more explicitly in another book co-authored with John Polesel (Teese and Polesel 2003).

4 See the body of work by Morais and Neves (2001, 2006) and Morais, Neves and Pires (2004) for the best outline of the 'mixed pedagogy' approach.

3 Evaluation and critique: a modified Bernsteinian basis for curriculum

1 For exceptions, see Fairclough *et al.* (2002). See also Carter and Sealey (2004) who argue that language is a 'cultural emergent property' which has causal properties of its own. See also López (2001) on the role of metaphor in structuring our understanding of the world.

2 Young also argues that Durkheim was fundamentally a rationalist in saying that: 'despite his criticisms of Kant, Durkheim was at heart a rationalist who accepted the idea that reason (and its specification as logic) was the unique quality that made people human (and different from other animals). Reason was also, for Durkheim, the basis of our objectively true knowledge of the world, and hence it was the foundation of science.'

3 See Horton (1982) for a distinction between primary (everyday) and secondary (esoteric) theory to argue for a similar relationship between the two kinds of knowledge, but from a materialist premise.

4 See Young (2007a: 57), who, in a sympathetic treatment of Bernstein, also says that he presents an over-idealized notion of science (particularly physics).

5 Sayer argues that Popper does not solve the problems of positivism. This is because Popper's method does not solve the problem of induction, for having proved a theory wrong one day, how are we to know that the world hasn't changed the next (Sayer 1992: 171)? Deductive logic doesn't tell us what it is *about* the properties that cause them to act in a particular way, and it cannot distinguish between relations that are necessary and those which are contingent (Sayer 1992, 1998, 2000). He argues that the more fundamental problem with Popper's approach is that he accepts Hume's nominalist theory of ontology – that the world consists of discrete and atomized objects and events (Sayer 1992: 155). Hypotheses are demonstrated to be 'not false' by the occurrence of constant conjunctions of events.

6 However, while there is a greater emphasis on knowledge, this is reflected in policy and in curriculum through the lens of vocationalism which uses genericism as the mode for organizing knowledge and results in an emphasis on generic attributes and employability skills rather than discipline-specific knowledge. This is discussed in Chapter 6 on the relativising of knowledge in curriculum and in Chapter 7 on the crisis of curriculum.

7 See in particular Gamble (2004b, 2006a, 2006b) and Breier (2004, 2005).

4 What does commitment to realism mean for curriculum?

1 See Bhaskar (1998d: 16–17) for a discussion of the ways in which critical realism can underlabour the social sciences.

2 The different properties of objects and our knowledge about those objects are discussed in more depth in the next chapter.

3 Critical realism postdates Polanyi, so I am not attributing the label critical realist to him, even though he presents an impeccable critical realist analysis of the nature of strata and emergence and uses many of the same terms and concepts.

4 See also Sayer (1992: 92).

5 Critical realists debate the role of inferential statistics, with some arguing for a greater role than others. See Nash (1999) and Williams and Dyer (2004) for more optimistic views about the role of predictive statistics, and Scott (2000), Sayer (1992, 2000) and Collier (1994) who argue for a more limited role, while not denying the importance of descriptive statistics (provided they are based on 'good' abstractions and not taxonomic categories that are not internally related). However, regardless of the position held, all start from a realist ontology about causal mechanisms.

6 See Collier (2001) for a discussion of the notion of absence.

7 And I think the term originated and is most associated with Giddens (1987: 20).

5 The role of the disciplines in curriculum: a critical realist analysis

1 Barnes and Bloor (1982: 29) give the following (extraordinary) example in the natural sciences:

> was the fact that living matter appeared in Pouchet's laboratory preparations evidence for the spontaneous generation of life, or evidence of the incompetence of the experimenter, as Pasteur maintained? As historians of science have shown, different scientists drew different conclusions and took the evidence to point in different directions. This was possible because something is only evidence for something else when set in the context of assumptions that which give it meaning – assumptions, for instance, about what is a priori probably or improbable. If, on religious and political grounds, there is a desire to maintain a sharp and symbolically useful distinction between matter and life, then Pouchet must have blundered rather than have made a fascinating discovery.

2 These two approaches are discussed in more depth in Chapter 7 'The crisis of curriculum'.
3 I am not attributing the label 'critical realist' to Chalmers (1999: 244–45) (he prefers structural realist or unrepresentative realist), but he is a realist and much of what he says is consistent with critical realism. It would be harder to find a clearer exposition than in his deservedly famous little book *What is this thing called science?*
4 See also Maton (2003) for a similar discussion of Bourdieu.
5 Margaret Archer (2004), another leading critical realist, disagrees with him. She argues that knowledge of the natural world is primarily non-linguistic and arises from embodied engagement. This is not an argument between them about scientific training, but about the extent to which our engagement in the natural world and in the 'practical' world is socially mediated. Arguably, Archer's approach leads to an under-socialized individual.
6 Collier (1997: 26) attributes post-modernist arguments that, for example, privilege the 'practical wisdom' of shepherds over the pretensions scientists trained in abstract science recruited by the Ministry of Agriculture, to a failure to recognize the limitations of the abstract sciences, and the need for social practices to be mediated by the concrete sciences: 'Yet the fault lies not with abstract science but with the tendency of its commercial and military users to apply science in its abstract state, rather than treating abstract sciences as contributory disciplines whose results must flow together into the sea of concrete science before they are in a fit state to be applied practically.'
7 See the previous chapter for a discussion about the similarities and differences between the natural and social sciences.
8 See, for example, the most well-known exponents of this in Michael Gibbons and his colleagues (Nowotny *et al.*, 2001, 2003; Gibbons, 2004) who distinguish between 'mode 1' and 'mode 2' science, with the former based on disciplinary distinctions and the latter on transgressing these boundaries.
9 Collier (1998b: 261–62) provides a lovely example when he illustrates the different insights the gods in Valhalla bring to understanding why a strike is on at a particular factory. Thor provides the physical description of why things have stopped but he needs Woden to analyse the social realities and to tell him there is a strike on, whereas Fey, the god of biology and Loki, the god of unconscious are needed to explain that 'the boss's daughter is going to elope with the chief shop steward, the boss is going to die of apoplexy, and the daughter [will] inherit the firm and turn it into a workers' co-operative.'
10 See footnote 8.

6 How knowledge was dethroned in society and displaced in curriculum

1 See Sinclair-Jones and Jureidini (2003) for an overview of debates.
2 Which possibly could be more accurately described as neo-Fordism, at least in liberal market Anglophone nations – see Moore (2004: 63) for the distinction between neo-Fordism and post-Fordism.
3 Lim (2008) argues that 'welfare to work' is a policy-tightening exercise rather than a labour market policy aimed at enhancing the skills of welfare benefit recipients. Barnett and Spoehr (2008) argue that current policies do not adequately distinguish between training for short-term, insecure employment and that required for high-quality employment.
4 Anglophone liberal market economies differ from the 'coordinated' market economies of Northern Europe. The economies of Northern Europe use social partnerships between employers, business and labour to match graduates to jobs in relatively stable labour markets, whereas Anglophone liberal market economies use the market as the mechanism for matching graduates and jobs in volatile labour markets (Hall and Soskice 2001). There are higher levels of investment by employers in the Northern European economies because poaching by other employers is less of a problem, and voluntary and involuntary staff turnover is lower (Culpepper 2001; Estevez-Abe *et al.* 2001).
5 This is illustrated by the City of Toowoomba in Queensland, Australia, which held a referendum on 29 July 2006 to determine whether the city should recycle water back into the city's dam in response to the unprecedented drought at the time. The dam level for the City of Toowoomba was 18 per cent at December 2006. The proposal was rejected by approximately 60 per cent to 40 per cent. In the lead up to the referendum, the media interviewed many residents, and a common reason given by those who were going to vote against the proposal was because they didn't trust the science. See: http://www.toowoombawater.com.au (viewed 21 June 2009).
6 See Grubb (2004, 2006) for an explanation of similar processes in the United States.
7 After the defeat of the previous conservative Australian government and the election of the Labor government in November 2007, the Department of Education, Science and Training was reconstituted as the Department of Education, Employment and Workplace Relations.
8 In Australia, generic skills are called generic attributes in higher education, and they were called generic skills in VET, but they are now called employability skills.

7 The crisis of curriculum

1 Donnelly (2004) is the most vocal and populist proponent of this approach in Australian school curriculum debates.
2 See the previous chapter for a discussion of pedagogic and competence pedagogic modes.
3 This means they need to know the lyrics. *Advance Australia Fair* replaced *God Save the Queen* as Australia's national anthem in 1984 (even though the British Queen remains Australia's head of state). While school children (especially primary school children) may know the first verse because they are required to sing it, the second is more problematic. Many of my generation do not know the lyrics to the first verse, and there are songs that parody this. The conservative government also required schools to have a functioning flagpole to fly the Australian flag when they sing the national anthem if they were to receive additional funding.
4 Rudd argues that markets are needed to solve problems such as climate change despite this being 'perhaps the greatest market failure in history'.
5 Market choice also disguises the *class*-differentiated outcomes in choosing different post-school pathways. James (2000, 2002) reports that aspirations for different post-school outcomes (work, VET or university) are differentiated by socio-economic background,

location and gender, with socio-economic background the major factor. Different class outcomes can thus be disguised as different choices consumers make.

6 See Billett (2004: 192–94) for an outline of some of the key cognitive and socio-cultural constructivist theories of learning and their commonalities and differences.

7 Guile (2006: 257) argues that Billett's work offers the fullest expression of the process-based approach to vocational knowledge.

8 See Colley *et al.* (2003) for a typology of approaches to the formal/informal distinction from largely socio-cultural frameworks.

9 See Devos (2002) for an excellent discussion of the absence of gendered power relations in the workplace learning literature.

10 And this, along with its emphasis on labour and tools (including ideational tools), makes it one of the better socio-cultural theories of learning. See Wheelahan (2007a) for an argument that there are possible synergies between activity theory and critical realism, while recognizing that there are important differences between them.

11 See Gale and Russell (2007) for an analysis the way in which deficit discourses are constructed in teacher education for school teachers as an excuse for increasing state intervention in teacher education programmes in Australia. Overt control is exercised in VET because all must have a *VET-specific* competency-based qualification at the level of certificate IV, regardless of the higher education teaching qualifications they may have (Smith and Keating 2003). Such overt control is not exercised over higher education but universities are required to implement student satisfaction surveys and indirect control is exercised through funding mechanisms (Wheelahan 2007b).

8 The appropriation of constructivism by instrumentalism

1 See Smith and Keating (2003) for a discussion of controversies in Australia, Young (2006a) and Wolf (1998, 2002) for a discussion of England, Strathdee (2005) for a discussion of New Zealand, and Allais (2006, 2007a) and Gamble (2003, 2006b) for a discussion of South Africa.

2 See Gale (2006) for a similar discussion about the deficit discourse constructed around school teachers in Australia.

3 See Mitchell, Wood and Young (2001a), Mitchell, Young and Henry (2001b) and Mitchell, McKenna, Bald and Perry (2006b) for illustrative examples.

4 This was one of the key problems identified in the high-level review of training packages by Schofield and McDonald (2004: 18) who argued that the balance between the regulatory and enabling functions of training packages was tied too tightly to the former. They argued that there should be less discussion of 'rules' and more discussion of 'design', while still supporting the basic aims for, and framework underpinning, training packages. This has not happened, and Hoeckel *et al.* (2008), in an OECD review of VET in Australia, criticized training packages for their complexity.

5 In fairness, Schofield and McDonald, while agreeing with the notion of an industry-led system, do not restrict this to employers. Their approach is far more corporatist and friendly to unions.

6 See Smith and Blake (2005: 3–4) for a particularly illustrative example of this.

7 And instrumentalism shares this feature with constructivism, as illustrated in the next section.

8 If confined to statements about correlation and constant conjunctions of events, statements that have been derived either through an inductive or deductive process (Hume 1921 [1777]: 27; Popper 1962: 55).

9 See Turner (1994) for a particularly clear example of this in his very individualistic version of constructionism. He insists on a foundationalist theory of knowledge as 'truth', insists on the constant conjunction of events as a prerequisite for the existence

of 'laws', finds it impossible, and therefore rejects the possibility of knowledge beyond the subjective.
10 This demonstrates how constructivist approaches can be a bridge to CBT. See Hager (2003: 9) where he argues that 'precision is possible and attainable for descriptions of performance and its outcomes' but no such precision is possible 'when it comes to the underpinning constituents of competence (capabilities, abilities, skills)'. This is because these constituents 'are attributes or properties of people' and we can only *infer* the extent to which people possess these attributes based on their performance. He also distinguishes between performance descriptors as outcomes and curriculum as processes of learning, and in so doing provides a theoretical basis for this distinction in VET policy, even if it gets mangled in the process (Hager 2003: 16).

9 Conclusion: what type of curriculum do we need? The social realist alternative

1 See Beck (1999, 2002, 2006) for a similar analysis which focusses on England, but which is also relevant more broadly to other Anglophone countries with similar systems.
2 Arguably however, the recent and pervasive skill shortage in Australia, which was a preoccupation of governments, employers and unions prior to the recent global financial crisis, has done much to improve the status of the traditional trades, particularly the highly skilled trades in the construction industry. Electricians, plumbers and carpenters became very sought after.
3 See also Young (2003a) on the 'process'-oriented models of qualifications in Northern Europe which are based on agreements by the social partners about the content and processes of learning, in contrast to the 'outcomes'-based approaches typical of Anglophone countries. See Clarke and Winch (2004, 2006, 2007) on the relationship between models of skills formation and their relationship to social and industrial conditions and the impact this has on pedagogy.
4 This does not mean that learning in educational institutions must take place on campus – rather it refers to structured, purposeful learning obtained by participating in studying for qualifications.
5 See Morais and Neves (2001, 2006), Morais *et al.* (2004), Gamble (2004a, 2004b, 2006a, 2006b), Bourne (2003, 2004), Arnot and Reay (2004, 2006, 2007), Muller (2006a, 2006b, 2008) and Daniels (2006).

References

Allais, S. M. (2006), 'Problems with qualification reform in senior secondary education in South Africa', in Young, M. and Gamble, J. (eds), *Knowledge, Curriculum and Qualifications for South African Further Education*, Cape Town: Human Sciences Research Council.

—— (2007a) *The rise and fall of the NQF: A critical analysis of the South African National Qualifications Framework*, PhD, Graduate School of Public Management and Development, Faculty of Commerce, Law and Management University of the Witwatersrand. Johannesburg.

—— (2007b), 'Why the South African NQF failed: lessons for countries wanting to introduce national qualifications frameworks', *European Journal of Education*, 42, (4): 523–47.

Archer, M. (1988), *Culture and Agency: The Place of Culture in Social Theory*, Cambridge: Cambridge University Press.

—— (1995), *Realist Social Theory: The Morphogenetic Approach*, Cambridge: Cambridge University Press.

—— (2000), *Being Human: The Problem of Agency*, Cambridge: Cambridge University Press.

—— (2004), 'Objectivity and the growth of knowledge', in Archer, M. and Outhwaite, W. (eds), *Defending Objectivity: Essays in Honour of Andrew Collier*, New York: Routledge.

Arnot, M. and Reay, D. (2004), 'The framing of pedagogic encounters: regulating the social order in classroom learning', in Muller, J., Davies, B. and Morais, A. (eds), *Reading Bernstein, Researching Bernstein*, London: RougledgeFalmer.

—— (2006), 'Power, pedagogic voices and pupil talk: the implications for pupil consultation as transformative practice', in Moore, R., Arnot, M., Beck, J. and Daniels, H. (eds), *Knowledge, Power and Educational Reform*, London: Routledge.

Australian Labor Party (2007a), *The Australian Economy Needs an Education Revolution: New Directions Paper on the Critical Link Between Long Term Prosperity, Productivity Growth and Human Capital Investment*, Australian Labor Party, Canberra <www.alp.org.au/download/now/education_revolution.pdf> viewed 7 July 2009.

—— (2007b), *New Directions for Early Childhood Education Universal Access to Early Learning for 4 Year Olds*, Australian Labor Party, Canberra, <http://www.alp.org.au/media/0107/ms290.php> viewed 6 June 2007.

Australian National Training Authority (2003), *Shaping Our Future: A Discussion Starter for the Next National Strategy for Vocational Education and Training 2004–2010*, 8 January 2003, ANTA, Brisbane, <http://www.dest.gov.au/sectors/training_skills/publications_resources/profiles/anta/profile/shaping_our_future_a_discussion_starter.htm> viewed 3 March 2004.

Avis, J. (2006), 'From reproduction to learning cultures: post-compulsory education in England', *British Journal of Sociology of Education*, 27, (3): 341–54.

—— (2007), 'Engeström's version of activity theory: a conservative praxis?', *Journal of Education and Work*, 20, (3): 161–77.

Ball, S. (2003), 'The teacher's soul and the terrors of performativity', *Journal of Education Policy*, 18, (2): 215–28.

Barnes, B. and Bloor, D. (1982), 'Relativism, rationalism and the sociology of knowledge', in Hollis, M. and Lukes, S. (eds), *Rationality and Relativism*, Cambridge, Massechusetts: The MIT Press.

Barnett, M. (2006), 'Vocational knowledge and vocational pedagogy', in Young, M. and Gamble, J. (eds), *Knowledge, Curriculum and Qualifications for South African Further Education*, Cape Town: Human Sciences Research Council.

Bates, I. (1998), 'Resisting "empowerment" and realizing power: an exploration of aspects of the GNVQ', *Journal of Education and Work*, 11, (2): 187–204.

Bates, I., Bloomer, M., Hodkinson, P. and Yeomans, D. (1998), 'Progressivism and the GNVQ: context, ideology and practice', *Journal of Education and Work*, 112: 109–26.

Beck, J. (1999), 'Makeover or takeover? The strange death of educational autonomy in neo-liberal England', *British Journal of Sociology of Education*, 20, (2): 223–38.

—— (2002), 'The sacred and the profane in recent struggles to promote official pedagogic identities', *British Journal of Sociology of Education*, 23, (2): 617–26.

—— (2006a), ' "Directed time": identity and time in New Right and New Labour policy discourse', in Moore, R., Arnot, M., Beck, J. and Daniels, H. (eds), *Knowledge, Power and Educational Reform: Applying the Sociology of Basil Bernstein*, London: Routledge.

Beck, J. and Young, M. (2005), 'The assault on the professions and the restructuring of academic and professional identities: a Bernsteinian analysis', *British Journal of Sociology of Education*, 26, (2): 183–97.

Beck, U. (1994), 'The reinvention of politics: towards a theory of reflexive modernization', in Beck, U., Giddens, A. and Lash, S. (eds), *Reflexive Modernization: Politics, Tradition and Aesthetics in the Modern Social Order*, California: Standford University Press.

—— (2006b), 'Living in the world risk society', *Economy and Society*, 35, (3): 329–45

—— (2007), 'Beyond class and nation: reframing social inequalities in a globalizing world', *The British Journal of Sociology*, 58, (4): 679–705.

Beckett, D. and Hager, P. (2002), *Life, Work and Learning. Practice in Postmodernity*, London: Routledge.

Benton, T. and Craib, I. (2001), *Philosophy of Social Science: The Philosophical Foundations of Social Thought*, Hampshire: Palgrave.

Bernstein, B. (1995), 'A response', in Sadovnik, A. R. (ed.), *Knowledge and Pedagogy: The Sociology of Basil Bernstein*, Norwood, New Jersey: Ablex Publishing Corporation.

—— (1996), *Pedagogy, Symbolic Control and Identity: Theory, Research, Critique*, London: Taylor & Francis.

—— (1999), 'Vertical and horizontal discourse: an essay', *British Journal of Sociology of Education*, 20, (2): 157–73.

—— (2000), *Pedagogy, Symbolic Control and Identity*, 2nd ed., Oxford: Rowman & Littlefield Publishers.

—— (2003), *The Structuring of Pedagogic Discourse, Volume IV, Class, Codes and Control*, 2nd ed., New York: Routledge.

Bhaskar, R. (1998a), 'General introduction', in Archer, M., Bhaskar, R., Collier, A., Lawson, T. and Norrie, A. (eds), *Critical Realism: Essential Readings*, London: Routledge.

—— (1998b), 'The logic of scientific discovery', in Archer, M., Bhaskar, R., Collier, A., Lawson, T. and Norrie, A. (eds), *Critical Realism: Essential Readings*, London: Routledge.

—— (1998c), 'Philosophy and scientific realism', in Archer, M., Bhaskar, R., Collier, A., Lawson, T. and Norrie, A. (eds), *Critical Realism: Essential Readings*, London: Routledge.

—— (1998d), *The Possibility of Naturalism: A Philosophical Critique of the Contemporary Human Sciences*, 3rd ed., London: Routledge.

—— (2008), *A Realist Theory of Science*, 3rd ed., London: Verso.

Bhaskar, R. and Danermark, B. (2006), 'Metatheory, interdisciplinarity and disability research: a critical realist perspective', *Scandinavian Journal of Disability Research*, 8, (4): 278–97.

Bhaskar, R. and Norrie, A. (1998), 'Introduction. Dialectic and dialectical critical realism', in Archer, M., Bhaskar, R., Collier, A., Lawson, T. and Norrie, A. (eds), *Critical Realism. Essential Readings*, London: Routledge.

Billett, S. (2002), 'Critiquing workplace learning discourses: participation and continuity at work', *Studies in the Education of Adults*, 34, (1): 56–67.

—— (2004), 'Co-participation at work: learning through work and throughout working lives', *Studies in the Education of Adults*, 36, (2): 190–205.

Bishop, J. (2006a), *The 2006 Sir Robert Menzies Lecture delivered by the Hon Julie Bishop MP: The Liberal Frontier, Building a Civil Society*, Friday 3 November, Commonwealth Minister for Education, Science and Training, Parliament House, Melbourne, <http://www.dest.gov.au/Ministers/Media/Bishop/2006/11/B001061106.asp> 10 December 2006.

—— (2006b), *Minister Bishop's Address to the Australian History Summit Dinner 16 August 2006 Forgetting Our Past, Failing Our Future: The Teaching of Australian History*, Commonwealth Minister for Education, Science and Training, Canberra, <http://www.dest.gov.au/ministers/media/bishop/2006/08/b001170806.asp> viewed 19 September 2006.

Bloomer, M. (1998), ' "They tell you what to do and then they let you get on with it": the illusion of progressivism in GNVQ', *Journal of Education and Work*, 11, (2): 167–86.

Boud, D. (2006), 'Combining work and learning: the disturbing challenge of practice', in Edwards, R., Gallacher, J. and Whittaker, S. (eds), *Learning Outside the Academy: International Research Perspectives on Lifelong Learning*, London: Routledge.

Boud, D., Rooney, D. and Solomon, N. (2009), 'Talking up learning at work: cautionary tales in co-opting everyday learning', *International Journal of Lifelong Education*, 28, (3): 323–34.

Bourdieu, P. (1984 [1979]), *Distinction*, New York: Routledge.

—— (1988), *Homo Academicus*, Stanford, Califormia: Standford University Press.

—— (1990), *The Logic of Practice*, Stanford, California: Stanford University Press.

—— (1998), *Practical Reason*, Stanford, California: Stanford University Press.

Bourdieu, P. and Wacquant, L. J. D. (1992), *An Invitation to Reflexive Sociology*, Cambridge: Polity Press.

Bourne, J. (2003), 'Vertical discourse: the role of the teacher in the transmission and acquisition of decontextualised language', *European Educational Research Journal*, 2, (4): 496–521.

—— (2004), 'Framing talk: towards a "radical visible pedagogy"', in Muller, J., Davies, B. and Morais, A. (eds), *Reading Bernstein, Researching Bernstein*, RoutledgeFalmer: London.

Braverman, H. (1974), *Labor and Monopoly Capital: The Degradation of Work in the Twentieth Century*, New York: Monthly Review Press.

Breier, M. (2004), 'Horizontal discourse in law and labour law', in Muller, J., Davies, B. and Morais, A. (eds), *Reading Bernstein, Researching Bernstein*, London: RoutledgeFalmer.

—— (2005), 'A disciplinary-specific approach to the recognition of prior informal experience in adult pedagogy: "rpl" as opposed to "RPL" ', *Studies in Continuing Education*, 27, (1): 51–65.

Bricmont, J. (2001), 'Sociology and epistemology', in López, J. and Potter, G. (eds), *After Postmodernism: An Introduction to Critical Realism*, London: The Athlone Press.

Butler, E. (2000), 'Knowing "now", learning futures. The politics and knowledge practices of vocational education and training', *International Journal of Lifelong Education*, 19, (4): 322–41.

Callan, V. (2008), *Accelerated Apprenticeships: Apprentice, Employer and Teaching Staff Perceptions*, 8 May, National Centre for Vocational Education Research, Adelaide, <http://www.ncver.edu.au/publications/1991.html> accessed 14 May 2009.

Carter, B. and New, C. (2004), 'Introduction: realist social theory and empirical research', in Carter, B. and New, C. (eds), *Making Realism Work. Realist Social Theory and Empirical Research*, London: Routledge.

Carter, B. and Sealey, A. (2004), 'Researching "real" language', in Carter, B. and New, C. (eds), *Making Realism Work. Realist Social Theory and Empirical Research*, London: Routledge.

Castells, M. (2000), *The Rise of the Network Society*, 2nd ed., Oxford: Blackwell Publishers.

Centre for the Study of Higher Education (2008), *Participation and Equity: A Review of the Participation in Higher Education of People from Low Socioeconomic Backgrounds and Indigenous People*, Centre for the Study of Higher Education, University of Melbourne, Melbourne, <http://www.universitiesaustralia.edu.au/documents/publications/policy/ equity/0308_Particip_Equity_CSHE_Final_Report.pdf> viewed 7 April 2009.

Chalmers, A. F. (1999), *What Is This Thing Called Science?*, Buckingham: Open University Press.

Chappell, C. (2004), 'Contemporary vocational learning – changing pedagogy', *Learner and Practitioner: The Heart of the Matter, 7th Annual VET Research Association Conference*, 17–19 March, Rydges Eagle Hawk Resort, Canberra, <http://www.avetra.org.au/ Conference_Archives/2004/documents/PA013Chappell.pdf> viewed 7 April 2009.

Chappell, C., Hawke, G., Rhodes, C. and Solomon, N. (2003), *High Level Review of Training Packages Phase 1 Report. An Analysis of the Current and Future Context in which Training Packages Will Need to Operate*, Australian National Training Authority, Brisbane, <http://www.dest.gov.au/NR/rdonlyres/38C2B125–31E1–4C2C-AA5A-532C63BD205B/11536/HLRTP_Phase_1_report.pdf> viewed 16 February 2004.

Clarke, L. and Winch, C. (2004), 'Apprenticeship and applied theoretical knowledge', *Educational Philosophy and Theory*, 36, (5): 509–21.

—— (2006), 'A European skills framework? – but what are skills? Anglo-Saxon versus German concepts', *Journal of Education and Work*, 19, (3): 255–69.

—— (eds), (2007), *Vocational Education: International Approaches, Developments and Systems*, London: Routledge.

Clayton, B. and Blom, K. (2004), 'Doing it well, doing it better: practitioners, pedagogy and training packages', in, *'Learner & Practitioner – the Heart of the Matter' The seventh Australian VET Research Association Conference*, 17–19 March 2004, Canberra, <http://www.avetra.org.au/Conference_Archives/2004/papers.shtml> viewed 18 October 2004.

Colley, H., Hodkinson, P. and Malcom, J. (2003), *Informality and Formality in Learning: a Report for the Learning and Skills Research Centre*, Learning and Skills Research Centre, Learning and Skills Development Agency, Department for Education and Skills, London.

—— (2006), 'European policies on "non-formal" learning: a genealogical review', in Edwards, R., Gallacher, J. and Whittaker, S. (eds), *Learning Outside the Academy: International Research Perspectives on Lifelong Learning*, London: Routledge.

Collier, A. (1994), *Critical Realism: An Introduction to Roy Bhaskar's Philosophy*, London: Verso.

—— (1997), 'Unhewn demonstrations', *Radical Philosophy*, 81: 22–26.

—— (1998a), 'Emancipation and explanation', in Archer, M., Bhaskar, R., Collier, A., Lawson, T. and Norrie, A. (eds), *Critical Realism: Essential Readings*, London: Routledge.

—— (1998b), 'Stratified explanation and Marx's conception of history', in Archer, M., Bhaskar, R., Collier, A., Lawson, T. and Norrie, A. (eds), *Critical Realism: Essential Readings*, London: Routledge.

—— (1999), *Being and Worth*, London: Routledge.

—— (2001), 'On real and nominal absences', in López, J. and Potter, G. (eds), *After Postmodernism: An Introduction to Critical Realism*, London: The Athlone Press.

—— (2003), *In Defence of Objectivity and Other Essays*, New York: Routledge.

Connell, R. W., Ashenden, D. J., Kessler, S. and Dowsett, G. W. (1982), *Making the Difference: Schools, Families and Social Division*, North Sydney: George Allen & Unwin.

Cox, E. and Caldwell, P. (2000), 'Making policy social', in Winter, I. (ed.), *Social Capital and Public Policy in Australia*, Melbourne: Australian Institute of Family Studies.

Cruickshank, J. (2003), 'Critical realism: a brief definition', in Cruickshank, J. (ed.), *Critical Realism: The Difference It Makes*, New York: Routledge.

Cullen, J., Hadjivassiliou, K., Hamilton, E., Kelleher, J., Sommerlad, E. and Stern, E. (2002), *Review of Current Pedagogic Research and Practice in the Fields of Post-Compulsory Education and Lifelong Learning*, February, The Tavistock Institute, London.

Cully, M. (2003), *Pathways to Knowledge Work*, National Centre for Vocational Education Research, Adelaide, <http://www.ncver.edu.au/publications/927.html> viewed 10 June 2004.

—— (2008), *Working in Harmony: The Links between the Labour Market and the Education and Training Market in Australia*, 28 May, National Centre for Vocational Education Research, Adelaide, <http://www.ncver.edu.au/publications/1993.html> viewed 28 April 2009.

Culpepper, P. D. (2001), 'Employers, public policy and the politics of decentralized cooperation in Germany and France', in Hall, P. A. and Soskice, D. (eds), *Varieties of Capitalism The Institutional Foundations of Comparative Advantage*, Oxford: Oxford University Press.

Danermark, B., Ekström, M., Jakobsen, L. and Karlsson, J. C. (2002), *Explaining Society. Critical Realism in the Social Sciences*, London: Routledge.

Daniels, H. (2006), 'Activity, discourse and pedagogic change', in Moore, R., Arnot, M., Beck, J. and Daniels, H. (eds), *Knowledge, Power and Educational Reform: Applying the Sociology of Basil Bernstein*, London: Routledge.

Department of Education, Science and Training (2002), *Striving for Quality: Learning, Teaching and Scholarship*, DEST, Canberra.

—— (2006), *Training Package Development Handbook*, November, Department of Education Science and Training, Canberra, <http://www.dest.gov.au/sectors/training_skills/publications_resources/profiles/Training_Package_Development_Handbook.htm> viewed 16 March 2007.

Devos, A. (2002), 'Gender, work and workplace learning', in Reeve, F., Cartwright, M. and Edwards, R. (eds), *Supporting Lifelong Learning: Organising Learning*, 2, London: RoutledgeFalmer.

Dewey, J. (1938), *Experience and Education*, New York: Touchstone.

—— (1997 [1910]), *How We Think*, Mineola, New York: Dover Publications.

—— (1997 [1916]), *Democracy and Education: An Introduction to the Philosophy of Education*, New York: The Free Press.

Dickens, P. (2003), 'Changing our environment, changing ourselves: critical realism and transdisciplinary research', *Interdisciplinary Science Reviews*, 28, (2): 95–105.

Donnelly, K. (2004), *Why Our Schools Are Failing*, Sydney: Duffy & Snellgrove.

Down, C. (2003a), 'The impact of training packages: what might we learn about substantial systemwide change processes?', *International Journal of Training Research*, 1, (2): 1–20.

—— (2003b), 'Training packages: the learning journey to date', in *The Changing Face of VET: The Sixth Australian VET Research Association Conference*, 9–11 April, Sydney, <http://www.avetra.org.au/abstracts_and_papers_2003/refereed/Down.pdf> viewed 14 April 2004.

Dumont, L. (1985), 'A modified view of our origins: the Christian beginnings of modern individualism', in Carrithers, M., Collins, S. and Lukes, S. (eds), *The Category of the Person. Anthropology, Philosophy, History*, Cambridge: Cambridge University Press.

Durkheim, E. (1960), 'The dualism of human nature and its social conditions', in Wolff, K. H. (ed.), *Emile Durkheim, 1858–1917: A Collection of Essays, with Translations and a Bibliography*, Columbus: Ohio State University Press.

—— (1967), *The Elementary Forms of Religious Life*, New York: The Free Press.

Edwards, R. and Miller, K. (2007), 'Putting the context into learning', *Pedagogy, Culture and Society*, 15, (3): 263–74.

Edwards, R. and Usher, R. (1994), *Postmodernism and Education*, London: Routledge.

—— (2001), 'Lifelong learning: a postmodern condition of education?', *Adult Education Quarterly*, 51, (4): 273–78.

Emy, H. V. and Hughes, O. E. (1988), *Australian Politics: Realities in Conflict*, South Melbourne: Macmillan.

Engeström, Y. (2004), 'The new generation of expertise: seven theses', in Rainbird, H., Fuller, A. and Munro, A. (eds), *Workplace Learning in Context*, London: New York.

Estevez-Abe, M., Torben, I. and Soskice, D. (2001), 'Social protection and the formation of skills: a reinterpretation of the welfare state', in Hall, P. A. and Soskice, D. (eds), *Varieties of Capitalism: The Institutional Foundations of Comparative Advantage*, Oxford: Oxford University Press.

Fairclough, N., Jessop, B. and Sayer, A. (2002), 'Critical realism and semiosis', *Journal of Critical Realism*, 5, (1): 9.

Fenwick, T. (2006), 'Inside out of experiential learning: fluid bodies, co-emergent minds', in Edwards, R., Gallacher, J. and Whittaker, S. (eds), *Learning Outside the Academy: International Research Perspectives on Lifelong Learning*, London: Routledge.

Field, J. (2006), *Lifelong Learning and the New Educational Order*, 2nd ed., Staffordshire: Trentham Books.

Foley, P. (2007), *The Socio-Economic Status of Vocational Education and Training Students in Australia*, National Centre for Vocational Education Research, Adelaide, <http://www.ncver.edu.au/publications/1690.html> viewed 7 April 2009.

Freebody, P. (2006), *'Obedience, Learning, Virtue and Arithmetic': Knowledge, Skill and Disposition in the Organisation of Senior Schooling*, Queensland Studies Authority, Brisbane, <http://www.qsa.qld.edu.au/syllabus_review/docs/report-Freebody.pdf> 6 February 2007.

Fuller, A. and Unwin, L. (2004), 'Expansive learning environments: integrating organizational and personal development', in Rainbird, H., Fuller, A. and Munro, A. (eds), *Workplace Learning in Context*, London: Routledge.

Fuller, A., Munro, A. and Rainbird, H. (2004), 'Introduction and overview', in Rainbird, H., Fuller, A. and Munro, A. (eds), *Workplace Learning in Context*, London: Routledge.

Gale, T. (2006), 'How did we ever arrive at the conclusion that teachers are the problem? A critical reading in the discourses of Australian schooling', in Doecke, B., Howie, M. and Sawyer, W. (eds), *'Only Connect …': English Teaching, Schooling, and Democracy*, Kent Town: AATE & Wakefield Press.

Gale, T. and Cross, R. (2007), 'Nebulous goobledegook: the politics of (re)learning how and what to teach in Australia', in Berry, A., Clemens, A. and Kostogriz, A. (eds), *Dimensions of Professional Learning: Professionalism, Practice and Identity*, Rotterdam: Sense Publishers.

Gamble, J. (2003), *Curriculum Responsiveness in FET Colleges*, Cape Town: HSRC Press.

—— (2004a), 'A future curriculum mandate for Further Education and Training Colleges: recognising intermediate knowledge and skill', in McGrath, S., Badroodien, A., Kraak, A. and Unwin, L. (eds), *Shifting Understandings of Skills in South Africa: Overcoming the Historical Imprint of a Low Skills Regime*, Cape Town: Human Sciences Research Council.

—— (2004b), 'Retrieving the general from the particular: the structure of craft knowledge', in Muller, J., Davies, B. and Morais, A. (eds), *Reading Bernstein, Researching Bernstein*, London: RoutledgeFalmer.

—— (2006a), 'Exploring the transmission of moral order as invisible semiotic mediator of tacit knowledge', in Sadovnik, A. R. (ed.), *Fourth International Basil Bernstein Symposium*, Rutgers University, Newark, New Jersey.

—— (2006b), 'Theory and practice in the vocational curriculum', in Young, M. and Gamble, J. (eds), *Knowledge, Curriculum and Qualifications for South African Further Education*, Cape Town: Human Sciences Research Council.

Gellner, E. (1982), 'Relativism and universals', in Hollis, M. and Lukes, S. (eds), *Rationality and Relativism*, Cambridge, Massachusetts: The MIT Press.

Gibbons, M. (1997), *What Kind of University? Research and Teaching in the 21st Century*, 1997 Beanland lecture, Victoria University of Technology, Melbourne.

—— (2004), 'Globalisation, innovation and socially robust knowledge', in King, R. (ed.), *The University in the Global Age*, Houndsmills: Palgrave Macmillan.

—— (2005), 'Engagement with the Community: the emergence of a new social contract between society and science', in *Community Engagement National Workshop*, 4 March 2005, Brisbane: Griffith University.

Giddens, A. (1987), *Social Theory and Modern Sociology*, Cambridge: Polity Press.

—— (1993), *Sociology*, 2nd ed., Cambridge: Polity Press.

—— (1994), 'Living in a post-traditional society', in Beck, U., Giddens, A. and Lash, S. (eds), *Reflexive Modernization: Politics, Tradition and Aesthetics in the Modern Social Order*, Standford: Standford University Press.

—— (1999), 'Risk and responsibility', *The Modern Law Review*, 61, (1): 1–10.

Giddens, A., Duneier, M. and Appelbaum, R. P. (2006), *Essentials of Sociology*, New York: W.W. Norton & Company, Inc.

Gillard, J. (2008a), 'Reforming education and skills: challenges of the twenty first century', in *The City Of London Corporation*, 30 June 2008 London, United Kingdom: Deputy Prime Minister Australia, Minister for Employment and Workplace Relations, <http://mediacentre.dewr.gov.au/mediacentre/gillard/releases/reformingeducationandskillschallengesofthetwentyfirstcentury.htm> accessed 21 November 2008.

—— (2008b), 'Speech Australian Industry Group', in *Australian Government Minister for Education, Employment and Workplace Relations*, 8 December, <http://www.deewr.gov.au/Ministers/Gillard/Media/Speeches/Pages/Article_081208_160434.aspx> viewed 4 May 2009.

Gonczi, A. (2004), 'The new professional and vocational education', in *Dimensions of Adult Learning: Adult Education and Training in a Global Era*, Crows Nest: Allen & Unwin.

Goozee, G. (2001), *The Development of TAFE in Australia*, Adelaide: National Centre for Vocational Education Research.

Granville, G. (2004), *Impact of the National Qualifications Framework after Ten Years of Democracy*, South African Qualifications Authority, Pretoria, <http://www.saqa.org.za/> viewed 13 September 2005.

Groff, R. (2008), 'Introduction', in Groff, R. (ed.), *Revitalizing Causality: Realism about Causality in Philosophy and Social Science*, London: Routledge.

Grubb, W. N. (2004), *The Anglo-American Approach to Vocationalism: the Economic Roles of Education in England*, Research Paper 52, October 2004, David Gardner Chair in Higher Education, University of California, Berkeley, USA.

—— (2005), 'Vocationalism in higher education: the triumph of the Education Gospel', *The Journal of Higher Education*, 76, (1): 1–25.

—— (2006), 'Vocationalism and the differentiation of tertiary education: lessons from US community colleges', *Journal of Further and Higher Education*, 30, (1): 27–42.

Guile, D. (2006), 'Learning across contexts', *Educational Philosophy and Theory*, 38, (3): 251–68.

Guthrie, H. (2009), *Competence and Competency Based Training: What the Literature Says*, National Centre for Vocational Education Research, Adelaide, <http://www.ncver.edu.au/publications/2153.html> viewed 7 July 2009.

Hager, P. (2003), 'Why we need to refurbish our understanding of learning – the strange case of competence', in Searle, J., Yashin-Shaw, I. and Roebuck, D. (eds), *Enriching Learning Cultures*, 11th Annual International Conference on Post-Compulsory Education and Training, vol. 2, Gold Coast, Queensland: Australian Academic Press.

—— (2004), 'Conceptions of learning and understanding learning at work', *Studies in Continuing Education*, 26, (1): 3–17.

Hager, P. and Smith, E. (2004), 'The inescapability of significant contextual learning in work performance', *London Review of Education*, 2, (1): 33–46.

Hall, P. A. and Soskice, D. (2001), 'An introduction to Varieties of Capitalism', in Hall, P. A. and Soskice, D. (eds), *Varieties of Capitalism The Institutional Foundations of Comparative Advantage*, Oxford: Oxford University Press.

Harris, J. (1999), 'Ways of seeing the recognition of prior learning (RPL): what contribution can such practices make to social inclusion?', *Studies in the Education of Adults*, 31, (2): 124–39.

—— (2000), 'Re-visioning the boundaries of learning theory in the assessment of prior experiential learning (APEL)', in, *SCUTREA, 30th Annual Conference*, 3–5 July 2000, University of Nottingham, <http://www.leeds.ac.uk/educol/documents/00001448.htm> viewed 7 July 2009.

Harris, R., Simons, M. and Clayton, B. (2005), *Shifting mindsets: The changing work roles of vocational education and training practitioners*, 10 March 2005, National Centre for Vocational Education Research, Adelaide, <http://www.ncver.edu.au/publications/1524.html> viewed 7 July 2009.

Hartley, D. (2007), 'Personalisation: the emerging "revised" code of education?', *Oxford Review of Education*, 33, (5): 629–42.

Hasan, R. (2001), 'The ontogenesis of decontextualised language: some achievements of classification and framing', in Morais, A., Neves, I., Davies, B. and Daniels, H. (eds), *Towards a Sociology of Pedagogy. The Contribution of Basil Bernstein to Research*, New York: Peter Lang.

Hickox, M. and Moore, R. (1995), 'Liberal-humanist education: the vocationalist challenge ', *Curriculum Studies* 3, (1): 45–59.

Hobbes, T. (1985 [1651]), *Leviathan*, London: Penguin.

Hodkinson, P. (1998), 'Choosing GNVQ', *Journal of Education and Work*, 11, (2): 151–65.

Hoeckel, K., Field, S., Justesen, T. R. and Kim, M. (2008), *Learning for Jobs OECD Reviews of Vocational Education and Training*, November, Organisation for Economic Co-operation and Development, Paris, <http://www.oecd.org/dataoecd/27/11/41631383.pdf> 18 March 2009.

Horlick-Jones, T. and Sime, J. (2004), 'Living on the border: knowledge, risk and transdisciplinarity', *Futures*, 36, (4): 441–456.

Horton, R. (1982), 'Tradition and modernity revisited', in Hollis, M. and Lukes, S. (eds), *Rationality and Relativism*, Cambridge, Massachusetts: The MIT Press.

Hume, D. (1921 [1777]), *An Enquiry Concerning Human Understanding and Selections from a Treatise of Human Nature*, Chicago: The Open Court Publishing Company.

James, R. (2000), *TAFE, University or Work? The Early Preferences and Choices of Students in Years 10, 11 & 12*, 11 June 2000, National Centre for Vocational Education Research, Adelaide, <http://www.ncver.edu.au/publications/441.html> viewed 7 July 2009.

—— (2002), *Socioeconomic Background and Higher Education Participation: An Analysis of School Students' Aspirations and Expectations*, April, Evaluations and Investigations Programme, Higher Education Group, Department of Education, Science and Training, Canberra.

James, R., Baldwin, G., Coates, H., Krause, K.-L. and McInnis, C. (2004), *Analysis of Equity Groups in Higher Education 1991–2002*, Department of Education, Science and Training, Canberra.

James, R., McInnes, C. and Baldwin, G. (1999), *Which University? The Factors Influencing the Choices of Prospective Undergraduates*, Evaluations and Investigations Program, 99/3, Higher Education Division, Canberra.

Jarvis, D. S. L. (2007), 'Risk, globalisation and the state: A critical appraisal of Ulrich Beck and the World Risk Society Thesis', *Global Society*, 21, (1): 23–46.

Jessup, G. (1991), *Outcomes: NVQs and the Emerging Model of Education and Training*, London: The Falmer Press.

Johnson, T., Dandeker, C. and Ashworth, C. (1984), *The Structure of Social Theory*, Hampshire: Macmillan.

Jones, L. and Moore, R. (1995), 'Appropriating competence: the competency movement, the New Right and the "culture change" project', *British Journal of Education and Work*, 8, (2): 78–92.

Keating, J. (2003), 'Qualifications frameworks in Australia', *Journal of Education and Work*, 16, (3): 271–88.

Kelly, D. (2005), *Reviewing Workplace Bullying: Strengthening Approaches to a Complex Phenomenon*, Faculty of Arts – Papers, Faculty of Arts, University of Wollongong, Wollongong, <http://ro.uow.edu.au/cgi/viewcontent.cgi?article=1023&context=artspapers> 7 March 2007.

Lave, J. and Wenger, E. (1991), *Situated Learning: Legitimate Peripheral Participation*, Cambridge: Cambridge University Press.

Lawson, T. (1998), 'Economic science without experimentation', in Archer, M., Bhaskar, R., Collier, A., Lawson, T. and Norrie, A. (eds), *Critical Realism. Essential Readings*, London: Routledge.

Lolwana, P. (2005), *National Qualifications Frameworks and the Further Education and Training/Higher Education Interface*, November, South African Qualifications Authority, Pretoria, <http://www.saqa.org.za> viewed 6 October 2006.

López, J. (2001), 'Metaphors of social complexity', in López, J. and Potter, G. (eds), *After Postmodernism: An Introduction to Critical Realism*, London: The Athlone Press.

—— (2003), 'Critical realism: the difference that it makes, in theory', in Cruickshank, J. (ed.), *Critical Realism: The Difference it Makes*, New York: Routledge.

Macpherson, C. B. (1962), *The Political Theory of Possessive Individualism*, Oxford: Oxford University Press.

Marginson, S. (1993), *Education and Public Policy in Australia*, Melbourne: Cambridge University Press.

—— (1997a), *Educating Australia: Government, Economy and Citizen since 1960*, Melbourne: Cambridge University Press.

—— (1997b), *Markets in Education*, St Leonards: Allen & Unwin.

—— (2000), *The Changing Nature and Organisation of Work, and the Implications for Vocational Education and Training in Australia: Issues Paper*, National Centre for Vocational Education Research, Adelaide, <http://www.ncver.edu.au/publications/432.htmlhttp://www.ncver.edu.au/publications/432.html> viewed 7 July 2009.

Marx, K. (1932), *Part I: Feuerbach. Opposition of the Materialist and Idealist Outlook. B. The Illusion of the Epoch*, Marxists Internet Archive, <http://marxists.org/archive/marx/works/1845/german-ideology/ch01b.htm> viewed 9 September 2007.

Maton, K. (2003), 'Pierre Bourdieu and the epistemic conditions of social scientific knowledge', *Space & Culture*, 6, (1): 52–65.

—— (2006), 'On knowledge structures and knower structures', in Moore, R., Arnot, M., Beck, J. and Daniels, H. (eds), *Knowledge, Power and Educational Reform: Applying the Sociology of Basil Bernstein*, London: Routledge.

—— (2007), 'Segmentalism: the problem of knowledge-building in education, work and life', in paper presented at *Explorations in Knowledge, Society & Education*, July, University of Cambridge.

Mayer, E. C. (1992), *Putting General Education to Work: The Key Competencies Report*, Australian Education Council, Melbourne.

Melles, G. (2008), 'Curriculum documents and practice in the NZ polytechnic sector: consensus and dissensus ', *Research in Post-Compulsory Education*, 13, (1): 55–67.

Michelson, E. (2006), 'Beyond Galileo's telescope: situated knowledge and the recognition of power', in Andersson, P. and Harris, J. (eds), *Re-theorising the Recognition of Prior Learning*, London: National Institute of Adult and Continuing Education.

Misko, J. (2006), *Vocational Education and Training in Australia, the United Kingdom and Germany*, 24 April 2006, National Centre for Vocational Education Research, Adelaide, <http://www.ncver.edu.au/publications/1670.html> viewed 7 July 2009.

Mitchell, J., Chappell, C., Bateman, A. and Roy, S. (2006a), *Quality is the Key: Critical Issues in Teaching, Learning and Assessment in Vocational Education and Training*, National Centre for Vocational Education Research, Adelaide, <http://www.ncver.edu.au/publications/1710.html> 14 May 2009.

Mitchell, J., McKenna, S., Bald, C. and Perry, W. (2006b), *New Capabilities in VET*, Reframing the Future, Adelaide, <http://www.reframingthefuture.net/docs/2006/Publications/0ALL_New_Capabilities_in_VET_06.pdf> viewed 14 May 2009.

Mitchell, J., McKenna, S., Bald, C., Perry, W. and Earls, S. (2007), *Human Capital Enhanced by VET*, Reframing the Future, Adelaide, <http://www.reframingthefuture.net/docs/2007/Publications/0ALL_Human_Capital_book_7may07.pdf> 14 May 2009.

Mitchell, J., Wood, S. and Young, S. (2001a), *Communities of Practice: Reshaping Professional Practice and Improving Organisational Productivity in the Vocational Education and Training (VET) Sector Resources for Practitioners*, Australian National Training Authority, Melbourne, <http://www.reframingthefuture.net/docs/2003/Publications/4CP_cop.pdf> viewed 14 May 2009.

Mitchell, J., Young, S. and Henry, J. (2001b), *A New Model of Workbased Learning in the VET Sector*, Reframing the Future, Adelaide, <http://www.reframingthefuture.net/docs/2003/Publications/0ALL_WBL.pdf> viewed 14 May 2009.

Moodie, G. (2006), 'Vocational education institutions' role in national innovation', *Research in Post-Compulsory Education*, 11, (2): 131–40.

Moore, R. (2000), 'For knowledge: tradition, progressivism and progress in education – reconstructing the curriculum debate', *Cambridge Journal of Education*, 30, (1): 17–36.

—— (2004), *Education and Society: Issues and Explanations in the Sociology of Education*, Cambridge: Polity Press.

—— (2006a), 'Hierarchical knowledge structure and the canon: a preference for judgments', in Christie, F. and Martin, J. R. (eds), *Language, Knowledge and Pedagogy: Functional Linguistic and Sociological Perspectives*, London: Continuum Press.

—— (2006b), 'Knowledge structures and intellectual fields: Basil Bernstein and the sociology of knowledge', in Moore, R., Arnot, M., Beck, J. and Daniels, H. (eds), *Knowledge, Power and Educational Reform: Applying the Sociology of Basil Bernstein*, London: Routledge.

—— (2007a), 'Going critical: the problem of problematising knowledge in education studies', *Critical Studies in Education*, 48, (1): 25–41.

—— (2007b), *Sociology of Knowledge and Education*, London: Continuum.

Moore, R. and Maton, K. (2001), 'Founding the sociology of knowledge: Basil Bernstein, intellectual fields and the epistemic device', in Morais, A., Neves, I., Davies, B. and Daniels, H. (eds), *Towards a Sociology of Pedagogy. The Contribution of Basil Bernstein to Research*, New York: Peter Lang.

Moore, R. and Muller, J. (2002), 'The growth of knowledge and the discursive gap', *British Journal of Sociology of Education*, 23, (4): 627–37.

Moore, R. and Young, M. (2001), 'Knowledge and the curriculum in the sociology of education: towards a reconceptualisation', *British Journal of Sociology of Education*, 22, (4): 445–61.

Morais, A. and Neves, I. (2001), 'Pedagogic social contexts: studies for a sociology of learning', in Morais, A., Neves, I., Davies, B. and Daniels, H. (eds), *Towards a Sociology of Pedagogy. The Contribution of Basil Bernstein to Research*, New York: Peter Lang.

—— (2006), 'Teachers as creators of social contexts for scientific learning', in Moore, R., Arnot, M., Beck, J. and Daniels, H. (eds), *Knowledge, Power and Educational Reform: Applying the Sociology of Basil Bernstein*, London: RoutledgeFalmer.

Morais, A., Neves, I. and Pires, D. (2004), 'The *what* and the *how* of teaching and learning: going deeper into sociological analysis and interventions', in Muller, J., Davies, B. and Morais, A. (eds), *Reading Bernstein, Research Bernstein*, London: RoutledgeFalmer.

Moran, J. (2001), *Interdisciplinarity*, New York: Routledge.

Mounier, A. (2001), *The Three Logics of Skills in French Literature*, Report for the NSW Board of Vocational Education and Training, March 2001, Australian Centre for Industrial Relations Research and Training (ACIRRT), University of Sydney, Sydney, <http://www.bvet.nsw.gov.au/pdf/threelogics.pdf> viewed 6 June 2004.

Muller, J. (2000), *Reclaiming Knowledge. Social Theory, Curriculum and Education Policy*, London: RoutledgeFalmer.

—— (2004), 'Introduction: the possibilities of Basil Bernstein', in Muller, J., Davies, B. and Morais, A. (eds), *Reading Bernstein, Researching Bernstein*, London: RoutledgeFalmer.

—— (2006a), 'Differentiation and progression in the curriculum', in Young, M. and Gamble, J. (eds), *Knowledge, Curriculum and Qualifications for South African Further Education*, Cape Town: Human Sciences Research Council.

—— (2006b), 'On the shoulders of giants: verticality of knowledge and the school curriculum', in Moore, R., Arnot, M., Beck, J. and Daniels, H. (eds), *Knowledge, Power and Educational Reform: Applying the Sociology of Basil Bernstein*, London: Routledge.

—— (2008), *In Search of Coherence: A Conceptual Guide to Curriculum Planning for Comprehensive Universities* January, University of Cape Town, Report prepared for the SANTED Project, Centre for Education Policy Development, Cape Town.

Nash, R. (1999), 'Realism in the sociology of education: "explaining" social differences in attainment', *British Journal of Sociology of Education*, 20, (1): 107–25.

National Centre for Vocational Education Research (2008), *2006 VET in Schools Statistics: A Report for the Ministerial Council on Education, Employment, Training and Youth Affairs (MCEETYA) Secretariat: Draft Report 1*, 10 October, NCVER, Adelaide, <http://www.mceetya.edu.au/verve/_resources/2006_MCEETYA_VET_in_Schools_report.pdf> viewed 8 March 2009.

Nelson, B. (2005), *Transcript of Iinterview with Jon Faine Radio 774 ABC Melbourne*, 25 August, Media Centre, Dr Brendan Nelson, Australian Government Minister for Education, Science & Training, Australia, <http://www.dest.gov.au/Ministers/Media/Nelson/2005/08/trans250805.asp> viewed 7 July 2009.

Neumann, R., Parry, S. and Becher, T. (2002), 'Teaching and learning in their disciplinary contexts: a conceptual analysis', *Studies in Higher Education*, 27, (4): 405–17.

Niiniluoto, I. (1999), *Critical Scientific Realism*, Oxford: Oxford University Press.

Norris, C. (2008), 'Meaning, truth and causal explanation: the "Humean condition" revisited', in Groff, R. (ed.), *Revitalizing Causality: Realism about Causality in Philosophy and Social Science*, London: Routledge.

Nowotny, H., Scott, P. and Gibbons, M. (2001), *Re-thinking Science. Knowledge and the Public in an Age of Uncertainty*, Cambridge: Polity.

—— (2003), ' "Mode 2" revisited: the new production of knowledge', *Minerva*, 41, (3): 179–94.

Olssen, M. and Peters, M. A. (2005), 'Neoliberalism, higher education and the knowledge economy: from the free market to knowledge capitalism', *Journal of Education Policy*, 20, (3): 313–45.

Onyx, J. and Bullen, P. (2000), 'Sources of social capital', in Winter, I. (ed.), *Social Capital and Public Policy in Australia*, Melbourne: Australian Institute of Family Studies.

Outhwaite, W. (1998), 'Realism and social science', in Archer, M., Bhaskar, R., Collier, A., Lawson, T. and Norrie, A. (eds), *Critical Realism: Essential Readings*, London: Routledge.

Polanyi, M. (1983 [1966]), *The Tacit Dimension*, Gloucester: Peter Smith.

Polesel, J. (2008), 'Democratising the curriculum or training the children of the poor: school-based vocational training in Australia', *Journal of Education Policy*, 23 (6): 615–32.

Popper, K. R. (1962), *Conjectures and Refutations. The Growth of Scientific Knowledge*, New York: Basic Books.

Porpora, D. V. (2008), 'Sociology's causal confusion', in Groff, R. (ed.), *Revitalizing Causality: Realism about Causality in Philosophy and Social Science*, London: Routledge.

Pusey, M. (1991), *Economic Rationalism in Canberra: A Nation Building State Changes Its Mind*, Melbourne: Cambridge University Press.

Reich, R. (1992), *The Work of Nations: Preparing Ourselves for 21st Century Capitalism*, New York: Vintage Books.

Robinson, C. (2003), 'Employment opportunities and needs for the future', in, *Skilling Australia*, 10 September 2003, Marriott Hotel Gold Coast.

Rudd, K. (2008), *Address to the Centre for Independent Studies – Consilium*, Hyatt Regency, Coolum, Queensland: Prime Minister of Australia.

Rumsey, D. (2003), *Think Piece on the Training Package Model*, Australian National Training Authority, Brisbane, <http://www.dest.gov.au/NR/rdonlyres/7B0ECA21–23AD0–4E50-9242-24FC87E54509/6341/TP_model_thinkpiece.pdf> viewed 6 May 2006.

Santiago, P., Tremblay, K., Basri, E. and Arnal, E. (2008a), *Tertiary Education for the Knowledge Society Volume 1 Special Features: Governance, Funding, Quality*, Organisation for Economic Development and Co-operation, Paris, <http://www.oecd.org/document/35/0,3343,en_2649_39263238_36021283_1_1_1_1,00.html> viewed 7 July 2009.

—— (2008b), *Tertiary Education for the Knowledge Society Volume 2 Special Features: Equity, Innovation, Labour Market, Internationalisation*, Organisation for Economic Development and Co-operation, Paris, <http://www.oecd.org/document/35/0,3343,en_2649_39263238_36021283_1_1_1_1,00.html> viewed 7 July 2009.

Sayer, A. (1992), *Method in Social Science: A Realist Approach*, 2nd ed, London: Routledge.

—— (1998), 'Abstraction: a realist interpretation', in Archer, M., Bhaskar, R., Collier, A., Lawson, T. and Norrie, A. (eds), *Critical Realism: Essential Readings*, London: Routledge.

—— (1999), 'Bourdieu, Smith and disinterested judgement', *The Sociological Review*, 47, (3): 403–31.

—— (2000), *Realism and Social Science*, London: Sage.

Schofield, K. and McDonald, R. (2004), *Moving on[…]Report of the High Level Review of Training Packages*, April, Australian National Training Authority, Brisbane.

Scollay, M. (2000), 'The VET reforms debate', *Campus Review*, March 22, Sydney.

Scott, D. (2000), *Realism and Educational Research: New Perspectives and Possibilities*, London: RoutledgeFalmer.

Sfard, A. (1998), 'On two metaphors for learning and the dangers of choosing just one', *Educational Researcher*, 27, (2): 4–13.

Sinclair-Jones, J. and Jureidini, R. (2003), 'Work', in Jureidini, R. and Poole, M. (eds), *Sociology: Australian Connections*, Crows Nest: Allen & Unwin.

Singh, P. (2002), 'Pedagogising knowledge: Bernstein's theory of the pedagogic device', *British Journal of Sociology of Education*, 23, (4): 571–82.

Skilbeck, M., Connell, H., Lowe, N. and Tait, K. (1994), *The Vocational Quest: New Directions in Education and Training*, New York: Routledge.

Smith, E. and Keating, J. (2003), *From Training Reform to Training Packages*, Tuggerah: Social Science Press.

Smith, P. and Blake, D. (2005), *Facilitating Learning Through Effective Teaching: At a Glance*, National Centre for Vocational Education Research, Adelaide, <http://www.ncver.edu.au/publications/byauthor.html? sub = Damian%20Blake> viewed 7 July 2009.

Spratt, P. (2003), 'Social research methods', in Jureidini, R. and Poole, M. (eds), *Sociology: Australian Connections*, Crows Nest: Allen & Unwin.

Strathdee, R. (2005), 'Globalization, innovation and the declining significance of qualifications led social and economic change', *Journal of Education Policy*, 20, (4): 437–56.

Taylor, C. (1982), 'Rationality', in Hollis, M. and Lukes, S. (eds), *Rationality and Relativism*, Cambridge, Massachusetts: The MIT Press.

Teese, R. (2000), *Academic Success & Social Power: Examinations and Inequality*, Carlton South: Melbourne University Press.

Teese, R. and Polesel, J. (2003), *Undemocratic Schooling: Equity and Quality in Mass Secondary Education in Australia*, Melbourne: Melbourne University Press.

Teese, R., Nicholas, T., Polesel, J. and Helme, S. (2006a), *The Destinations of School Leavers in Victoria*, Communications Division for the Department of Education & Training, Melbourne, <http://www.sofweb.vic.edu.au/voced/ontrack/pdfs/destinations_2005.pdf> viewed 8 March 2007.

Teese, R., Robinson, L., Lamb, S. and Mason, K. (2006b), *The 2005 On Track Longitudinal Survey: The Destinations of 2003 School Leavers in Victoria Two Years On*, Office of Learning and Teaching, Department of Education & Training, Melbourne, <http://www.sofweb.vic.edu.au/voced/ontrack/default.htm> viewed 9 March 2007.

Thompson Klein, J. (2004), 'Prospects for transdisciplinarity', *Futures*, 36, (4): 515–526.

Trow, M. (1974), 'Problems in the transition from elite to mass higher education', *Policies for Higher Education*, OECD, (Paris): 51–101.

Trow, M. (2005), *Reflections on the Transition from Elite to Mass to Universal Access: Forms and Phases of Higher Education in Modern Societies since WWII*, WP2005–4, Institute of Governmental Studies, University of California, Berkeley, Berkeley, <http://repositories.cdlib.org/cgi/viewcontent.cgi?article = 1046&context = igs> viewed 13 February 2009.

Tuck, R. (2007), *An Introductory Guide to National Qualifications Frameworks*, Skills and Employability Department, International Labour Office, Geneva, <http://www.ilo.org/skills/what/pubs/lang – en/docName – WCMS_103623/index.htm> viewed 7 July 2009.

Turner, S. (1994), *The Social Theory of Practices*, Cambridge: Polity Press.

Unwin, L., Felstead, A., Fuller, A., Bishop, D., Lee, T., Jewson, N. and Butler, P. (2007), 'Looking inside the Russian doll: the interconnections between context, learning and pedagogy in the workplace', *Pedagogy, Culture and Society*, 15, (3): 333–48.

Usher, R. (1996), 'A critique of the neglected epistemological assumptions of educational research', in Scott, D. and Usher, R. (eds), *Understanding Educational Research*, London: Routledge.

Victorian Workcover Authority, The (2006), *Incidence of Workplace Bullying in Victoria: Summary Findings*, 16 November 2006 The Victorian Workcover Authority, Melbourne, <http://www.worksafe.vic.gov.au/wps/wcm/resources/file/eb256a4ee88245d/summary_of_bullying_incidence_reports.pdf> viewed 6 May 2009.

Vygotsky, L. S. (1978), 'Mind in society. the development of higher psychological processes', in Cole, M., John-Steiner, V., Scribner, S. and Souberman, E. (eds), *Mind in Society. The Development of Higher Psychological Processes*, Cambridge, Massachussets: Harvard University Press.

Wanrooy, B. v., Oxenbridge, S., Buchanan, J. and Jakubau, M. (2007), *Australia at Work: The Benchmark Report*, Workplace Research Centre, University of Sydney, Sydney, <http://www.wrc.org.au/free-download.php?did = 6&sid = 1381> viewed 30 April 2009.

Wenger, E. (1998), *Communities of Practice: Learning, Meaning and Identity*, Cambridge: Cambridge University Press.

Wexler, P. (1995), 'Bernstein: A Jewish Misreading', in Sadovnik, A. R. (ed.), *Knowledge and Pedagogy: The Sociology of Basil Bernstein*, Norwood, New Jersey: Ablex Publishing Corporation.

Wheelahan, L. (2002), 'Post-compulsory education and training in Australia and citizenship', in Searle, J. and Roebuck, D. (eds), *Envisioning Practice – Implementing Change. Proceedings of the 10th Annual International Conference on Post-Compulsory Education and Training*, vol. 3, Park Royal Surfers Paradise, Gold Coast: Centre for Learning and Work Research, Faculty of Education, Griffith University.

—— (2003), 'ANTA directs research effort', *Campus Review*, June 10, North Sydney.

—— (2004), 'What are the alternatives to training packages?', in, *Learner and Practitioner: the Heart of the Matter, 7th Annual VET Research Association Conference*, 17–19 March 2004., Rydges Eagle Hawk Resort, Canberra, <http://www.avetra.org.au/Conference_Archives/2004/documents/PA022Wheelahan.PDF> viewed 7 July 2009.

—— (2005), 'Talking about process', *Campus Review*, 17 August, North Sydney, 7.

—— (2006), 'The Clayton's review', *Campus Review*, 22 February, North Sydney, 15.

—— (2007a), 'Blending activity theory and critical realism to theorise the relationship between the individual and society and the implications for pedagogy', *Studies in the Education of Adults*, 39, (2): 183–96.

—— (2007b), 'How not to fund teaching and learning', *Australian Universities Review*, 49, (1 & 2): 31–38.

—— (2009), 'What kind of access does VET provide to higher education for low SES students? Not a lot', *Student equity in higher education: What we know. What we need to know*, National Centre for Student Equity in Higher Education, 25 and 26 February, University of South Australia, <http://www.unisa.edu.au/hawkeinstitute/events/default.asp> viewed 10 March 2009.

Wheelahan, L. and Carter, R. (2001), 'National Training Packages: a new curriculum framework for vocational education and training in Australia', *Education and Training*, 43, (6): 303–16.

Williams, M. and Dyer, W. (2004), 'Realism and probability', in Carter, B. and New, C. (eds), *Making Realism Work. Realist Social Theory and Empirical Research*, London: Routledge.

Winch, C. (2002), 'Work, well-being and vocational education: the ethical significance of work and preparation for work', *Journal of Applied Philosophy*, 19, (3): 261–71.

Winch, C. (2006), 'Rules, technique, and practical knowledge: a Wittgensteinian exploration of vocational learning', *Educational Theory*, 56, (4): 407–21.

Winch, C. and Hyland, T. (2007), *A Guide to Vocational Education and Training*, London: Continuum.

Wolf, A. (1998), 'The training illusion', *Prospect*, 33, (August/September): 12–13.

Wolf, A. (2002), *Does Education Matter? Myths about Education and Economic Growth*, London: Penguin.

World Bank, Th (2002), *Constructing Knowledge Societies: New Challenges for Tertiary Education*, Washington, DC: The World Bank.

Young, M. (1998), *The Curriculum of the Future*, London: RoutledgeFalmer.

—— (2001), *The Role of National Qualifications Frameworks in Promoting Lifelong Learning*, Discussion paper, Organisation of Economic Co-operation and Development, Paris.

—— (2003a), 'Comparing approaches to the role of qualifications in the promotion of lifelong learning', *European Journal of Education*, 38, (2): 199–211.

Young, M. (2003b), 'Curriculum studies and the problem of knowledge: updating the enlightenment?', *Policy Futures in Education*, 1, (3): 553–64.

—— (2005), *National Qualifications Frameworks: Their Feasibility for Effective Implementation in Developing Countries*, Geneva: International Labour Organization.

—— (2006a), 'Conceptualising vocational knowledge: some theoretical considerations', in Young, M. and Gamble, J. (eds), *Knowledge, Curriculum and Qualifications for South African Further Education*, Cape Town: Human Sciences Research Council.

—— (2006b), 'Endword', in Andersson, P. and Harris, J. (eds), *Re-theorising the Recognition of Prior Learning*, London: National Institute of Adult and Continuing Education.

—— (2006c), 'Reforming the further education and training curriculum: an international perspective', in Young, M. and Gamble, J. (eds), *Knowledge, Curriculum and Qualifications for South African Further Education*, Cape Town: Human Sciences Research Council.

—— (2007a), 'Durkheim and Vygotsky's theories of knowledge and their implications for a critical educational theory', *Critical Studies in Education*, 48, (1): 43–62.

—— (2007b), 'Qualifications frameworks: some conceptual issues', *European Journal of Education*, 42, (4): 445–57.

—— (2008a), *Bringing Knowledge Back In: From Social Constructivism to Social Realism in the Sociology of Education*, London: Routledge.

—— (2008b), 'From constructivism to realism in the sociology of the curriculum', *Review of Research in Education*, 32, (1): 1–28.

Young, M. and Muller, J. (2007), 'Truth and truthfulness in the sociology of educational knowledge', *Theory and Research in Education*, 5, (2): 173–201.

Index